RAROTONGA

RAROTONGA

A Novel

CHRISTIAN WILLIAMS

East Wind Press
A division of East Wind Productions, Inc.

This book is a work of fiction. Any references to historical events, real people or real locales are used fictitiously.

Printed in the United States of America.

ISBN-13: 978-0-9972531-3-9
ISBN-10: 0-9972531-3-4

Inquiries: Phyllis@olmsteadwilliams.com
Olmstead Williams Communications, Inc.
10940 Wilshire Blvd, Suite 1210
Los Angeles, CA 90024
310-824-9000

For M.C.W.

"Are not half our lives spent in reproaches for foregone actions, of the true nature and consequences of which we were wholly ignorant at the time?"

—Herman Melville

A glossary of nautical terms appears on Page 331.

CHAPTER ONE

Southwest of Midway Island

On the 87th day, having rested, the multimillionaire Bobby Ayers woke as he often did with a remnant of a smile, residuum of a dream perhaps, or the memory of having outfoxed them all. It could linger all morning, the smile. It could maintain. Robert Allington Ayers, as he was called in court documents, at the moment lay supine, feeling in the fluids of his gut the rolling motion of a yacht moving effortlessly across a vacant sea. No alarm had roused him, nor phone call or periscope of doubt. Ayers woke when rested. Automatically.

In the soft light of dawn he padded through the salon, no handholds necessary today. The ship's galley was still unfinished, but the exposed wiring bundles above the six-burner swinging stove only accentuated the perfection of the Aurelia II in its alcove. The Aurelia was the best espresso machine in the world, and Ayers could see his reflection distorted in the stainless body as he ground the beans and filled the single portacup. It had a capacious boiler tank and a milk steamer that spun the liquid in a certain pleasing way, clockwise, notwithstanding what side of the equator you were on. It made a lot of noise, hissing and puffing. It put on a little show, which was all right. Good marketing. He pressed into his face a wash rag from one of the sinks, discovered sawdust in it, ran pressure water on it, shook away the wood chips and twisted it damp and cool. Twisting was one of the motions that hurt his fingers. A touch of arthritis, not uncommon in a man of 61. The feeling took a moment to go away so he leaned against the bulkhead behind him, waiting. On the April calendar taped to the door of the wine locker he marked the number of days since departure. "Eighty-seven" fell on a Tuesday, but Ayers had long lost interest in what day of the week that might be.

The sliding door of the refrigerator behind him opened with the push of a button. Inside was a tray of varnished mahogany. He transferred it to the marble of the counter, where its detent clicked home. This device José had made for him, after three design consultations, to hold a sterling service of sugar, cream and spoons. Each fit snug in a niche, as did the tray in the marble. No spillage, even in a heavy seaway. He swallowed a single espresso shot, put the tiny cup into the dishwasher, and chose a handled bowl for the cappuccino that would be breakfast. Again the machine whirred and steamed with more vigor than the lazy Pacific passing outside the galley portlights.

Well, good morning.

And good morning to you.

From a drawer he pulled a saxophone reed, and with that tucked in his mouth moved through the dangling conduit of the uncompleted main salon to the settee, a 10-foot curve of cherrywood that wrapped the cabin like a comforting arm. From a weathered case he began the ritual assembly of the sax. For today he chose a Jody Jazz mouthpiece, husky but forgiving. Lubricate the section corks. Put strap around neck. The big main cabin was quiet, rectangles of dawn sun playing on the teak and holly floorboards under his bare feet. He blew patterns in thirds and then in sixths. They honked raw and the tones seemed to cling to the padded ceiling above. The cork wax spread a familiar scent of roses. He put the instrument down, laying it across the velvet of its box, and went back to make another cappuccino.

Après Vous was the name of the yacht which coursed easily across the surface of the morning ocean. In hardly eight knots of wind she still made an easy four miles every hour. From any vantage a few miles away, *Après Vous* appeared as little more than a speck against the horizon. But at 60 feet overall she was in fact quite large, with a towering mast that could spread more than 1500 square feet of sail. She had begun life as a luxury sailboat designed for prince and princess, and unusually capable of sailing waters both vasty deep and worrisome shallow. Her draft ranged from a mere 6 feet to twice that with her keel extended for stability and pointing close to the wind. Her hull was long and sleek and brand new, or had been new, before the anchors of a dredge failed in a winter gale and the windblown barge entwined itself with the newly launched yacht and carried them both ashore. For 18 hours the rusty dredge ground the yacht's hull under its enormous weight, violating her on a bed of mud. When the waters retreated she lay scandalized and broken, a $3 million loss. Ayers bought her sight unseen by text message from Barcelona, directing salvation to begin immediately at a boatyard in Mexico.

* * *

3

By habit, Bobby Ayers ran through scales after breakfast. He played phrases, not whole melodies. Morning was a reminder of the space between notes, and the role of distance in artful relations. As soon as he felt musical—the reed working, the breath coming—he stopped. Nighttime was for music, and he preferred to wait for it like an assignation. The anticipation could carry him all day, meeting to meeting, airport to airport, deal to deal. As fast as he ran or as glorious the chase, the day was only a deferment of something better to come: the world of chords and tunes and signatures of time, the circle of fifths in his head and his mouth and his hands. It was a reunion always waiting.

Ayers put the instrument away and climbed the salon stairway to the deck. He knew what he would see: a gentle oceanscape, the big boat hardly heeling as she loped across the wavelets. There was one reef in the mainsail and only the staysail set. The huge genoa jib remained furled on the forestay. That had been sail enough for darkness, and today he could set more if the mood allowed. The horizon showed no tropical cumulus yet, they would grow as the day wore on. As usual, there was nothing made by man on the far horizon or the dome of the sky. In this world he was the only one, and had been for months.

The deck check complete, he returned below and found his way aft to the master's cabin. It contained a massive double berth and private access to a separate cockpit above. The only decoration was a taped-on postcard of a dog catching a Frisbee. The compartment was appointed in rosewood joinery, with a large en suite bath and shower. He passed through its elegant space to the engine room, where rough oak planks lay stacked in sawdust under a rusty chain hoist. Ayers surveyed the mess with satisfaction. He had made it himself by personally installing, at sea, a 500-pound diesel generator that for months had sat on its pallet, filling his cabin. It was a task for three mechanics in a well-equipped boatyard, and he had done it alone using wedges, a hydraulic jack and this hoist crane built from its shipping pallet. He had fitted and connected the seawater source, wired the engine panel and vented the exhaust. He had been able to work in this sweat-hole, covered in grease, only when the weather was mild. If the seas rose to slam the boat around an unsecured quarter-ton of engine could be dangerous, especially if his tremors returned at just the wrong time.

Now, seven days later, all that was left to do was connect the electric starter, but nowhere on board could be found the cables shown on the inventory list. They were probably still in José's shed in Mexico. Well, in fairness, departure had been somewhat rushed. He couldn't blame his old foreman for that, and it was not in his nature to blame himself.

By afternoon Ayers discovered that by disconnecting the service wires from the ship's main engine he could lead them to the generator. By five o'clock he had the fluids in and the installation checklist complete. It started immediately, rumbling quietly at 1800 rpms under its soundproofing, and after five minutes he shut it down. Job complete. And who the hell else could have accomplished it alone, with only the available tools in a cramped bilge 2,000 miles from land? Nobody else. The sensation of accomplishment was heightened because the powerful generator was not even necessary. The yacht's electrical needs for air conditioning, bow thruster and power winches were already supplied by solar panels and the windmill generator on the stern. He had installed the thing just to check it off his list. A triumph of will without even the need for necessity.

Ayers backed out of the engine room and stripped off his oil-stained shirt and tattered shorts. They went into a cinch bag marked "reuse". In the master's shower he stood for a long time under the hot, fresh water, scrubbing his hands and arms with Borax. When he emerged the watermaker turned itself on. He had installed that, too, solving all the complications, and now it was a part of him. He could feel, as if in his own body, the watermaker's permeable membrane pressurize to 20,000 pounds per square inch and begin to forcibly separate the salt from the sea around him. It was his will at work, topping off the 400-gallon fresh water tank.

Still naked, because it was 88 degrees in the cabin, he climbed the stairway of the main salon to the enormous center cockpit with seating for 12. Whitecaps decorated the afternoon around him. Overhead, a white fulmar hovered above the mast, watching him the way it always did. The fulmar remained in place even as fog advanced rapidly from all around. A squall, perhaps, although they tended to come after dinner, not before. The fog grew thick and the bird disappeared.

* * *

Ayers returned to consciousness sometime later to find himself on hands and knees. He checked for injury but found not even a bruise. The event, as he assessed it, was the result of a sudden rotation of his head as he surmounted the shadow of the companionway stairs into blinding sunlight. He had worked all day in the confines of the dim engine room. To spin and scan when emerging on deck was prudent, but it did interrupt the communication of the inner ear with the cerebellum. Balance was a system like any other and he could conceive the plumbing in his head as easily as the plumbing in the boat. He had looked it up a year ago. Everyone's equilibrium was maintained by fluid-filled tubes in the cranium. In the tubes were sensing hairs. Among the hairs were crystals of calcium carbonate called otoconia, evolved to signal movement. Sometimes they got disrupted if you turned your head.

When he had told Arnie Stein that, Dr. Stein had just nodded. An occasional misfire was not unusual, he agreed. He had himself puked within 20 minutes the one time he was on a sailboat, despite an anti-seasick wristband. And you're right, Bobby, if a golf course didn't hold still I could never sink a putt. Still, let's do some tests. Ayers found Stein's analogy unpersuasive and his medicine cautionary. As a service provider, his first act was always to refer to his subcontractors. All he did was to ask questions, and questions were easy. To beat them you only had to say nothing, and wait. That turned the tables. That made Arnie and everybody else shift in their chairs, lose concentration, and quickly move on. To resist confession without torture worked in business and pleasure and marriage. Say nothing. Smile. Look in their eyes and watch them abandon the field. It had made Bobby Ayers rich.

Dr. Stein gave him some dizzy pills. He had a year's supply on board, but had stopped taking them months ago after the gale off Mexico had proved his balance to be as good as ever. He took a few now, as insurance.

* * *

On an evening like this Ayers liked to sit in his enormous cockpit with a cocktail. In good weather he left the deck cushions out for him and as many as 10 guests. The guest list varied with memory and mood. They were old friends or enemies or lovers or abominations from dreams. Some were true and some were fictions in togas or stovepipe hats. He could summon them, but usually they came of their own accord. They had been with him long before this voyage, in foreign hotels or inside a clanking MRI machine or in the back seat of a rental car. They were the natural companions of a solo life and now the inevitable apparitions of a singlehander long at sea. But this evening there was no one. No figure from a book, no lover untouched by time, no specter of memory or phantom of the unresolved. Ayers had always been alone but seldom without his companions. He waited.

The martinis tonight were Hendrick's gin. He enjoyed the rattle of cubes in the shaker and the icy, transparent pour. The cold nose of juniper and cucumber. The first wetting of lip and tongue, the catalog of occurrence and remembering, of people and places and that balcony in Tangier where Sondra, the fake countess, had taken off her pearls and said—what was it she had said? She would remember. But she was not here. Well, he had himself. Good company always.

It's a pretty sunset, don't you agree?

I do. Red sky at night, sailor's delight.

Ayers had not glanced at the navigation chart nor altered sail all this day, and still they continued on course 160 magnetic, latitude 12 degrees north of the equator, far from any shipping lanes or aircraft routes or anybody's navy, and where, in this season at least, the weather today was the same as tomorrow's. If rain squalls came, his response would be the touch of a toggle on an electric winch and the mainsail would automatically furl. In fact, he could push one button and the yacht would sail on whatever course he set, forever.

From the salon below came the fabulous Bill Evans playing the ship's Yamaha piano. If you didn't look, Evans was there in the flesh at the height of his powers. If you did look, the keys were being pressed by invisible fingers. Ayers looked away, so Bill would stay. His own saxophone was a solo act of music. But Evan's keyboard was a chart of the harmony of the spheres and a window to the mystic structure of jazz.

It was getting dark, so he went below for his instrument. As a project 20 years before he had commissioned a radio producer to remove the saxophone track from a dozen recorded standards. It was before digital and the extractions had not been entirely successful, so sometimes remnants of Charlie Parker or Coleman Hawkins remained as he performed in their place. It was like being with them, almost. He had played this horn almost every day for how long? Fifty years? As a kid in pickup bands, and then for a while pretty good, but never with a gift. A gift would have changed everything.

Number 19 was Billie Holiday, "Good Morning Heartache" of 1946, with Bobby filling in. He leaned back against the bulkhead and started the session. The opening bars were his to play, and after that she always came in.

Good morning heartache, you old gloomy sight
Good morning heartache, I thought we said goodbye last night.

He stayed under, buoying her up, not letting her fall.
I turned and tossed until it seemed like you had gone
But here you are with the dawn.

In the next riff he stopped and she went on without him. The tremor began in his right hand and moved up his arm to his shoulder. He unhooked and laid the instrument down as the salon filled with fireflies. He pressed his back against the bulkhead so as to steady the way of the ship through the sea.

Too many of Dr. Stein's pills. This is what they do, and the answer is to just stop taking them.

CHAPTER TWO

Laura

"I'm Laura," she said.

"I see that," said Eleanor Szabo through the screen door. "Come in. I made coffee."

A resemblance to her father was often cited to Laura, and often the first thing said in introductions and the most unintentionally irritating. The directedness of her speech. The controlled tension in her bearing. The absence of the smile lines that predict personality or permit interpretation. Yes, yes, yes. She bore it.

"You look like him," Eleanor said.

"I don't see it."

"Take it from me."

Laura smiled and relaxed her leather bag onto the floor. She hadn't known what to expect, although her father's first wife had been pleasant on the phone and not apparently surprised to hear from her.

"Let's make it a glass of wine."

"Gladly," Laura said.

Professor Szabo had a scholarly chair with an unpronounceable name and according to the University of

Pennsylvania math department, an international reputation in big data. She was 58, still with the welcoming features and thick, cropped hair in the two pictures of her that Laura possessed. Her old farmhouse was snug, with a scent of books and earth.

"How long have you been here?" Laura asked.

"Almost 30 years. It's a good commute, and I only teach three days now."

"I went to Penn, you know. I was class of 2004, so you were there the whole time. I never got anywhere near the statistics department though, too scary for me."

"Me too, sometimes," Eleanor said. "Now, why did you call? Bobby's not dead, I'd know that. Last I heard he might be going to jail, but I'd know that, too, if he actually went."

Laura had rehearsed this moment. She withdrew from her bag a handful of folders, opening one on her lap.

"My father has a trust, the Robert Ayers Living Trust, of which I'm the trustee, which is more or less the same as executor of a will. He named you as a beneficiary specifically included, and the lawyers feel it's a good idea for all the people named to know about his wishes for them in advance of his actual death."

"OK."

"So, he intends for you to receive approximately one-quarter of his assets, we don't know what that figure is yet but it's very substantial. And also, Eleanor, he wants you to have a certain kind of a historic car called a Lotus Esprit turbo, in the color yellow. His lawyers have to find you one, which they will do, or if you prefer, the equivalent in money. I guess, obviously, the car has some meaning, and my job is to answer questions and so on and work out the details as best we can."

"Where is he, Laura?" Eleanor said.

"Well, we don't know. He's at sea on his yacht and he hasn't checked in. It's been three months now."

"How worried are you?"

"Some. A little. A lot."

Eleanor grunted. "Listen, nobody ever knew where Bobby was until he wanted them to. He was a ghost then and he still is now. And that sports car was a piece of crap from the wrong James Bond movie—a Roger Moore James Bond movie, and I'm sure the only James Bond car with a ski rack. Do I get a ski rack?"

Laura shuffled papers. "It just says the car or equivalent—"

"You need to stay here with me tonight," Eleanor said abruptly.

"Thanks, but I already have a reservation—"

"Cancel it. The guest room's all set and the bathtub's huge. You've got a heavy load in that bag of documents and some of that weight is me. I think this is what is supposed to happen."

Laura had not had an actual bath in months. Her apartment shower was a plastic booth with mold on the curtain. She had almost missed the plane from Hartford to Philadelphia and then waited in line 90 minutes for a rental car and right now, needed to pee. This trip was her first attempt at following the crazy requirements of her father's living trust, which had turned her into an inspector general of his past against her will ever since his lawyers had dragooned her into it. She had been only vaguely aware of his first wife, to whom he now promised an antique car and a fortune. Well, here she was. And Eleanor had a bathtub.

"Thanks, I accept."

"So where is Bobby, really?"

"We don't know and I don't think he wants us to. This sailboat of his is big, he could be anywhere. Or dead, which I don't think he is."

"You know," Eleanor said, "we should have been introduced a long time ago."

"How so?"

"Did you know about me when you were at Penn?"

"Sorry, no."

"Don't be sorry. When your father visited you on campus, he stayed with me. We consulted on your courses and teachers. I kept track of you for him, wherever he was. I was your advocate, in fact. When you changed majors from business to art history he wanted to talk you out of it, but I said you were right. You didn't know me, but I knew you. I checked out your roommates, your friends, and I know why Bobby didn't tell you about us. It was spying and we knew it."

"Shit," Laura said.

"Hey, you did well. It was a pleasure knowing you. And, probably wrong."

"You and my father—stayed together? And we never met?"

"Don't be too upset. Bobby and I had history that didn't include other people. We did the best we could with it and didn't always succeed. Anyhow, he only came to visit me so he could take you out to dinner."

Laura knew then that forever she would see this woman behind every bush of her undergraduate years, that whole confused and suppressed era of eager young men, weed and Adderall, her past suddenly reclassified from Secret to Limited Distribution.

"Shit," Laura said again. "So you looked through my windows?"

"Never did that. I collected data. Believe me, data has no intrinsic meaning, I just handed it off to your father for analysis. I did go to a couple of your swim meets. You were good, but I was sort of glad when you quit. Waste of time, in my opinion. You mad?"

"Your secret, not mine," Laura said.

"So let's move on. I happen to know that your father is into the IRS for a bundle, and the case is in tax court, and he's got five or six other lawsuits against him, and where do you stand on that?"

Laura stared at her.

"Relax, I didn't dig that up, it was brought to my attention. The IRS came to me because we were married three years, and I have a security clearance so I'm in the computers. They asked about you. They think he skipped. Did he?"

"I don't know."

Eleanor leaned back in her chair. "I like Bobby as a yachtsman," she said, "in one of those hats."

"What did you tell the IRS?"

"Nothing, why make it easy for them? But expect a visit."

Distinguished Professor Szabo, now with her feet up, looked 18, third wine glass cradled in her lap. Laura liked her despite the awkward history. She was forthright, not judgmental and with a nice factor of hidden guilt about unauthorized surveillance, a guilt probably long nurtured. What was uncomfortable was the way Eleanor looked at her with what seemed to be personal interest. Weird.

"So maybe you can tell me why my father quit school like he was Bill Gates or Zuckerberg or somebody. And why he quit you. And why he quit my mother and me and all of us, no goodbyes, no nothing."

"Why anything?" Szabo said. "His father was a roofer, he had only a partial scholarship, and he thought Penn was a bad financial deal, so he walked. I wasn't there, he was three years older and already working for Mr. Sullivan when we met. Big construction business in South Jersey. I asked him, why not finish school? and he said, 'this is faster.' And he had this incredibly rapid rise from mud on his boots to black suits and meetings and phone calls all the time. Mr. Sullivan gave him a Lincoln as a company car and then a year later, he bought the yellow Lotus himself. It was all wrong for an executive in construction, and he knew it.

"Your father and I met in a laundromat. No words, just underwear tumbling. At the time I was in a study group with nerds and he was smarter than them, quicker, older, and one look was all it took for both of us. My friends were graduate students, they were impressed when he picked up the dinner tab. Every day I went to class, he went to work, and at night—well, not to gross you out, but we didn't need any other entertainment. When we got married I didn't even tell my parents. The thing was, with Bobby and me, no questions was the deal. So after the second year, with all this money coming in, he stopped coming home every night. Trouble at work. Yeah, little did I know. You're aware there is some pathology in your father?"

"My mother says he's nuts."

"Let me keep going," Eleanor said. "I met Mr. Sullivan and his family, great people, you'd think Bobby was his son. They owned all this equipment, front loaders, bulldozers. Bobby was the salesman, young guy on the way up. Of course what did I know, it's construction, it's New Jersey, it's the Mafia, right? But Bobby said it was just normal business issues. He could talk to anybody if it was business, he was the big solver. They had equipment stolen, set on fire, it was in the papers. He didn't tell me anything and I didn't ask. You look at me like that, but that's me. I am not distracted. You give me computer time in a big lab and my own project to work on and nothing else exists. I was getting my name on papers. I was doing original research. I got to go to a conference in Switzerland with two Nobels and when I came back after two weeks he was gone and cops came asking about him."

"Cops? Eleanor, what was going on?"

"It had to do with the arson going around. I didn't know anything, stupid me. That's when your father disappeared. We had $22,000 in our bank account and he didn't take any of it out. He just—went. I didn't see him again for three years, when he came back from Europe to formalize our divorce. We did that in a bed at the Morris House Hotel in Philadelphia. Signed the papers, made love, and in the morning he was gone again. I see your look."

"It just makes no sense to me."

"Anyhow, that was the end of Bobby and me until 20 years later, when you went to college. That brought him back and I was still there. I was married to a crazy Spaniard physicist who didn't understand. Bobby used to take Eduardo and me to dinner and talk about you. I said, 'Eduardo, be patient, when Laura graduates he'll be gone.' Physicists are supposed to be beyond Isaac Newton nowadays, right? They have to deal with uncertainty in the universe, right? He was Spanish, that was his problem. Bobby and I confused him."

"I imagine," Laura said.

"You want everything to make sense?"

"Yes," said Laura.

"No, you'd be disappointed."

They talked until late. At midnight Eleanor went to the bookshelves that lined the big living room. The top three tiers were Laura's father's books. They were all autobiographies of famous men. "That's all he would read," Eleanor said. "Anything he could steal from and use. He had no intellectual interest at all. He just went one success story to the next, scribbling in the margins."

Laura used a stepladder to scan the spines: Ben Franklin, Andrew Carnegie, Fred Astaire, Lowell Thomas--there were a hundred, the authors random, the pages dog-eared.

"You want them?" asked Eleanor.

"I don't have the room."

"Neither do I, anymore," Eleanor said. "I have a conference in Washington tomorrow, you can drive me to the train station. I'll wake you. Enjoy your bath."

* * *

Robert Ayers had come into Eleanor Szabo's life early, and into Laura's life late.

He arrived in the first grade, when Ed Newman sat with Laura in the classroom of her school on Parents' Day. The teacher's assistant, a young woman new to Meadow Country Day School, had knelt beside them to say, "Oh Mr. Ayers, your daughter is such fun to work with every day."

"Stepdaughter," Ed said. "I'm Newman, she's Ayers."

It was the tizzy afterward that Laura remembered: the stony face of Mrs. Utecliffe as she drew the assistant away, a nuance not lost on Laura. And the apology to Edward, made quietly but not beyond her hearing. That night she had asked her mother what a stepdaughter was.

"You, sweetheart," Julia Newman told her with a hug.

Laura called Ed Newman "Dad" until she was 13, then nothing for a few years, and by the time college came she had shifted to "Ed," which seemed natural to them all by that time.

She concluded early, from overhead remarks and casual instruction, that her real father had abandoned her and everyone else and was therefore beyond the reach of language or imagination. Ed, who was actually more attentive than most fathers, served to complete the family photographs. It worked.

On her 13th birthday, her mother and Ed invited Laura into his study to tell her that her birth father wished to meet her. By that time she knew she had one, it just never came up. However, Ed and Julia had decided that a meeting was now a good idea. They explained about what to expect, about the value of withholding judgement, about how nothing would change at home, and how this was inevitable in a good way, and how God loves every one of us equally and without discrimination for cause, including Robert Allington Ayers.

Laura recalled herself saying, "Except for the Japanese, which He killed something like 100,000 of them with Truman's atomic bomb," a topic discussed in school the day before.

"He's a good man," Ed had said. "And he's your biological dad, kiddo." To which her mother added, "Not your real dad."

In fact, Laura had already met the biological Bobby Ayers two years prior and had just come back from 10 days in Europe with him courtesy of Aunt Sarah, who believed her sister Julia to be a world-class control freak. So it was that young Laura learned the value of a secret--the power and the glory of knowing stuff other people didn't, and keeping your mouth shut about it. It was actually easier to love your mother, and to appreciate Ed, if you had a vast realm of information that they didn't, and knew they would stroke out if they knew you did.

But age 32 was not age 13.

And Eleanor Szabo, in whose bed she lay, wasn't her mother.

* * *

At 7 a.m. they were out the door, each dragging an overnight bag across the noisy gravel of the driveway, each slinging hers into the open trunk of Laura's anonymous rental car. It was raining, the Pennsylvania air thick and cold, but they kept the windows open until the highway ramp and the line of trucks required encapsulation with each other.

"Well," Eleanor said after a while, "we have something in common."

"We do." Laura said. "A hangover."

"I meant your father."

"I know what you meant."

"He always comes back this way. I go along just fine and then the phone rings, or he shows up--in this case as you."

Laura was conscious of Eleanor staring at her. It made her uncomfortable.

"You know why we really got married? To get into married student housing--a garden apartment. We weren't looking ahead, why should we? We were young and ambitious and I was flexible, as long as nothing got in my way, and Bobby didn't get in my way. I loved him for that. I loved us for being free. So naturally, I got pregnant right away."

Laura turned to find Eleanor illuminated in the head-lights of an enormous 18-wheeler overtaking them.

"Stay in your lane," Eleanor said. "I picked breakfast to tell him. I mean, why tell the guy at all, really, if you're going to do what I knew I was going to do. But I did tell him. Let me finish, Laura. And he said, 'whatever we want.' Those were his exact words, and from anybody else it's probably a cop-out but it wasn't from him. He would've been fine, I think. Whatever problems arose, he would have solved them. But of course I took care of the problem, and that was that. Nobody knew. I cried, but not much. Not enough, probably. Your father never mentioned it at all, but sometimes we'd see a young family with a kid in a stroller or something and he'd just sort of squeeze my hand. And I thought, no, don't communicate with me, I am a blackboard erased."

Laura drove through the rain, feeling herself studied. A glance showed tears streaking Eleanor's face, or perhaps it was a reflection from the streaming windows. Laura felt obliged to say something, but no something came.

There was silence for the next half hour until finally the car descended an off-ramp and Professor Szabo expertly directed Laura through confusing turns into a crowded Kiss & Ride lane. Cops gestured her forward, rain pattering on cars, until they bumped a high red curb and Eleanor sprang out towards the trunk.

Sidewalk figures hurried past, suitcase wheels rattling, raincoats swishing, as Eleanor hauled out her bag. Laura was unprepared for the suddenness by which she was pulled into the other woman's parting embrace, and unprepared to feel the tears still on her cheek. Eleanor had been beautiful. She saw what her father had seen, but felt none of it. The intimacy in the eyes and the proprietary grip on her shoulders made her uneasy.

"Do you miss your father?"

"Yes, of course." Laura said. "Looks like you do, too."

"No, I miss the half of you that could've been me," Eleanor said. "Friends, now. Keep in touch."

CHAPTER THREE

Inge-Lise

The boat had arrived in Ensenada, Mexico, before Bobby
Ayers did, transported on the deck of a ship down the
winter Atlantic shore, across the Gulf of Mexico, through
the Panama Canal and then north to its shipyard destination. When he got there *Après Vous* rested on land in an
enormous cradle, mast and boom still secured flat along
her deck and flecked with seaweed from her ignominious
piggyback voyage. Her transport wraps were torn and
ragged, and her hull still bore the jagged scars of grounding.

Ayers arrived in much better shape, which was good
news to Luis Alfaro, the boatyard manager. The shipping
of the project vessel from New York had been complicated,
with an undercurrent of mistrust caused by two pending
lawsuits. Alfaro did not have to deal with that, the boatyard owners did. And no doubt Mr. Ayers had put up a
substantial bond for the work to be done, since his yacht
was questionable collateral in its current state. There was no
doubt why he had chosen them. The yard had a reputation
for low labor prices compared to San Diego, which was

true. What signified more was that Alfaro's teams were good at their jobs. Mexicans took pride in their skills, and the yachting community gave them respect in turn. It was why they brought their boats here.

It took a month for Sr. Alfaro to fully adjust himself to the nature of the client. Mr. Ayers was lodged in a good hotel on the embarcadero, dined at the best restaurants, and was well known to be a famous millionaire. He was recognized by the women as an *hidalgo*, a gentleman in the old sense, because of his formality of dress and bearing. He used fewer words than most of the Americans. Even so, he did not descend immediately to the point or issue or demand, as everybody did these days, but greeted you first with his eyes. The voluntary exchange of respect was unusual. Usually you had to beg for it.

Mr. Ayers was at the yard every morning with his big iPhone. The iPhone had on it that day's jobs, their progress and materials, which they worked out together. As yard manager, that was actually Alfaro's job, and at first sharing it had made him uneasy. But not for long. The American was responsive to input. You checked over his lists and if you said it wouldn't work, he amended or made a deletion as you watched. The workers loved him. Here was a client who understood procedures, instead of just shouting. All disappointments of schedule fell on Alfaro, of course, but behind his office door. Mr. Ayers did not betray a manager to his workers. For once, yard and owner worked together—a miracle. Alfaro knew this to be the fruit of Mr. Ayers' long experience in the construction trades, where he had gained not just knowledge of schedules and supply, but of the power of *respeto* to move men. Respect. When Luis Alfaro got some, he gave it back.

Mr. Ayers was a millionaire, and nobody at the yard had ever seen one with work gloves on. It was worrisome, yes, that the client knew as much about what was going on with his boat as he did. So Alfaro had concluded they were partners. There were lines not to be crossed, and both knew them. In the end, it was about the boat, and if the boat was on schedule Luis could keep his job. Which was far from secure.

Sometimes they disagreed. After the first month, when the mast had been painted but was not yet fully cured, Alfaro had resisted installing it. Mr. Ayers listened, and said, "Let's put the mast in the boat today." Alfaro had stood his ground. He was emphatic in his warning that the paint job could be ruined. The American had nodded, and said again, "Let's put the mast in the boat today," this time in English. His Spanish was pretty good, but Alfaro had learned that when this client spoke in English it was no longer a consultation. The work crews figured that out, too. In fact, Alfaro began giving his own commands in English, because they hopped to faster and without the usual impertinent familiarities.

So the mast went in that day, and did suffer a few scrapes, but nothing that couldn't be touched up. Millionaires are all in a hurry, Alfaro told his wife that night.

"That's why they're millionaires and you're not," she said.

* * *

That November in the pleasant seaside town of Ensenada there were half a dozen yachting families awaiting preparation of their boats for the "puddle jump," the long cruise to the islands of the South Pacific and beyond. They recognized each other immediately as a complement of like souls whose numbers changed but whose goals were the same, and found themselves dining together, drinking together and exchanging precious information, every piece of which was filed in a learning bank as insurance against disaster. The bond bound remarkably disparate crews. There was the O'Connell family of Morro Bay, headed around the world on a thick-waisted cruising ketch: Father, mother, and three sons aged five, seven and 10. A near gale on the sail down had broken half their tired gear but not their spirits. They walked arm in arm—all of them—in Hawaiian shirts and flip flops, although the climate a mere 60 miles south of San Diego was that of winter, by local standards.

There was "Ford," a 25-year-old eccentric on a wooden folkboat, his mast bare wood and his steering gear made out of the old automobile parts by which he got his name. And to whom Ayers slipped $200, so he could eat. Hank and Sherry were a quiet couple with two cats who were readying their Catalina 44 sloop for paradise. She was the sailor and he was, as he put it, along for the ride. Subsequent familiarity revealed Hank's pocket Constitution, doubts about global warming, and a strong belief that real estate, which he had formerly sold, was intended by God only for the worthy. Others came and went: sport fishermen bound for the fertile banks offshore, retirees checking out Baja California as a place to live cheap, crazy surfers hoping to ride the gigantic waves on the seamount 100 miles offshore, and a 55-foot Beneteau sailboat crewed by three Swedish couples and a Dane named Inge-Lise Sorenson.

They took meals together, played cards together and studied weather maps together. They discussed charts, sailing directions, notices to mariners, satellite phones, Grib files, watermakers, halyard chafe, gale procedures, solar panels, ampere hours and all the many challenges promised by what would be 6,000 miles at sea, for those intending Fiji, or 23,000 miles for Ford, who was bound around the world.

Ayers was student and teacher. Each night, as they came together at the Cantina del Mar, new possibilities were argued. Perhaps it was not necessary to sail first to the Galapagos Islands, 600 miles off the coast of Ecuador, before on to the South Seas. Perhaps it was best to head directly for the Marquesas. But why was it necessary to rush? Why not spend a year in the Sea of Cortez a mere 1500 miles south, reputed a wonderland of marlin and unspoiled beaches. Yet they must make Tahiti by summer, and then Fiji or Samoa by September, before the cyclone season set in. Their yachts were going nowhere at the moment, because the boatyard was behind schedule and new gear, once ordered, took a very long time to arrive. Time seemed to stop. What was the rush, they were already cruising. Life was good.

When Tom from Whangarei passed through, New Zealand became the topic for a week. He was a dashing traveler with only a backpack whose mother had an avocado and passionfruit ranch there. They would all meet again in Whangarei by Christmas next year, all their boats bobbing at anchor in Town Basin. Tom slept boat to boat, or on any floor handy, and then one day he was gone. The armada of group imagination then altered course to Nuku Hiva, in the Marquesas island chain. That was where Bobby Ayers said Melville had gone and left a path for all to follow. The potential destinations were endless. Pick a place on the watery chart of the world. Getting there was just a matter of a well-found yacht and the confidence that comes of thinking it through. Often they retired to their rooms after such long and encouraging colloquies more certain than ever that paradise was in sight.

One night, after such an evening, Inge-Lise Sorenson followed Ayers back to his suite.

* * *

She was in her 50s, hair short and graying, with a complexion of mating freckles under fine lines that enhanced unblinking hazel eyes. She and Ayers had sat at the group table for weeks, never side by side, and among the voluble complement of the Cantina they had talked the least of all. She was one of seven aboard the Beneteau, the yacht owned by her old friends Max and Claudia. Aside from one overnight sail on the Baltic, Inge-Lise had never been offshore. But the Beneteau was a comfortable boat, and her hosts liked good company. Which she was.

Ayers paused at the stairwell of his hotel, sensing her behind him. She wore a yellow foul-weather tunic wet from the light rain outside.

"Hi," said Ayers, who knew she wasn't staying in his hotel. It was almost 11 o'clock.

"Do you have a moment that I could ask you questions?" Inge-Lise said. There was no place to sit in the hotel foyer.

"Come up," said Ayers.

His suite was the largest of the hotel. It had a large sitting area, a sort-of kitchen, a bedroom with balcony overlooking the harbor. They hung their jackets on wooden pegs behind the door. Ayers offered beer and tequila. She asked for water. He poured two glasses of Perrier and gestured for her to sit down. She chose a hard chair.

"You have a really big boat," Inge-Lise said. "And lovely. Built in Europe?"

He smiled. "New Jersey."

She nodded so politely that he laughed.

"It's a Ted Hood design, or it was until it got wrecked in a hurricane. We're just finishing the rebuild and it's been a long project, but I enjoy projects. How's it on the Beneteau? You sailed down from San Francisco, isn't that right?"

She nodded. "Even with a new boat there were some problems. The watermaker, the engine alignment. Not my problems, I'm just a guest. I don't know a lot, but I'm learning."

"We all are," Ayers said.

"You will be with us on the puddle jump, right?" Ayers liked the way she said "puddle jump," as if it were out of a children's book. The slight accent helped. She wore wool, not the typical fleece, and he could smell its dampness. Her wrists were smooth, jointing hand to arm like the fine woodworking he admired. Her Topsiders were soaked.

"What route will you take?" This had come up a lot, and Ayers had never committed to a destination, in group conversation at least.

"Not sure. What do you think?"

"I am in favor of the Galapagos route," she said emphatically. "My reasons are that if you go there, you see what Charles Darwin saw, which isn't to be missed. And then, the trade winds carry you to Nuku Hiva. And on west from there, as far as you want to. Tahiti. Australia. Ford is going all the way around the world, he says."

Ford, with his homemade wind vane, struck Ayers as unlikely to make it through tomorrow, much less around Cape Horn. His charts were Xeroxed and his navigation system was a cell phone.

"Good, he can lead us all," Ayers said.

"He's almost an idiot, I think," she said, looking down.

Ayers burst out laughing, which startled her. He rose and walked to his bathroom.

"Don't you think that?" said Inge-Lise, standing up herself.

From the bathroom Ayers brought a clean white towel. He gestured for her to sit down. He bent and placed the towel at her feet.

"Dry off, wet feet are no fun. And I have some good Hennessy. I don't think there's any heat at all in this hotel."

He poured the brandy into monogrammed hotel glassware as she pulled off her wet socks and scrubbed her feet with the towel. He watched as she did a sitting dance, slapping both feet as if to pound life and warmth back into them. Then, after a swig of the brandy, she took three steps toward the bathroom and hurled the wet towel 20 feet expertly into a hidden corner.

"Really, how far are you going, Robert?" Inge-Lise asked. Everyone else called him Bobby. That was how he introduced himself, and always had.

"I haven't decided."

"You might go all the way around, though?"

"Am I being interviewed?" Ayers said. His questions were often rhetorical. It kept some people at arm's length, but not Inge-Lise.

"Yes, you are being interviewed. I am going to school on you. I have decided I need to learn the jobs on a boat. I don't want to be just a supernumerary, I want to be a real crew person. I didn't know that before, but now it seems wrong just to be along for the ride."

"Good."

"You're a singlehander, OK." She sat straight in her chair, bare feet under her. "You have a self-steerer, you don't need a crew. But what is the appeal? I guess that there are no people." She laughed. "But there are seven of us on the Beneteau, and they're my good friends, and we get along well, and we talk over everything. I like the night watches with a different person every night, and seeing the sun come up together and cooking the meals and so on. I wouldn't like to be alone, especially when we had a gale off San Francisco on the way down and I was seasick. So, as a singlehander, why do it? Help me understand. I don't ask you at the dinners because it is a little bit intimate, but I would like to know. My captain, Max, says your boat is supposed to have a big crew, and even our boat is a lot of work for us, so how does it work? How do you sleep? Or maybe I shouldn't ask this, tell me."

"I don't foresee problems," he said.

"It takes two of us just to pull the mainsail up!" she said, challenging.

"*Après Vous* has electric winches," Ayers replied. "Also, electric steering, with another whole back-up unit. Electric foresails and reefing. Bow thrusters for docking. Power windlass for the chain and the anchor. Redundant radar, satellite TV, weather forecasts. A piano. A custom circular staircase being built in Italy right now, if it ever gets finished in time. So you see, it's all taken care of. The boat does the work, I'm just the supervisor, and in my world one boss is all you need."

"I'd be lonely," she said without emphasis.

"How do you know?"

"I think I would be."

"Having a lot of people around doesn't solve that."

"No, of course not."

"So maybe you wouldn't be," he said. Ayers reached for a bag on the floor and withdrew a battered volume. "This guy, a Frenchman, Bernard Moitessier, sailed with people and also alone." He handed her the book. "He was alone when he sailed around the world, and when he got to the end of his circumnavigation he started around all over again. He found something out there. He talks about it better than I can."

He watched as she turned pages, bent over. Curiosity in others was seldom of use to Ayers, and he preferred his own. Curiosity without real interest was prattle from which he abruptly fled. Fast reader, he noticed. It had been a while since he had been alone with anybody, and although there were good reasons for that he recognized himself as out of practice. He had been watching Inge-Lise for weeks across tables and while walking in groups or poring over laptops as they ordered gear and scoured their combined knowledge of maintenance, preparation and anticipation. He had collected her information automatically: the easy walk, boyish hips, curve of breasts, the haircut that looked homemade but probably cost $300. Her teeth were slightly snaggled. She was attached to her friends but unattached to any man of them. She no doubt saw him as a puzzle to be solved. Good, he liked being a puzzle and took pains to be one. Yes, for weeks he had observed her. Now, he looked at her. He saw that she fit in, and had a place.

"Can I take this?" she said.

"Sure. There're lots of books, Chichester and Slocum and the Johnsons—" She was looking for a pencil, but he stopped her hand. "One at a time. Anyway, we're not like them and we don't have to be. Sailing is much easier with modern gear. And look, we'll all stick together across the ocean. We'll see each other on the radar, we'll talk every day on our satellite phones, we'll share the weather information. They call it a puddle jump, and the distances are far but I don't see it as anybody being alone. We'll all make the crossing together."

"I think to have your mind set on something is the appeal," she said.

They finished the brandies at the same time.

"You know as much as I do," he said.

"I doubt it, Robert. But I will learn."

She put her wet socks in her pocket and slipped into her shoes. She rose and took her weather jacket off the peg. The room was cold and the light from the bulbs harsh. It was after midnight. Ayers put his glass on the counter and his hand on the doorknob. He was close to her, the wool and her scent.

"Stay here tonight."

"I don't think so," Inge-Lise said pleasantly. "Thanks for the book."

Ayers nodded and helped her into the wet jacket.

She went out the door and down the corridor. Ayers poured another brandy and reviewed the yard schedule for the next day, with attention to the replacement of the hydraulics for the steering system, and when he got into bed the sheets were clammy. His last thoughts were of incompatible fittings, because if the new hydraulic lines wouldn't connect it would be a month before new ones could be shipped in by DHA, with a good chance they would never reach Mexico at all.

He turned the lights out and was asleep in less than a minute, satisfied that progress was being made.

* * *

The hydraulic lines did fit together. The work was in the cramped engine room, where Ayers was in the way. Luis Alfaro was proving to be a good foreman, so when satisfied that the schedule would be met Ayers slipped away out the unguarded gate at the end of the yard and followed the muddy path to town. The rain had stopped and the first hint of a wind from the desert was in the air, purifying it. His destination was a bodega owned by Sr. Schultz, a heavy man whose father had been a German hippie, or anarchist, depending on who you asked. Ayers sat on a bench outside his store, eating a churro and waiting for the boys to come home from school. Sr. Schultz did not approach him. Each week he got a $100 bill, almost a whole day's receipts, for not bothering the millionaire with questions.

When five kids appeared in the alley they waved in recognition and Ayers ambled after them, tossing the churro wrapper in a can. They traversed a number of alleys to a small warehouse with a padlock on the door, which Ayers opened with a key. In the dim light inside, Mikey Garcia, age 13, took from a peg on the wall a clipboard and a stub of pencil and brought it to him.

On the clipboard was a printout of foodstuffs imported and local. Ayers compared the boxes to the lists of stores. Most of it had come through Schultz's bodega, bags of rice and beans and canned specialties from *pozole* to *menudo* and scores of guavas, papaya, mango and the sweet milk caramel his flan required. The piles slowly rose each week as the boys moved new boxes in. They did a good job, and quietly. On Fridays each was paid his fee by Mikey, as Ayers watched. On Friday they also all counted the bottles of beer, of which there were 288, and the 30 liters of whisky, and especially the two bottles of Courvoisier, each in a rosewood box. Each boy was required to touch each bottle as they counted, so the ritual took quite a while. If any were missing, the employment would end. The counting was a game, and when the counts agreed there were high fives all around. And when not, they had to start over. Bobby Ayers liked watching them count.

Security had been arranged by Sr. Schultz through his wife's brother, a policeman who had agreed to assure the sanctity of the warehouse, declaring that a matter of civic pride quite apart from the weekly compensation.

This day, Ayers brought Sr. Schultz a new order, many pages long, for review. Schultz, reading it, said it might present certain questions at the customs house. What questions? Mainly questions about the pheasant and the elk medallions and the Kobe beef from Japan, which Sr. Schultz said his bodega clientele rarely or seldom or never ordered, or even knew existed. Ayers stared at him for longer than he had ever been stared at, so long that he wondered if maybe the millionaire was having a seizure or something. But he didn't want to say anything wrong, so he just waited. He didn't bring up money. In fact, nobody knew where the money for this stuff came from, it was all prepaid before it arrived on the DGH from the border or from the airport. His wife did not like the requirement for such discretion. She worried that *el gran hombre* Mr. Ayers was a child molester, luring boys into warehouses. Including his own son! But Mr. Ayers was not like that, assuredly. He was a businessman, except that unlike other businessmen you didn't have to wait forever to get paid.

"OK, then, no problem," Schultz said, concluding that customs had been taken care of. Ayers then removed his hand from the bodega counter to reveal a fan of hundred-dollar bills. Schultz discretely removed them as two women with shopping carts walked in. "When is this shipment coming?" Schultz asked, lowering his voice.

"The boys will know," said Ayers. "Now let me have a *piña*."

Schultz smiled broadly and snatched from a tub of ice a colorful bottle of pineapple soda. The women who were watching the rich American smiled.

"No charge, señor!" Schultz said theatrically, popping the cap off with a flourish.

Ayers took a swig, nodded gracefully to the ladies, and glided out the door. Such a handsome rich American.

That they all should shop local, is it not true, Sr. Schultz?

That they all definitely should, Sr. Schultz agreed.

* * *

The rains continued, slowing the work on the boats. Time slowed too. The earliest departure for the South Seas was the month of January, and so there was no rush. The rush the puddle-jumpers had felt upon their scattered arrivals had given way at first to impatience, then acceptance and eventually to the recognition that their dream had already begun, here in this semi-exotic Mexican port.

So, they relaxed. They had read about the camaraderie of the cruising life and now it was all around them. Without a job working for somebody else, their only job was the planning and execution of their own dream. Life was a few things to do each day, and even those few things were not altogether necessary because, it turned out, the day progressed anyway, lunch and dinner arrived as usual, and then sleep came, and another day. The clock moved at its own pace. You couldn't slow it down or speed it up. That was a revelation.

Captain Max of the Beneteau had the idea to go horseback riding on the beach. They hired a bus to Rosarito for riding and dinner. The expedition was a success, and Ayers picked up the tab. They toured the local wine country, which was a far cry from Napa or Provence, but interesting in its own way. They flew drones and watched the footage of themselves. They went to the movies and on hikes together. Their organizing principle was to form and reform according to who felt like doing what, who was not working on their boat that day, who was available for bridge or for trading paperbacks or for just watching TV. They took care of each other's comfort and education. They gave Ford a can of deodorant. Max gave him a haircut and then presented him with the clippers, saying that by the time he had sailed around the world he'd need them again.

The crews noted the changes in each other. It was obvious now that two of the couples on Max's boat, which was Inge-Lise's boat, found each other a bumpy road. They moved into separate hotels and sat at opposite ends of restaurant tables. Perceptions of Hank and Sherry, the cat owners, evolved 180 degrees: opinionated Hank was now universally recognized as a 240-pound servant to his wife, bashfully obedient, corrected at every turn, and led by the hand as if blind. He questioned universal health care, but not her. The O'Connells, after six weeks, put their boat up for sale and took their three sons back to Morro Bay without goodbyes or explanation. The visiting American fishermen never seemed to fit in. Too drunk. The packs of dirt bikers arriving to crash the Baja deserts were compatible and oddly well behaved, although when they roared off at dawn it woke everybody up. Ford's boat sank at the dock, with him in it. Faulty toilet valve. Ford pumped the boat out, had the toilet removed, and used a bucket.

With one exception, Ayers remained as he had at first meeting. He still wore his suits and expensive shoes all day, and only at dinner changed to casual. He was helpful, generous, friendly and distant. Googling him didn't help much. He had been a developer of malls and hotels internationally. His Wikipedia entry was short and drab, citing no wives or children or university and footnoted with articles in French and German. The Chicago Tribune called him "the $60 Million Man." Forbes, "a roofer's son out to roof the world." Quoted in a Guardian article about offshore tax shelters he said that United States policy was to steal the pennies off a dead man's eyes. Wikipedia had frozen his entry after a two-year edit war.

The exception was Inge-Lise Sorenson. Everybody knew she and Bobby were a thing but nobody mentioned it. She wasn't chatty and he would just stare you down. The only obvious change was that they now sat next to each other in the restaurants. And she smiled more.

Claudia, her best friend, went on and on about her, as best friends do. Inge-Lise had had been vice president of VIP Services at Braniff for many years. She was Wonder Woman. She had endured and flourished. She had set the form for executive women all over Europe. She was a role model. She was a fashion model. Look at her waist. Her hips. Look at her skin, which seemed to glow more every day, a reference to Bobby Ayers that the others let pass.

Inge-Lisa would listen and correct. True, at her retirement dinner she had been declared *wunderbar hochwirksam und sympathisch* by her boss, the same boss who had tried to pull her clothes off in an Uber the night before. She had been *wonderfully effective* at stopping him, but not *sympathetic* to his needs at all. The greatest fame of her employment had been the emergency diversion of a charter flight to a remote farmhouse in Bavaria so Paris Hilton could pee—and then discovering the toilet seat for sale on eBay the next day. Yes, she had been a model—but only of gloves and wristwatches, as Claudia well knew but always forgot to mention. For 20 years Claudia had been bugging her to get her teeth fixed. Well, it's not too late, honey.

The puddle jumpers stuck together because the biggest threat to long-distance cruisers, they had all heard, was not sticking together. They needed each other, but in close quarters as time dragged it made sparks. When the crew of her yacht came almost to blows, Inge-Lise was shaken.

That was the first night she stayed with Robert. They talked in his room until after midnight. That is, she talked and he listened. They avoided the past, as was their habit. The present was plenty. She had finished four of his offshore sailing books and could now discuss steering gear and weather files and why coating eggs in Vaseline preserved them, unrefrigerated. The scene in the restaurant—a platter of shrimp had been thrown—stayed with her. It brought back memories of her own partings and their challenge to assuage and forgive. Ayers listened. She woke next to him in bed at 3 a.m., his leg over hers, aware she had been snoring. So she had a lover again. A light was still on. She turned to see that Ayers had been watching her sleep. She overcame a weightless feeling of contentment and safety and took his hand where it lay on her stomach.

"I am thinking about something, Robert, can I tell you?"

"Sure," he said.

"I would like to see your boat. You showed me the outside, but I would like to see the inside, where you'll live.

"It's not ready. We're still working on it."

"I know that."

He laughed and kissed her. "It's a big mess, crates and junk and sawdust and paint and wires and five guys drilling and hammering and a plastic radio playing mariachi music over the chop saws."

She put her nose against his.

"I want to see it."

"OK," Ayers said.

"Tomorrow."

"OK."

"And you know why."

When he nodded she sat up, legs crossed under her.

"You know that my shipmates are getting along terrible. It's not going to work, they will never survive the voyage. The boat is owned by Max and Claudia, but the others are paying a share. I don't pay, I'm a guest. Already on the night watches coming down here, before I knew anything, there was tension.

"About you not paying?"

"No, Claudia calls it unbalancing."

"How?"

"The friendships are unbalanced.

"Say what you mean."

"All right, one of them thinks her husband looks at me. And yes, he does. But worse is that in our group I'm never wrong. I am listened to, the cocktail is made for me first, even Claudia notices it. I'm trapped between these marriages, I'm like ammunition for people to use against each other. Oh, I could explain much better in French—"

He kissed her.

"OK, tomorrow we'll go aboard."

"Stop. Robert, you know you have a lot of space and I am only seven stone 10 and I will fit very well. I'm strong for a woman and I know things now. I know how to make a rolling hitch and a bowline and I am familiar with reefing. All I need is experience. I know how to work and I can cook better than you can and you like me, right? Therefore, I want to come on your boat, and get off the boat I am on. Well?"

"Good idea. I had the same idea myself."

"No you didn't, I had to ask."

"I was waiting for the time."

"And I will get off at the first stop if we get tired of each other," she said.

"OK."

"There," she said. "I asked you and you said yes or you had to say yes, and so that's it. I will tell Claudia and Max tomorrow that I'm changing boats. They'll be relieved, I think."

"Come here," Ayers commanded, opening his arms.

"No thank you. Sleep when you can, that's what you always say. Right now you can, I can't."

She bounded off the bed, pulled on Ayers' heavy robe, lifted Adlard Coles' "Heavy Weather Sailing" off the night table and disappeared into the living room, closing the bedroom door behind her.

Ayers could sleep. He lived in the present, and the present was where he wanted to be.

CHAPTER FOUR

Maurice

Laura returned to the Hartford airport in a grey drizzle. She picked out Maurice easily as he approached among the ranks of cars in the parking lot. He was six feet four inches tall, and all the more noticeable with The Wall Street Journal spread over his head. As a rain cell descended he dashed in a sprint toward Baggage Claim. She gave him time to notice her, jettison his wet paper and smooth his head with one hand. An admirable figure with a purposeful stride. But, wet.

They embraced and he led her to his car, which was aromatic with leather preservative. An Audi, it was. Or a Mercedes. One of them, anyway.

"So, how was it?" Maurice asked.

"OK, if you like paying $700 round trip."

"You value your time," he said.

They rode to dinner in silence, which was him reading her mood. He was good at it. He accelerated rapidly in accordance with the powerful engine, but then leveled off for passenger comfort. Pretty thoughtful, since the guy loved to drive fast. She was not hungry, but accompanied him to luncheon at Szechuan Palace where he wolfed down a plate of deep fried seafood with flashing chopsticks and talked. A new possible client. A survey of their near, middle and far futures together, realistic but general enough not to cause friction. The debatable value of houses as investments, which she was too tired to debate. Maurice lived in Hartford. She lived in Fairfield, 50 miles away. He frequently drove them back and forth, a two-hour round trip.

"I'll drop you at my place and tonight we can watch a movie."

"I need to get to my mother's house for dinner."

"Julia will understand. Stay over and we'll go out tomorrow night and I'll take you back Saturday morning."

So she did. On the phone her mother not only understood but was pleased, which was irritating. Julia liked Maurice. Julia thought Maurice was God. Julia would be happy to plan their wedding without Laura at all if, well, whatever.

The apartment of Maurice Charles was a second-floor walk-up in what had once been a fire station, and to which entry was made by a broad stairway adjoined by a historic ladder truck on display. His rooms occupied the entire top floor of the structure, and except for a large bedroom at either end was entirely open. Couches faced a central fireplace from which radiated freestanding bookcases demarking dining and kitchen areas. The movie he had selected was black and white and Russian, and she was asleep with her head on his lap before the third subtitle.

* * *

In the morning he made eggs and sausage, delivered with a lingering kiss on her neck.

"Sex tonight," Laura said. Maurice was a morning person and this morning she was not. He accepted the delay with aplomb and turned it to advantage, the next subject being delicate.

"I think you should tell your mother that the will has changed and her share is reduced," he said, sinking easily into a chair. "You're in charge, but it was his idea. I think what works in awkward situations is to get stuff out of the way so that later on people don't feel like there was a time when, you know, looking back, they got blindsided or something. You're just following your father's instructions, and we all know he's complicated. So, defuse it, right? Put everybody on the same page, especially Julia. She'll support you, and the more forthcoming you are the easier it is for everybody." Maurice was in the insurance business. Or, specifically, the re-insurance business. And also, with her, the reassurance business.

"Meh," Laura said.

"OK," he said. "We won't talk about it. Time for me to go to work."

She kissed him and adjusted the $200 necktie she had provided when they first met. "Go forth and flourish."

That night they made love, which by being scheduled with time to anticipate was sexier than if spontaneous during breakfast, which proved she was getting old. She wasted all day Friday reading job ads and writing half-interested emails before Maurice took her to dinner with his master-of-the-universe friends in Hartford, and then Saturday morning drove her back to Fairfield.

The Connecticut landscape outside the car passed like a black and white Russian movie. In summer, this familiar route was verdant walls of trees that turned roadways into veins in a universal organism. In winter, as now, it was gray bones of trees rising from the dead land. Vegetable myth, sure, that explained it all. In spring, it would all come back in green resurrection. When she was a kid the seasons had come one at a time, always new. Now they repeated like a looped cat video on YouTube. The hum of the tires. The drone of NPR. Thirty-two years old. How will the seasons look when she was 40, or 50. Or really old. She looked at Maurice, who had come into her life the Christmas before last. Large, amazing, two-year-old Maurice.

The car stopped in the driveway 20 miles later. "Thanks for the ride," she said. Their goodbyes were shortened by the sound of her mother coming across the gravel. Maurice unfolded from his vehicle to greet her.

"Hi Julia." They embraced.

"You're lovely to drive her all the way back every time, and Laura knows it."

"It's our time to talk," Maurice said.

"She talks? Lucky you."

Maurice was already pulling the overnight bag out of his trunk.

"Can you stay?" Julia said.

"Gotta go," Maurice said with peck at her cheek. Backing out, he was already on the phone. Mother and daughter crunched up the driveway together, the wheels of Laura's overnight bag dragging trenches behind them.

"How was Philadelphia?"

"It was fine."

"Would you have to move there?"

"It was just a job interview, mom. They have to see and I have to see and we'll all have to see."

"I'm just wondering what Maurice has to say about you moving 200 miles away."

"I'm not, because it probably won't happen," Laura said. "Is there any word from dad?"

"If there was, you'd get it first."

"Not necessarily."

"Believe me, Laura, this is just what he does. He likes people to worry. Don't sit waiting for the phone to ring. By the way, did you invite him to your wedding?"

Laura said nothing.

"Well, you two have your little secrets. Fine with me. I'm willing to share you and I guess Maurice is, too. And I'm used to living out on the end of a tree limb never knowing anything that's going to happen next or be able to plan for it. And—look at you, standing there, and I don't have a clue. You say nothing."

It had been like this always, with her mother: a need, a demand, for transparency, for pure connection in a mother-daughter dream of shared time, of shoulder-bumping holidays, of grandchildren running in summer grass, as if family had an endless umbilicus capable of oxygenating parent and child across the decades. Did it? Should it? Anyway, their current relationship was in most ways the best it ever had been, certainly better than those high-school years of foot-stomping and the armistice of college. Now there was Facebook and Instagram and email, instruments of diplomacy available to assuage misunderstanding. Laura rarely knew what daughterly crimes she had committed until afterwards. Then she set about repairs as best she could.

"Laura?"

In response, she enveloped her mother in her arms and held her immobile. It felt good.

Julia said in her ear, "I'm not bugging you. I just love you."

"Me too," Laura said.

"So listen, what's really up? How can you keep your apartment without a job? Can you move in with Maurice? Did you ask him?"

Laura just smiled at her.

"I don't know why God gave me ears," Julia said. "Come on, then, I'll make us lunch."

* * *

That evening, when Julia and Ed went to a fundraiser in Stamford, Laura carried a bottle of Sancerre and a glass up to her mother's bedroom. Then she went back down to the laundry room and got a stepladder. The stepladder was necessary to draw down the eight banker boxes from the high shelves of Julia's Closet #3, which had missed the latest remodel and so remained dusty and poorly lit. The boxes contained green hanging folders repeatedly reorganized over the years. Inside were pounds and pounds of snapshots of herself, negatives included, from the world before digital. She spread them out on the table in the adjoining sewing room, lingering more than she intended. In them she was a beautiful child. The child progressed in the albums from tricycle to bicycle to behind the wheel of Ed's TR-3, the Sunday-only sports car in which he had taught her to drive a manual transmission. Boyfriends appeared, their names imprinted on her memory like tattoos. That bikini she still had somewhere, probably. Ed in a beard she'd forgotten. A thousand pictures of her mother, all of them flattering. None at all of Bobby Ayers. Those were in a secret metal box under the cellar stairs which she had discovered at age 16, and from which she had purloined a dozen she liked. The souvenirs of her own past meant little to Laura—team rosters, swim medals, party invitations, foreign currency from family trips. Those memories were Julia's, not hers. Ah, here was a draft of her college application essay. It was "Laura" applying to Plato's Academy, and as Cicero's student in Rome, and to Aquinas for admission to a medieval university, and to Mount Holyoke Female Seminary in 1835. The ironic tour of women applicants through the centuries had been her own idea, and it had worked for three of her six target schools. Nice job, her father had said, but unnecessary. She already had had a "mortal lock," as he called it, on Penn, the result of his campaign of annual giving since her birth. She had then browbeat him with her GPA, national merit scholarship, swim championships and overall personal sufficiency until he backed off and wished he'd never opened his mouth. But Penn it had been, deserved or not. She put her mother's files back where they were stored. She was stalling, and knew it.

Most of the bottle of wine was gone before Laura drew down the last box, alphabetized "S-W". There she found what she was looking for: the Last Will and Testament of Robert Ayers. It was dated 12 years before and left his entire estate to Mrs. Julia Newman, formerly Ayers, to dispose of as Julia pleased. Their daughter Laura, still in school at the time, was to be taken care of in the best judgement of her mother.

The lawyers had warned Laura that there was probably a former will now rendered obsolete by the new Ayers Living Trust. She made sure all the storage boxes looked undisturbed, wondering if her mother had any idea how fast fortunes can change.

CHAPTER FIVE

Parting

After weeks of new intimacy with Inge-Lise, Bobby Ayers disappeared. She looked for him at lunch, but he was often at the boat at that time, or in one of the work sheds. When he missed dinner that night no one else noticed. But she did, given their new status as lovers with discretion, and the agreement that she would sign aboard as crew when the time came. Broaching the request had caused her uncharacteristic hesitation. The resolution had been clean and sure, and Robert had not mentioned it again. Now it seemed to lack confirmation. She wondered if she had made one of her mistakes of boldness.

The front desk of Ayers' Ensenada hotel was manned by a small, formal man who had seen Inge-Lise come and go several times and each time failed to smile. At noon of the second day of the disappearance she approached him in a businesslike manner, set her purse on the floor, and asked if Mr. Ayers were in his room. The man thought not. She asked when he might return. The man suggested calling him on his cellular phone. She had done that, she explained: the issue related to a birthday dinner than evening to which Mr. Ayers was invited, and for which his attendance was unconfirmed. The clerk dialed his room, waited, and hung up. No answer, *señorita*.

Inge-Lise examined his impassive face. At 51 years old she was *señora*, not *señorita*. The choice of address could be flattery or commentary. She thought it probably related to the clerk having observed her following Mr. Ayers up the stairs many times after dinner and then returning down the stairs alone at midnight to return to her own hotel. Perhaps the clerk now saw her as an intruder upon his guest—a prior affection now cooled. So she just turned and walked up the stairs without looking back.

Suite 204-5, Ayers' suite, was down a hall and around a crooked corner that projected toward the sea. She had not been there in daylight, and noticed the runner worn threadbare and the walls to be of an uninviting ochre. There was a smell of cooking oil. Turning the corner she came to his door and found on it a heavy brass padlock of the type common at the boatyard, which was vulnerable to pilferage. The hasp was newly installed. No sense knocking, so she returned to the front desk.

"Has Mr. Ayers changed to a better hotel?"

The small man straightened.

"Of course not. His suite is the best in the city." Then, archly: "as I think you have seen."

"Why is there a padlock on the door? Do you have robbers?"

She leaned in, bringing her face close to his, an invasion of space only a *gringa* would dare. To regain the offensive the clerk withdrew from a drawer a sheet of guest stationery upon which a single line was written in black marker. He spread it in front of her, pinning it to the counter with both hands.

It said, "Out of town on business, will return in 2-3 days. R. Ayers."

"Thank you," Inge-Lise said, picking up her bag. And as she turned, "Make sure no one tampers with the lock."

By dinner that night Ayers' absence was known and every member of their group, even the tourist girl currently hanging on Ford's arm, had asked her where Bobby was. So much for discretion. Out of town for a few days, she explained, adding unnecessarily that he had business to attend to, and even more unnecessarily that he had said they should all carry on without him. She noticed that the dissention aboard her former boat had eased, and the warring couples seemed on good terms again. Well, she was on Robert's boat, now. However, that plan, so firm in her mind for weeks, was now not so firm after all.

For the next two days, Inge-Lise read books and watched blurry TV and confined herself to one glass of wine and a salad for dinner. She evaluated her time with Robert, which had been day-to-day, exciting, careful and with no strings attached—although agreeing to take her aboard was certainly not trivial. She had pushed, but not hard. He had agreed that her plan made sense. She was surprised to feel it likely now that the whole thing was off. She was surprised to find that she was not in fact surprised.

At dawn on the third day of Ayers' disappearance came a call from Claudia. Before Inge-Lise answered it she saw smoke through her window. Claudia said the boatyard was on fire. By 6 a.m. they were all there, watching the fire brigades setting up. At the head of the marine railway where boats were launched a machinery shed burned intensely, fed by drums of fuel. They watched as burning diesel flowed like a mountain stream off the bulkhead, falling into the harbor and still flaming on the surface of the water. The fire had already spread to the wooden sheds where the panga fishing boats were serviced. Its tin roof bulged over jets of fire visible through the windows. There wasn't much wind and it was cold and there was nothing to do but watch as the firemen hosed down adjoining structures. Columns of smoke rose straight up. The scene resisted belief as if a dream, as if it happened every night but the familiar buildings were all magically returned to normal each morning. Not this morning. Then Claudia tugged Inge-Lise's arm and when she turned Robert was standing next to her.

He looked terrible. His face was pale and he was bleeding from a shaving cut on his chin. He had dressed hurriedly, the belt of his cashmere overcoat twisted in the back and his hands stuffed deep in its pockets. He put his shoulder against hers.

"Well, this ain't good," he said.

"Robert! My God, were you in the fire? You're shaking!"

She peered at his face as she pulled him close.

"No, I'm fine. I just got back in town, I've only had a few hours' sleep. When did it start?"

She told him what she knew, which wasn't much, and in a few hours the blaze was substantially out. Ayers' yacht was in the water and had not been harmed. None of the sailboats had been. But the boatyard was savagely transformed, its railway a twisted wreck and half the work and storage sheds smoldering under streaming fire hoses. Everyone knew what the fire meant. It meant that every boat's refit schedule would be delayed and every departure postponed, perhaps for months. The only recourse was to retire to the Cantina for coffee and lick their wounds. Ayers withdrew his arm from Inge-Lise's.

"Not coming with us?" she said.

"You go. I need to clean up. Have dinner with me tonight, just us. I'll have the hotel bring it in."

"You look awful," she said.

"You look great," he said, kissing her cheek.

So she joined the others as they checked over their boats, found nothing amiss except soot on deck, and then trudged up the hill to breakfast together like the family they had become.

* * *

Ayers found Luis Alfaro smoking a cigarette alone in the remains of the paint shed, where smoking was strictly forbidden. He was slumped in panic and despair.

"How bad?"

"I don't even know yet, Mr. Ayers. We're fucked is all I know. And I'm the one whose fault it will be. Any excuse to get rid of me and now they got one. The owners already got my replacement lined up, they told me that last month, a guy from their yard in Cabo, big tall Anglo guy. They brought him up here and made me show him around. Well, he can take a look around now, it's his problem not mine. But your boat's OK, none of the boats in the water got hurt."

"Better put that out," Ayers said of the cigarette in Alfaro's hand. "Did you start this fire?"

"What? No sir!"

"So act like it."

Ayers directed Alfaro to project assurance. He was to get his hands out of his pockets. He was to follow Ayers' lead. They went outside, stepping over crisscrossed hoses and into the first work shed. It housed three fishing boats in for repair and a woodshop that featured an antique belt-driven lathe. Smoke hung in the air and water dripped from the high east windows, which had broken under the flood of fire hoses. It had survived.

They emerged into Shed #2, which no longer had a roof. A dozen yard workers stood with coffee, half of them wearing their work respirators. This had been the fiberglass and resin shop, with laminations in progress. Tins of acetone had exploded and the floor was dotted with molten statuary which had once been coach roofs and custom bait wells. A forklift sat blackened, its seat cushion still smoldering. The 12-foot-high steel racks along the east wall had toppled, and amid their jumble of piping lay a hundred bags of sails, all of them melted, the names of their owners on yellow tags that now suggested tombstones. The entire west side of the building was missing, a black void beyond which firemen could be seen filling sandbags to contain the ruptured diesel oil that stood in black pools.

The yard crew hardly noticed Alfaro and the American millionaire in the expensive topcoat. They had arrived at work to find disaster. They watched the firemen like a movie. They stood drinking coffee with nothing to do. Ayers heard a laugh, and the end of an off-color joke. Heads shook. Smiles were exchanged. Fate or God or something had done all this, which at the moment had nothing to do with them.

"My gear was in those racks, wasn't it?" Ayers said to Alfaro.

"Yes, your spare sails were there." He pointed to heaps of blackened rubbish. "Your electronics, there—all gone now.' His tone was flat. "I should send these men home. Can't pay them to stand around with nothing to do."

"No," said Ayers.

"Sir, we are so fucked up right now—"

Ayers punched him hard in the arm, hard. Alfaro was startled. Mr. Ayers had never touched him before. He rubbed his arm.

"Give them something to do."

"To do what? The owners are on the way to fire me and the crews know it. That's why they don't even look at me. I'm a dead man, it's bad luck."

"Luis. This is not my first construction emergency. You're in charge, so give them something to do."

To Luis Alfaro, Mr. Ayers looked at that moment like part of the fire. His eyes were red and his hands were jammed into his coat pockets as if to contain them. He could hear the workers' Spanish, their gallows humor. The big cheese and the little cheese, that's what the men called them. It was disrespect, but understandable. Sure, give them something to do, when there is nothing to do because they're fucked, we're fucked, everybody's fucked and they know it."

"Do it," Ayers said. So Alfaro blinked, and obeyed.

"*Aye, cabrones!*" The men turned toward them, startled. "What're you standing there for! Get out there and help the *bomberos* make sandbags! And put down the fucking coffee! Anybody drinking fucking coffee today, you don't have a job tomorrow!"

As they scattered to the task, Ayers added: "And the one who calls you the little cheese? Fire him this afternoon."

"I'll do it now," Alfaro said, moving after the man. Ayers stopped him with his arm.

"No, give him time to show off some more. And don't tell him why he's fired. Let the others figure it out, and they will."

They spent the morning inspecting damage, then met in Alfaro's office where he tended two landline phones ringing constantly. Ayers took the time to assay his losses. *Après Vous* was undamaged but the elaborate schedule of preparations had suffered grievous loss. The fitting-out would be delayed for months. New equipment aboard was uninstalled. He had lost three custom headsails and all the protective canvas on the boat. Destroyed were his spare standing and running rigging. The new light-weight spinnaker pole and custom twin whiskers for the trade-winds rig were now $20,000 carbon-fiber puddles melted on the floor. The radar and elaborate satellite TV system, neither yet installed, lay in pools of salt water from the fire hoses. Some critical equipment was already aboard the boat, but still in crates. His entire manifest of spare parts, collected from manufacturers all over the world, was gone.

Alfaro, meantime, was under siege. By noon he turned the phones off and sank into his battered swivel chair.

"Where do we stand," Ayers asked him.

"Where do we stand? I'll tell you, Mr. Ayers. The insurance wants me not to do anything till they get here, the owners are coming from Texas, the firemen say we got violations, everybody wants to know how it started, how could this happen, and Sr. Faraday, the big owner, he just asked me, did we sweep up recently? Every time he comes here, it's that we should sweep up more frequently. And why? Because of the risk of fire! Thank you Sr. Faraday. Let me get a broom and sweep up this whole piece of shit boatyard, this whore of an electrical grid, this mother of a 70-year-old diesel winch that overheats every time, let me sweep up every corrupted thing I have told them about, but which to replace is not an economic necessity, so make it work, Alfaro! Make it work or you can go back to grinding the paint off the bottom of rowboats!" It was the voice of a victim, innocent and doomed.

Ayers proposed that they examine together all the existing work schedules. Delay was evident, but for how long? Alfaro predicted eight weeks at least. Ayers estimated longer than that, based on his experience of putting things right after site fires, a common event in the construction industry. Alfaro was to double all his estimates. A full assessment would take weeks and the insurance company would stall and drag it all out. The trick now, when there was uncertainty, was to forge ahead. In confusion, aggressive certainty was required.

Alfaro's cell phone erupted with seven new text messages scrolling and beeping. He shook his head. There was no hope. He was finished. He would just go home. It was good. The fire had saved him. He was no longer enslaved by cheapskate investors. He was no longer the butt of jokes, the fool who had done the best he could when nobody else could've done anything at all. He was glad of it. He would go home and die a free man while watching his children starve.

"Look at what the owners are saying now," he said, passing his cell phone to Ayers. Ayers took the phone and threw it 10 feet across the room to bounce off the wall.

"Come with me."

Twenty minutes later they were sitting in the window seat of the most expensive tourist restaurant in Ensenada. The window put them on display for everyone passing by on the sidewalk of the promenade. It was the table of honor, a table for two, the table for millionaires.

Ayers approved the bottle of wine, then waited till their glasses were filled. He smiled at the owner, who bowed and beamed. He waited as a waiter returned and gently placed Alfaro's napkin in his lap, where it belonged. And then he began to explain why, in his experience, there would be no immediate push to change leadership at the boatyard. That would come later, true. But for the moment, and for the next several months, Luis Alfaro was in fact indispensable and should therefore act like it. He knew the schedules. He knew the workers. He might someday be the goat, but at the moment he was god. In the days ahead, Ayers asked, what was Alfaro's primary fear?

"They're not going to pay."

"The Insurance company will pay. They have to."

"I mean the boats," Mr. Ayers. "Our income is the boats, and boats aren't going to come here if we can't work, and the sailboats that are here will get mad and leave, and the commercial fisherman will go to San Diego and pay more because otherwise they can't fish. Do you think the owners have cash reserves? They don't. No income for three months, they're dead. And I'm dead. Forty years old and three kids, and dead. Nobody can change that."

Ayers drew out a checkbook from his overcoat and wrote a check for $100,000. Alfaro just looked at it.

"Sir, you should go somewhere else."

"This money will keep you open."

"I'm just the manager. You should talk to the owners."

"The owners? Do you see them here? I'm talking to you. This check is to work on my boat, right? But you won't do that, you will misuse the funds to save the yard. You will keep the other paying customers and put me off. Don't worry, I'll sue the owners eventually, and I'll get interest and a penalty too. But if the yard goes bankrupt, I get nothing, understand? Believe me, this is the way it's done. And when these absentee owners push you around, when they speak harshly to you, you wave this check in their face. You tell them you have their boatyard in your hands. You, Luis Alfaro. Because you do."

As Alfaro held the check the faces of two women appeared in the window, large and close as if in a one-way mirror. They watched the millionaire pour wine into his glass. They were surprised to see him there, indistinct through the obscuring reflections of the bright day outside. They pressed close, noses almost against the glass. Yes, it was Luis Alfaro, from their church, dining with the rich American. One of them rapped sharply on the glass.

Inside, Alfaro jumped nearly out of his seat. Ayers laughed.

"Say hello," Ayers said.

Alfaro tapped the glass back. The women, unaware of their proximity, leaped back as if suddenly exposed. Their faces hurriedly withdrew, one drawing a shawl across her face.

Alfaro sat rigidly, check in hand. It was true that the American knew things that he never would. It was true that with this check to empower the general ledger he could carry the yard for months. He could add a dozen laborers to speed the cleanup. His influence would be enhanced. It already was, just to be seen in the window. That word would spread fast, the two of them dining as equals. As he and Ayers returned to the fire cleanup plan the wine lifted his mood and he saw what he had not seen before, which was that success was to willfully enter the darkness, and be the one with the candle.

"I'll do it, Mr. Ayers. "And if we survive, I will say to everybody in the world that you saved us all."

The American rose and laid down cash for the check. He made no move to shake hands, as most of the Americans did without any warning at all.

"The less you say about me the better," Ayers said as he walked out. "Remember that."

When he returned to the boatyard, Luis Alfaro found his phone and turned it on again. For the rest of the day, when the voices on it yelled at him, he reminded them that if they wanted to get anything done he was the solution, not the problem.

* * *

Because the grocer Diego Schultz was the most successful of his family, and because his success was due, he thought, to taking action rather than the popular pastime of just talking about it, he felt a certain private kinship with Robert Ayers. In their few months of acquaintance he had observed the American's surety of decision-making, brevity of speech and general lack of explanation. He tried to make those attributes his own.

So when Sr. Ayers called that afternoon and said he needed the boys tonight, and for all night, and to be at the warehouse at midnight, Schultz did not ask why. He just said that he and his son Mikey and the other boys would be there. Schultz had asked for no explanation. This new way of doing business was efficient and reflected the trust of men in men.

That night, when his son put on a jacket at the time he usually went to bed, Adele Schultz demanded to know from her husband where he was going.

"There is work, and that's all you need to know," Schultz said with dignity.

"The boys are loading supplies on the American's boat," she said, "that I already know. But why are *you* going, you who has not lifted a crate with his own hands in 10 years?"

"I don't have to explain to you," he said quietly.

Schultz stared her down. And it worked. To say nothing, that was the power. To establish the fortress of yourself.

"What are you, deaf?" Adele Schultz said. "Answer me!"

She was leaning at him with hands on hips such that Schultz involuntarily backed away, lowering his eyes.

"I don't explain," he said to the ground.

"Well if you throw your back out, you'll explain! You'll explain to me if the store is not open on time in the morning! You'll explain if our son is one minute late for his school tomorrow!"

Schultz felt his son slip out the door behind him, leaving him without a witness.

"Now go! And hurry up, Mr. Big Shot, so you don't have to explain to your millionaire boss how you didn't know he cleared this job with me before he even told you. What do you think, I would let Michael go unless the American came to me for permission? Why do I even have to explain these things to you!"

It took Schultz a block to catch up to Mikey, who was a fast walker. When they got to the warehouse Ayers was waiting and the other boys were already loading the carts. They took the first loads down the sloping street and onto a bike path that led to the boatyard. The night guard saw them, but he had been taken care of and turned conveniently away. They rolled the carts past the charred ruin of the marine railway, down the long pier and onto the gangway to *Après Vous*. There Ayers and two of the boys remained to stow the stores as the others went back for the next load. Schultz had a flashlight, but the boys made him turn it off: they had rehearsed the procedures and knew them in the dark. Schultz helped carry boxes for one trip, but the hill was steep and thereafter he supervised from a chair, where he was the next morning when the rays of the sun woke him. It was already 8 o'clock and the boys had gone directly to school, each with a new $100 bill.

Schultz took the short way home along the embarcadero, and when he looked for the American's yacht at the end of the long pier, the yacht was no longer there.

* * *

The dinner in Ayers' suite was catered by the Italian restaurant next to his hotel and carried in by the owner himself about 7 o'clock. There was an aperitivo of Campari and soda and antipasti of roasted peppers stacked to make a boat on a sea of whitecaps, the whitecaps being zucchini. The primo was angel hair, light with mushroom and cilantro and fragrant with truffle oil.

By the time of the shrimp course Inge-Lise could eat no more, and only watched Robert. He seemed rested and his color had returned. As usual it was no good to inquire about his mood, or to attempt small talk toward no particular end, as most people did to fill the space between them. She had no interest in bringing up the state of the yacht or its preparations, now obviously delayed like everyone else in the aftermath of the fire. One thing she knew without asking: this lovely dinner was apology for his abrupt absence for three days and his return without explanation. Apology accepted. They dined by candlelight, and after the Italian brought the coffee and some sweet cakes he took all the plates away with him and left a bottle of the first grappa she had ever tasted. Despite what she had heard it was smooth as skin and left upon her tongue the taste of pears.

Robert was open this night as seldom before. They discussed the Galapagos route to paradise. He thought it the best route because it allowed a stop in Acapulco along the way. From there, the cruise across the equator to the Galapagos, to be followed by a straight shot of 2,500 miles to Nuku Hiva in the Marquesas Islands, first landfall in the South Seas. From there, Tahiti was an open book. They went over, as they had many times together, the Ensenada friends they would reunite with along the way, the unlikelihood of storms, and the night watches they would keep, together and apart, under tropical skies. There would be flying fish and rainbows and in the month-long passages time would stop, or so everyone said it would, or seem to, and either way, they agreed, was all right with both of them. Time was all there was in the world. Not beginnings or endings, but the current that carried them, undivided by any ticking clock.

He answered her questions more fully than before, and now the syntax included her. It was "we," not "I" or "you," as it had once been. She asked if he were sure he would not regret giving up his solo adventure, and he said that everybody went through life singlehanded whether they knew it or not, even the two of them. Her feet were getting cold and the grappa was warm, and it was good to know she would be in bed with him soon. It seemed she knew him, even if she knew she did not. She knew enough not to need more. He was a handsome man, and her men had not always been handsome, because that didn't matter much. He was rich, but she had always been among people who lived comfortably and in fact, looking back, were, yes, rich. It was her luck as a woman to be considered desirable, and Danes were not known for a lot of talking, which was probably some of the attraction, for him. The whole world talked too much, and that was true. She said his name to herself: Robert.

"You must have been married," Ayers said, startling her.

"Yes, of course. Two times."

"Children?"

"No. I was working, travelling, and the time went. I regret, but not too much. I'm selfish, I think." She didn't know where to go next. Robert sometimes didn't react at all, and conversations just—stopped. "My first husband was a pilot for Icelandair, we met in language school. You know, they want you to speak three or four. He was German and we were together not very long. Because I flew away." She smiled when he grinned. "My second, Phillip, was a good guy. A Dane, like me. He died, but we had 20 years. Now, how about you? if you want to tell me."

Ayers held up three fingers.

"Three times? Oh my, that beats me. I'm glad it does."

She sipped the grappa. Then:

"Now let me say what a wonderful dinner this is, Robert. It's your Prince Charming side, for sure. So tell me, how is the boat, and what we must do to get it ready. Everybody is being delayed, Claudia and Max for at least a month, they think. I can stay here to wait, but can you? I know you have businesses, can you make trips and come back? Well, you just did, obviously. I saw the lock on your door. But certainly, if you must go away during the delay of the boat, I can look after things for you and supervise the schedules. I'm good at it, I did it for my company for a long time."

"I do have a child," Ayers said. "A daughter."

"You do. Good, I like knowing that. "

"She's like you. She has energy. Laura is her name."

Inge-Lise felt a chill. It was unintelligible but worth noticing, because a chill, or whatever she should call a sudden unexpected awareness, was always her best signal that something was up. Sometimes it was the recognition of an escape route fading. Sometimes it portended a revision of the world.

"I like the name Laura very much."

"You'd like her."

"I'm sure of it, Robert."

"She lives in Fairfield, Connecticut. That's where her mother lives, too."

"Would I like her mother, too?"

"I wouldn't be surprised."

"Would her mother like me?"

Ayers stared at her. He was not always attentive to signs, even when he was paying attention, as he was now.

"It's a joke, Robert." She laughed. "I am putting you on the spot, and there you are, right on the spot. You look like a little boy who just accidentally told a secret. Don't worry, I have secrets, too, so I don't mind yours. Do you know what matters to me? It is that when you looked at me that first night, I looked back. I knew right away what would happen, didn't you? Of course you did. And so here we are after a wonderful dinner, and I'm glad we are, I am glad of this accident we became and I am very glad that you have a daughter named Laura in Connecticut."

She got up and draped herself around him like a coat.

"My feet are cold," she said.

She squealed as he picked her up and carried her to the bedroom. They lay wrapped in each other for a long time until their extremities warmed and then made love in the way they had found was best for each of them.

She awoke a few hours later and according to her habit dressed quietly in order to return to her own hotel. Robert was still asleep when she kissed him. He opened his eyes and smiled, but she put her fingers to her lips and stole away into the hallway, down the stairwell, through the night and into her own hotel bed. The chill remained until the blankets warmed to their work.

* * *

At breakfast, Claudia asked Inge-Lise to accompany her to the boatyard office to consult with Sr. Alfaro about the revised schedule for the Beneteau. It was at that time that she broached the subject of her affection for Robert. "I approve," Claudia said with a grin. "Plus which, the guy is rich as hell so play your cards right and you're set for life." They had been friends since boarding school in Lausanne, so all Inge-Lise said was, "That's not it."

Sr. Alfaro was busy, and while waiting in the smoky office Inge-Lise noticed through a window that Robert's boat was not at its usual place at the dock.

Alfaro was telling Claudia that he could no longer guarantee any schedule but that the yard would give the puddle-jumpers high priority when Inge-Lise inquired why Mr. Ayers' boat was not in its usual place.

Alfaro said Mr. Ayers had taken the boat on a sea trial to test the hydraulics of the self-steering.

When the boat was not at the dock the next morning, either, Alfaro informed Inge-Lise that sea trials could take days. And that in fact, Mr. Ayers might be on a 400-mile singlehanded training cruise, which was in fact the recommended thing to do. Recommended for what, she asked.

"You don't take a yacht alone to the South Seas without testing the systems first," Alfaro said. "It is standard practice, as anyone who knows will readily agree."

A week later, Mexican port authorities came to Inge-Lise's hotel seeking to know if the girlfriend of the millionaire had received any communication from Mr. Ayers, who had left port bound for the Galapagos Islands without a *zarpe*, the required departure permit, an act that was strictly prohibited.

They were informed that Señora Inge-Lise Sorenson had checked out the day before, departing by air Tijuana-Los Angeles-Seattle, and had left her telephone number and a request for any further information available about Robert Ayers or his yacht.

The winter season lingered. At the cantina and the hotels, the ever-changing tribe of cruisers waited for February or March or whenever the vagaries of boatyard fires, pension checks and the wind patterns of the North and South Pacific oceans should conspire to permit their departure for paradise. Ford's boat sank again, and he gave up and went home to Oklahoma. He was replaced by Gerard, a bearded giant in a sailboat he had built himself out of cement, but which floated quite buoyantly anyhow.

Claudia sold Inge-Lise's empty bunk on the Beneteau to a photographer named Nora, who took pictures of everyone, was eager to learn more about the cruising lifestyle, and fitted into the dinner bunch at the cantina right away.

CHAPTER SIX

Trust

Ayers' original will had left everything to Julia, Laura's mother. The new trust divided her father's assets among the three ex-wives, Laura and various other creditors.

Hi, Mom? Guess what?

That was not a conversation Laura looked forward to having. So, against Maurice's advice, she had put it off for two weeks, then three. That entailed one long dinner at her mother's house, and a Sunday shopping trip during which enormous effort was required to keep the secret. Worse was that her mother was a paranormal investigator of souls, Laura's in particular, and knew something was up but was too clever to let on that she did. Or, she let on that she did know something was up, but intentionally didn't ask what it was. If so, that meant that her mother was now ahead in the game, as usual.

Hi mom, guess what?

Maurice, being a man, had no clue. He was for full and immediate disclosure. Not that he gave advice, he was too smart for that. He just loomed, nodded, listened, and offered to go over the alternatives again. He gauged her mood as the weight of responsibility, stoically borne. Ha. It was simpler than that. If her father weren't already probably dead, she ought to kill him for sticking her with this trust thing. Had he ever mentioned it? Nope. Had their relationship ever been anything but perfect? Nope. Had he not always been the one force in her life, distant but crystal clear, that demonstrated for Laura who she actually was, namely: independent without explanation and if other people don't get it, so what? Right, dad? Oh, and by the way, your first wife, Eleanor, is really cool and congrats to both of you for spying on me back in college. And there must be a lot more in this treasure hunt into your past for the loyal daughter to find and enjoy.

Hi mom, guess what I found out?

There was a hard line in Laura that surprised those who encountered it. She was gracious and easy, and then you hit the line. Our Girl in Connecticut she was not, for reasons, well, reasons she herself didn't know. The hard line was just in her and she kept it hidden as best she could, until she didn't.

An hour before, at 11 p.m., the telephone had rung and a woman's voice asked if she were Laura, daughter of Robert Ayers.

Yes, she was the daughter.

The voice asked if there were news of Robert.

When Laura inquired who was calling there was a silence and then a dial tone. When she tried to redial, the source was blocked. The voice knew who she was, and how to find her, and what questions to ask.

But the voice had hung up.

So Laura decided to hang up, too. The whole Trust thing.

* * *

The next afternoon she appeared at the law offices of James R. Barnet & Son, estate planners. The founder was about 70 and looked at first glance like a funeral director. A month before, Mr. Barnet, rhymes with garnet, had taken several hours to lay out for Laura the terms of the Robert Allington Ayers Living Trust, of which, she had been surprised to learn, she was the sole trustee.

Mr. Barnet had begun with the difference between a will and a trust. A will distributed holdings only after death. A trust took effect while the settlor, its creator, was alive and contained any instructions, wishes or requirements he deemed appropriate. The trustee carried them out. As trustee, Laura was in a position of substantial power because there was no oversight of any kind. Any redress of grievance against her could come only through the courts, by long and expensive litigation. Laura, he had said as if guiding her to a top-of-the-line casket, was solely in charge of the execution of her father's wishes, and the entire firm was at her disposal. His son Adam, who was about her age, had been assigned to guide her through the process.

Now she called upon Adam Barnet, rhymes with garnet, for help.

"I don't want to do this," Laura said, dropping into the client seat in front of his big desk.

"Tell me," Adam said, tilting back in the executive chair to rock with fingers clasped behind his head. The stretch of his silk shirt exposed the lateral musculature of a six-pack above his narrow belt. "We'll figure it out."

"I saw Eleanor, the first wife. I went to Philadelphia, I met her, she signed the papers, she knows what she's getting. It took two days. I don't know these people, Adam. It's really awkward for me. Eleanor thinks my father is all right, but it feels weird going around like some kind of operative of the not-really-dead-yet. Also, everybody thinks I know where he is, which I don't, so I'm the messenger of what? 'Sorry, I don't know any more than you do?' What I need to be doing is looking for a job, not this."

"One down," Adam said.

"And how many more beneficiaries to go? No way. I met the third wife only once – Vivian —and she doesn't like me. This business guy he owes money to, Mr. Sullivan? I can't even find him. Somebody from the IRS has my number now, they left a message and it's like what—they're on my trail? Is it true that I'm responsible for everything about my father? Bank accounts, investments, stuff in foreign countries, personal notes?"

He nodded. "Yes, you're the sole trustee. You're in charge of the assets."

"I don't want to be in charge of the assets! My father will come back with a suntan next week, and then what?"

"I understand your concern," Adam said. "And probably he wants this done before he does come back. Done deal, everybody knows everything. That's the job that he asked you to do, and it's smart. With a scale of assets like this, the trouble comes when beneficiaries get surprised. It's always better to let them know in advance. That's the thinking, and we believe it's sound."

"Then I want to hire somebody to do it. I'll help them."

"Well, your dad chose you. My guess is that you two have a special bond."

Adam folded forward, origami like, over his desk. She felt him reading her face. He had no wedding ring. Hands big. Confident.

"I didn't know my father as well as you think."

"None of us really knows anybody," he said, the offhanded wisdom left to hang in the air.

"I'm saying that I don't want to be the trustee. So what are the options, please?"

It took Adam Barnet 15 minutes to run through the options, of which there were essentially none. No trustee, then no Trust. Invalidation. Probate court. Ten or 20 percent of the Ayers fortune lost to shark lawyers, and that was the baseline. Hiring a professional fiduciary was possible, but Laura had been assigned certain delicate negotiations with remote beneficiaries and the implication of blood spilled in the past.

Laura stared at him.

"These things are a big responsibility," Adam said. "There are always revelations along the way. But there's not really any rush, the pace is entirely up to you."

"Do you know if my father had an earlier will in place?"

"Not written by our firm," he said. "We designed this structure for him six months ago, but, yes, most people would have set something up previously. We often run into that."

Laura already had. In her mother's closet under cover of darkness and fortified by a bottle of wine.

"Anyhow, it doesn't matter," Adam said, "because the Trust supersedes any prior will completely. That's very clear in the law, and I'm a lawyer." He nodded at the framed Juris Doctor degree from the University of Virginia hanging prominently behind his desk.

"I'm not," Laura said.

"No, art history, wasn't it? At Penn? I went to USC undergraduate, and I took a few art courses myself. Art's about people, and that's what this business is. A trust paints a portrait, in a way. It casts a light on who a person is and how they want to be remembered. For example, tilt your head right now, put on a pearl earring, you'd be a Vermeer. It's the way the light strikes you this moment."

"I want to get out of the Trust," Laura said, "so get me out."

He nodded. "You know, I thought when I got into this business it would be cut and dried, but it isn't. These things we create, for your dad in this case, are more than paper. People think their lives through with us. They look back and they see somebody to reward, or something to correct, or, sometimes, someone to exclude. Or they see it as a chance to complete their work on earth."

"I'm not my father's work on earth, Adam," Laura said.

"Literally, you are, and that's my point. A trust is the story of a life, and when a life goes on for a long time there are lots of chapters in it. Every day here I deal with old friends, ex-wives, children nobody knew about. Confessions, sometimes that's what it feels like. Corrections and messages. A 'living trust'—the words have power, and everybody feels it. The legacies go back in time and they project into the future. To be chosen to participate is to get to see who people are and who they were and what they've done, or want undone. To be a trustee is an honor. I know it's heavy, but he chose you."

She said nothing. Adam paused. This was the best part of the job, to be of use.

"You mentioned looking for a job? Frankly, you don't need to right now. The estate knowns the burdens of the trustee and you're expected to draw compensation. We have set aside expenses, the documents are in your folder.

It's essentially a straight $150,000 draw, but there's really no limitation. There's money for whatever it takes for you to do your job."

"I don't want money," she said.

"It's not about money." It was getting dark. He looked at his watch. "Laura. It's six o'clock. I pick up my son from soccer at 8. Let's continue this at Morrie's Steak House. We can have a drink, and we both have to eat."

"Who takes him to soccer?" Laura asked.

"She does. My ex, or soon-to-be."

"You make a good case, but I'm not there," she said.

So Adam recapitulated the complications of her withdrawal from the Trust, and the resultant family unrest, accusations, confusion and misunderstanding. Lawsuits untempered. He shared with her that her father referred to her as 'the competent one.' Without her participation the Trust was a war waiting to be fought. With her it was a road map of family redemption. His sympathetic tones lingered in the air between them, held aloft by professional concern and the broad shoulders of his expensive suit. Finally he fished the key to a Tesla out of a drawer and laid it on the desktop.

"Shall we continue this at dinner?"

"Are you serious?" Laura said.

"I am," he said. "A martini would do us both good."

"I'm the daughter, Adam, not the widow," she said, watching him blanche. "But I'm glad you're on the job, and I'll let you know what I decide about the Trust."

* * *

To the world, the status of Robert Ayers was not that of a missing person but of a millionaire gone sailing. His point of departure was Ensenada, Mexico. His destination was the South Seas. His lack of communication was typical. His cellular phone had always said, "I really want to talk to you," followed by a beep. But he didn't really want to talk to you. In a mini-profile in Forbes Magazine nine years before his pull-quote across the page had been, "I don't take calls, I make them." It was presented as a strategy practicable by the bold. It also meant that you could never get hold of the man.

Ayers' last known call was from Ensenada to James R. Barnet, rhymes with garnet. It was to amend an offshore account number, and he had spoken only to an assistant.

That was three months ago, so Laura started there. She had decided to take her father's bait and put him back on his own hook.

Her call to his boatyard in Mexico resulted only in the news that he had left, bound south, with all bills paid in full. She talked to Sr. Alfaro, who declared Mr. Ayers to be very educated, well equipped and highly skilled. Alfaro knew men, he said, and Mr. Ayers was a man, and his daughter would be well to significate his needs and not to include in them uninvited burdens of interference. She had difficulty understanding his English, which was delivered with formal condescension interrupted by bursts of vulgarity in Spanish directed at the workers around him. What an asshole.

She contacted the Mexican Navy, who had no news but who invited her to stop by the Manzanillo base, 500 miles south of Acapulco, to fill out paperwork.

The United States Coast Guard in San Diego was less polite. Her Internet research had uncovered an official form called a "float plan," a USCG document on which all intended ports of call were to be listed by the departing vessel. Had her father by any chance filed such a form, as required?

A lieutenant named Strabo, Leonard C., seemed irritated. Why did people think the Coast Guard kept records of departing yachtsmen? The Coast Guard was border security with guns, ma'am, drug interdiction with guns, ma'am, also antiterrorism with guns, and yes, ma'am, the Coast Guard also rescued 'yachtsmen' if they were drowning, but couldn't be expected to keep an eye on all of them like baby ducks, not in the face of an increasingly insufficient budget from Congress and overwhelming public misunderstanding of the basic Coast Guard mission.

Laura, who had a blank form in her hand, said it looked mighty official to her, had "USCG Float Plan" written all over it in big letters, and why publish such a form if the underfunded U.S. Coast Guard with all of its guns didn't require anybody to file it? His tone changed after she requested his name and rank and to speak to the officer of the day, who that day happened to be him.

"Look miss," Lt. Strabo said. "Your dad was supposed to send the float plan to you, not to us. So everybody would know where he's going. Why he didn't do that, how do I know?"

To locate her missing father Laura considered skip tracers, private eyes, and even a police missing-person report, but rejected them all as potential boomerangs, con jobs, public oversharing or violation of the Episcopalian Code of Family Silence, which held that you kept such things quiet until the actual indictment. So Laura sat and stewed, accommodating herself to the reality that she was stuck with the job of being her father's daughter and trustee of his impossible life, hitherto distantly entertaining but now up-close and uncomfortably her own. All their weeks and months together, the shared moments, the comfort of proximate genetic biology, the tradition of nothing needing to be said, where were they now? She could see him before her with that private smile, that intimacy that needed no name, just father and daughter.

Yo dad! Say something for once in your life!

She could deal with silence because that was his thing. Hers, too, maybe, or anyhow that's what Maurice said. What she couldn't deal with was the ring of a phone in her apartment and a woman's voice asking for 'Laura,' and news of "Robert,' and then hanging up. Everybody, even his enemies, called her father 'Bobby.' 'Robert' was too intimate. Also, a request for "news of" suggested currency. You don't call from five years ago, or 20 years ago, asking for "news." Plus which, Laura's cell phone number was not easy to find, so somebody had given it to her.

And the caller had hung up. If a cell phone call goes dead, people call right back. If they didn't want to talk to you, why call at all? And women do not hang up on people. That is never discourtesy, it is always something more. Way more.

There was intimacy in the voice, and she knew voices.

When she called Maurice at the office—"Hi, this is Laura, can I talk to Maurice?"—that was one voice. It didn't tell the other end whether you had slept with him last night.

But when Maurice came on the line, your voice changed. Its edges were different, it had history in it. And the history Laura had heard in the voice on the phone that had asked her for news of 'Robert?' That voice knew her father personally, and recently.

And as a woman.

The missing Bobby Ayers had last been seen by living human beings in the Mexican port of Ensenada. Laura's research folder by that name was an inch thick, full of maps and printouts and newspaper links about sailboat crews lodging there. The folder contained the most recent photo of her father, under the headline *Iluminan Mar con Luces Navideñas*. It was a picture montage from a waterfront restaurant called Cantina del Mar showing celebrants after a Christmas boat parade and dinner. He could be dimly seen in a photo raising a glass at a table of eight. A woman was at his side. There was one menu between them, as if they were sharing it. She was pretty. The caption listed first names only: Claudia, Max, Sam, Hank, Sherry, Bobby, Inge-Lise. So: Inge-Lise was her name. That name might account for the touch of accent on the phone.

It happened to be dinner time in Mexico, so she called the restaurant. She declared herself to be Bobby Ayers' daughter and asked to speak with anyone named Claudia, Max, Sam, Hank, Sherry or Inge-Lise. In a moment Claudia came on the line, delighted to speak with the daughter of Bobby Ayers. A band was playing behind her. No, Inge-Lise Sorenson was not there, she had returned to Seattle long since. But Claudia had her phone number, and Claudia thought it would be great for Laura and Inge-Lise to talk, and that such a talk might ease Inge-Lise's mind considerably.

But Inge-Lise Sorenson didn't want to talk to Laura Ayers. When Laura called the number, she hung up. When Laura called back five times, five times she was hung up on. To locate her, Laura typed "Inge-Lise Sorenson" into the search box of her LinkedIn account. Nothing. She searched "Xing" and "Opportunity," her other job-seeker sites. Nothing. She tried "Meetup," "Ryze," "Gadball" and "AngleList" too, the other links where her own curriculum vitae lay dormant. Nothing.

However, when Laura returned to LinkedIn, a search window remained open to a candidate named Inge-Lise Persig. The photo was right, the last name wrong. A married name, of course. Ten Internet minutes later she discovered Inge-Lise Persig to be a former public affairs employee of Braniff Airlines, pictured in the employee magazine with Angelina Jolie, Elon Musk and two Red Hot Chili Peppers, whose lost luggage by the efforts of Inge-Lise so quickly recovered had been, as the machine translation from German put it. Subsequently she had been an executive at Lufthansa, where one call to a night desk in Frankfort scored an address in Seattle for Inge-Lise Sorenson, the new name of the person who liked hanging up on other people's daughters.

Now what? To Seattle from JFK was $690, cheapest she could find, and it made two stops. Book it. That felt good. It was action. It was movement of her own accord. Wait, credit card rejected. She was over her limit again.

Outside the winter light was beginning to fade. She did not feel well. She had not eaten anything. She was oppressed and isolated and fed up with all the bullshit and the nobody-knows-anything and the waiting, mostly the waiting, and the doing, or actually the not doing anything at all.

She dug out the accordion folder called "Robert A. Ayers Living Trust" and found the leather case of checks in her own name. Next to the checks was a silver American Express Card in the name of the Trust and of Laura Ayers. She activated the card, rebooked herself in First Class on the redeye to Seattle, and called for an Uber. The flight was in three hours.

Maurice called while she was packing. He wanted to chat about the weekend.

She said, "not now."

There wasn't time to explain and her stomach was upset and he would give her a pass and she knew it.

* * *

She met Inge-Lise Sorenson at 9 a.m. in a sidewalk coffee shop. The Seattle sun was out. The city was clean, big, cool, far and Laura had not slept in 24 hours and felt like crap. She explained that she was the trustee of her father's living will and was acting on his behalf.

"Is Robert dead?" Inge-Lise asked.

"No, he's not dead, of course not."

"So why are you here? Because I doubt very much if I am mentioned in his will."

"You're obviously not in his will, but I know you were with him. And I need to find him."

"So do you think I have your father here? I am hiding him perhaps in my barn, under a pile of hay?"

They sat across from each other, toe to toe. The meeting was not going well. Inge-Lise felt interrogated. Laura exuded suspicion. Neither knew what the other wanted, or exactly why they were there. The young woman bore a striking similarity to her father: pretty, tall, distant. So Inge-Lise imposed distance back. She let Laura talk. She listened to the cadences of fiduciary duty, diligence of a daughter, regret to impose, matters of importance to the family. Inge-Lise was nibbling the scone they were supposed to be sharing, content to wait the meeting out. She observed perspiration on Laura's face. This isn't easy for her. What is she, 30 years old? No makeup. Wary. That is Robert's chin, all right. The ears, not so much.

"Sorry to be blunt," Laura said, "but I have to be. My father's an unusual man, very successful, many businesses, and therefore is obviously vulnerable to threats, retaliation, blackmail and—

"I'm not blackmailing him," Inge-Lise said. "Laura? Are you all right?"

Laura had both hands flat on the glass of the sidewalk table. She felt her rate of breathing increase. She saw the other woman looking at her. She felt the movement of passersby, and the vibrations of the traffic through her palms.

"Are you ill?" Inge-Lise asked.

"No."

But she was, yes. Definitely. And suddenly. And on her knees, into the gutter of the street. Horrible, horrible, the Inge-Lise woman holding her forehead as people edged past with coffee cups and plaid shirts and shoes treaded like Humvees, a trickle of yesterday's rainwater carrying her guts away in shreds of airplane eggs and bacon and a honey roll she would never eat again as long as she lived. The gutter carrying it away as she watched. Horrible, horrible. People stopping to inquire if she were all right. More being sick, her head being held again, a paper cup of water arriving to rinse her mouth. An Uber arriving, black Nissan, driver Ali, who helped her in. Lying on his seat. Fabric seat. They have towels for this, for people being sick in Ubers. Ali had a towel. The woman's legs near her head. A hand on her back, steadying her. Her head now on the woman's thigh, horrible, horrible. The car stopping. The door opening. A new Seattle gutter also running with water to carry her retching away. The car resuming its endless travel, tires humming.

"Does she need to stop again?" Ali asked from the front seat.

"No, keeping going, we're almost there," said Inge-Lise.

Laura's head was on the woman's lap, which was all she remembered about the rest of the ride.

* * *

She woke up in the second bedroom of a condo overlooking Puget Sound. The ninth floor, high above trees and with mountains in the distance. Tea and toast were on the night table and a cotton sweatsuit folded at the foot of the bed. Inge-Lise sat beside her.

"I am so sorry."

"Don't worry," Inge-Lise said, "You never have to go back to that place again."

Laura forced a smile.

"Thank god."

She took a shower and found Inge-Lise waiting at her counter, doing a crossword puzzle in French. She sat across from her, sipping cold tea.

"Do you know why I called you?" Inge-Lise said. "I called you because on the day before he left, Robert wrote your number down for me. A little unusual, since I never saw him again."

"I tried to call you back."

"I felt I had made an error," Inge-Lise said. "Please understand that there is no problem. Your father and I did not elope, we didn't rob a bank, we didn't have entanglements or even bad feelings. I may tell you that you are certainly his daughter, and that your mother was beautiful."

"Is," Laura said.

"Is, of course. So you haven't heard from him. How worried are you?"

"I don't know how worried to be. Everybody says he comes and goes." Laura gathered herself. "What happened in Mexico?"

The culture of the puddle-jumpers was new to Laura. She knew nothing of her father's boat, or of yacht passage-planning or the seasonal weather patterns that dominated it. Inge-Lise's picture of him supervising the yacht restoration did match her memories of construction sites, where as a girl in a hardhat she had followed as he nodded, pointed, and seemed to direct workers without words. She had seen him lecture a foreman about tools left out in the rain. She had seen him put kneepads over an expensive suit and kneel to inspect the placement of rebar before concrete was poured. Her time with him had been limited but in college she was the only female who knew what rebar was. She had never seen him more engaged, and that engagement was what Inge-Lise had seen in Ensenada. She felt a pang of envy.

"He didn't say goodbye to you?"

"No."

"You were going to go with him, though, as crew? Which by the way I would have liked. The whole idea of him going off alone I don't understand at all. So did he leave early because of the fire?"

"I think so. Why he left without me, I don't know. He just did."

"That was cruel."

"Yes, maybe so. I thought it was. But then, I wanted to get off the boat I was on, and it was my idea to join him since he had more room, and I sort of cornered him, he couldn't really say no. We probably both knew what we were doing all along. Anyway, you can't make somebody do what they don't want to do. I knew your father only for a few months. That was the entirety, and there were things we never asked each other. He seemed happy but sometimes he looked old, or tired, and I saw his hands shake. But whatever pain you have, you hide from yourself as much as anybody else. I believe that as soon as your father and I met we knew right away we would be together."

Inge-Lise's face was a mask of freckles pasted together that gave prominence to her cheekbones and the sweep of her neck. Her hair was overdue for coloration. But she was in control.

"Yes, I cried when he departed, but more from pride than surprise. Where did Bobby go? everybody asked me. But I didn't know anything more than they did, I was not consulted. I looked the fool, I can tell you that, saying to everyone that he would return soon. He wasn't returning soon, he wasn't returning to me at all. Well, I am not such an open book myself. My culture is not so expressive, either we have more secrets than others or we have less. But, Laura, you might want to think why it is that I know so much about you, which I do. And all of it from our last night together. An excellent swimmer with a flaw in the stroke, here." She touched her right shoulder.

"A fast student, a skeptic, a skier who goes through moguls like nothing, you should see it. He couldn't keep up with you and he loved that. The one who understood him, with no necessity for words. The one most like him, the only one like him. Oh, and by the way, it is his belief that Maurice will be good. That's the name, Maurice, right? Of Maurice he greatly approved."

Laura stared at her.

"Isn't that the correct name?" asked Inge-Lise,

"Yes, it is. My fiancé, Maurice Charles. He and dad only met once."

"So you see, for a man who talks almost not at all, your father talked a lot about you. Robert and I told each other nothing, but we knew everything. Words are not so important. People are wrong to want all the words. So, when are you going back?"

"Tonight."

"Tonight? Yes, that's what I would do."

"I need to leave soon."

"I'll drive you to the airport. Don't worry, I won't ask questions. But tell me, do you approve?"

"Of what?"

"Of me, now that you understand what happened. The way you are looking at me, I'm not so sure."

"I'm thinking of the mess I made on the sidewalk," Laura said.

"I'm glad you came. Now at least I'm not a mystery."

She moved to the stove to put the teakettle on, and Laura followed. She touched her shoulder.

"Where is my father, Inge-Lise? Even if you don't know, you must have a guess."

"I am sure Robert didn't go south," she replied. "That's what everybody thinks, but he didn't. He talked about it too much, he was too free with his plans, sharing the pilot charts, saying how we would all meet in the Marquesas, Fiji and Bali Hi. For him that was too much telling. I probably knew it at the time, I just put it aside. I didn't want to doubt his plans, or interfere in any way. When it came down to it, I was really never in his plans at all."

"So if he didn't sail south, where is he now?"

"Away from us," Inge-Lise said. 'That's all I know.'

She took her car keys from a peg and they went out together. The flight east was much shorter than the flight west, and barely had Laura snuggled down in her seat than it was time to land at JKF.

* * *

Three days after Laura returned she received a voice message from Adam Barnet requesting that she come to his office.

The Internal Revenue Service had been in touch, and after consultation Adam and his father both agreed that Laura should initiate contact immediately, as a gesture of goodwill.

Also, a package of documents had arrived from Mexico. It had been damaged by fire and repackaged by the US Postal Service, causing a long delay. Adam spread the papers out on his desk, turning each for Laura to examine. A new beneficiary had been named for the Ayers Living Trust. The gift was substantial, and the recipient was to be added to the list for contact and sign-off.

Did Laura know an "Inge-Lise Sorenson of Seattle, Washington?" Adam asked.

CHAPTER SEVEN

Alone

Because the respirator filled so often with water, Ayers periodically took it off. It was in effect a gas mask, and the water was the sweat from his own soaked headband. Ninety-two degrees in the cabin today. The fumes of the clear penetrating epoxy he was applying were pernicious, but necessary if the bases of his new cabinets were to last. After another hour he was finished, and lay back. Too long head-down in the bilge, but now finished. He stripped off the nitrile gloves and lay back against the cherrywood settee. Slight nausea. Bright light, flooding from the skylight. In the hanging stench of the epoxy rose a cross-referenced smell of burning sheds in Ensenada and simultaneously the scent of coconut lotion on Inge-Lise's neck.

He felt her leaning against him, as she did while reading in bed. No, it was a bulkhead, not Inge-Lise. But let the bulkhead be her. Nothing he had said was untrue. What had he said? That things would come out all right. That things moved toward completion, as they were designed to. Like him, she had journeyed beyond expectation, and that was the bond that had held them for the allotted while. Her role in the thing was minor but she had made it larger than written, and beginning that first night in the cantina when she had declined to meet his eyes. The novelty of her name: Inge-Lise, double and resistant to abbreviation, as if requiring attention and the savor of pronunciation.

What had he said that was true? That everything would be all right. The rest had served the intended purpose of establishing his probable route as southbound, with the rest of the puddle-jumpers. Every uncorrected assumption, every invitation to conclude, projected a probable future. It had been in his power to alter tomorrows and he had done that. Calculations of his current position based on recollections would put him well south of the equator by now, bound to Fiji. Had he lied? No, a lie with consequence only to the liar is no lie at all. He smiled. Deception requires faith. So, dear Inge-Lise, have faith.

Ayers was certain by now that nobody had the slightest idea where he was. He was lost to the world but not to himself, because his longitude and latitude scrolled this moment on the nearby GPS screen to an exactitude of 60 feet. He knew exactly where he was. A similar series of calculated ruses, none of them defined by French lawyers as outside any law, had won him and his partners ownership of a lucrative hotel in Deauville, near the racetrack. And also in New Jersey, and California, and Winnipeg. There is no consequence to dissembling if everything comes out fine.

He missed Inge-Lise without regret. He missed her warmth and her curiosity and the way she snuck up his stairs and through his door like a burglar. And her embrace. Let the bulkhead be her, what did that hurt. If he didn't turn his head, it was her.

In the matter of Alfaro and the boatyard, he was satisfied enough. The manager would survive. The fire was the best thing that could have happened to him. The owners would need him, and he would emerge from obscurity stronger, and probably as an arm-waving martinet. But modest power corrupts only modestly. As for the grocer Schultz and the cops, he had lined their pockets and kept the receipts. The boys had had an adventure, and done well that hurried night. Waifs were often a good investment.

By now, of course, everybody in Ensenada would think the millionaire Mr. Ayers was lost at sea, sunk by the weight of his own moneybags. And if they thought it was true, it was, for them. Just not for him.

* * *

Ayers was cleaning up after dinner when the VHF radio blared a loud voice that filled the boat.

"You're crazy, I don't see anything out there at all," the voice said.

The accent was eastern European, and the words were clear and startling but not intended for him. Ayers kept the ship's radio on all the time, even though in this sector there was never any traffic. There hadn't been a word over the speakers for at least a month. The world here was empty, as it should be.

He went on deck. Far to the north was a dim white point on the horizon. The sky was all stars, high and bright or low and hazy in the evening mist. The light was a ship, and unexpected. The world's shipping lanes were well established—direct sea highways between the harbors of the world plied by thousand-foot containerships for which time was fuel and money. He reflexively checked the Automatic Identification System at the yacht's navigation station. It was turned off. Disconnected, in fact. AIS was the new radar. It identified vessels to each other in great detail—course, speed, size, destination—and made possible instant communication between bridges. It removed the mystery of vessels passing in the night. For a singlehander like Ayers, an AIS ship alarm was the best defense against being sunk while sleeping, since he had no lookout of any other kind. But his own AIS transponder had been turned off since Ensenada, and the circuit breaker taped over to make sure it did not accidentally give his position away.

To confirm his intended stealth he ran the mental checklist: running lights? Off. Steaming light? Off. Cabin lights? He flipped off the master switch. The other vessel was at the limit of vision, and in fact beyond it. The curve of the earth meant an object rose on the horizon about 11 miles away. A ship's lights could be seen farther than that, because they were often five stories above the surface. They appeared first as a pinpoint, pale as a low star. At about eight miles, multiple white lights could be distinguished. At about six miles, color appeared: red, if the vessel's left side were observed, green if its other side appeared. To see both running lights at once, red and green, meant only one thing: a ship heading directly toward the observer.

This one dim light far away was only an invitation to watch, and see what happened. Even at 20 knots closing speed, half an hour would elapse before evasive action was required. So Ayers made an espresso and waited. It seemed likely that the fragment of voice that had filled the salon was an accident of transmission, a push of an unintended button. No one was looking for him here.

"Hello little sailboat how you doin' out there this lovely night?"

The voice filled the cabin again, buoyant and too loud. Ayers had not heard live speech in months, and immediately reduced the volume on the VHF. The yacht slid silent through the darkness. A flashlight rolled across the chart table. He glanced at the clock: 20:12 hours, 8:12 p.m. He climbed the ladder to the center cockpit and looked again. Same light, possibly brighter. There was no moon yet this evening, although by midnight it would rise, almost full, to illuminate the deck and the whiteness of his towering mainsail. Then he would be visible 20 miles away.

Ayers returned to the chart table and opened the memoirs of John "Dizzy" Gillespie, a founder of modern jazz and the style called bebop, joining him and Charlie Parker and Max Roach on 54th Street, one of those jam sessions with Charles Mingus on bass, Mingus, who got mad so fast you were never sure if he'd hit you. Charlie Parker, a heroin addict, was nodding off again on his chair, which always made Diz worried for him. Ayers could sit in with them any time just by opening the book.

"Little boat, little boat, little boat, this is *Yusha Flying Fish* out of Busan for Panama Canal, little boat, little boat out dere on the deep blue sea."

He heard, or imagined, laughter in the background and the tinkling of ice in glasses. A bottle of slivovitz perhaps, there being nothing else to do out here if the temperatures in the refrigerated containers were holding steady, and the engine room reports were as usual, and the company was not on the phone with some schedule change or weather advisory. Nothing to do most of the time, so any diversion welcome. Ayers went back to his book. It was common for yachts not to monitor the radio, as theoretically required. Even ships didn't. Many times in the past Ayers had hailed passing vessels and never had the courtesy of a reply.

"OK, little boat out there, this is First Officer Semiac and I am wondering this fine night if you got worries because I see you on the radar but there is no AIS signal, so —whazzz up!"

Laughter again. Must be a real party on that bridge. Ayers had another look through the binoculars. The light might have moved a degree to the right in the past 10 minutes, but there was no reference point for confirmation and she was too far away for her running lights to show her course. Was the ship closer? Hard to say. Maybe, maybe not. So he waited. Somebody had to hear a VHF transmission for there to be a reply, and as far as he was concerned nobody on his boat had heard anything.

"OK, little boat, coming over for a look. We're passing close anyhow, no problem at all."

Ayers reached for his microphone and pressed the transmit button.

"Ship calling sailing vessel *Margarita*, go ahead."

He made up the fictitious name on the spot and intentionally transmitted on 1-watt power, which was minimal and unlikely to be heard well.

"Go to 25 watts" the voice said, its tone suddenly professional. Ayers quickly complied.

"That better?"

"Hi. I just been watching you a while and wondering if everything is OK and why don't you use the automatic I.D. system?

"We do, captain," Ayers replied easily. "But it's on the blink right now. We lost it a couple days out of Seattle."

"How big do you have and folks on board?"

"We are a 45-foot sloop with a crew of three, my wife and her sister. How about you, sir?"

The cord for the radio microphone just reached the cockpit, where Ayers had climbed again. He could see that the white light ahead was brighter. He thought he could see the beginnings of red and green, the eyes of a big ship heading directly toward him at 20 knots.

"Cars is all we've got, couple thousand of them. No wives and no sisters."

Ayers paused a moment. Then:

"Well, captain, we're just starting up dinner here, and my wife Sheila says we would like to invite ya'll aboard to join us."

The other tone changed, softened.

"Thank you, sir. Believe me, I would like that very much if it were possible."

Yes, Ayers could now distinguish red and green dead ahead. And above them, the loom of deck lights against the clouds.

"Captain, we are making five knots on two zero zero magnetic. There is no reason to alter course for us, we're not in any distress. Sheila is listening and she would like to send you her regards and thank you for your concern."

In a moment the reply came:

"My wife Henrika says backatcha missus, even though she is far away. Captain, your radar signature very strong and so you don't got to worry about loss of AIS signal right away but probably you should get it fixed when you get there, OK?"

"Understood," said Ayers. "We will do that."

"It is lonely trip without your own people."

"I know it must be. Godspeed then, this is Sailing Vessel *Margarita* out.

"OK, *Yusha Flying Fish* says goodbye and good luck this fine evening for us all."

Ayers heard the other mic click off and the silence return to his cabin. From the ladder he watched the red light slowly disappear, leaving only the green as the vast bulk of the containership, 900 feet long, engines throbbing with 10,000 horsepower, resumed her original course to pass well away on his starboard side.

Would First Officer Semiac write the sighting of a yacht in his log? Probably not. No one would care about such an encounter, certainly not the shipping company. And if he did report it, the log would record a fictional boat called *Margarita*, of fictional size, populated with a fictional crew just sitting down to a fictional dinner.

What was dinner again?

Pasta. Yes, and he would pretend to eat it. He poured a glass of Chianti and let fall a head of garlic on the floor to squash it with the metatarsophalangeal joint of his foot. As the cloves spread he trod them, too, separating the papery skins with a toe. Efficient, if not for public display. He had learned the technique in Bilbao from a new French acquaintance who was younger than she looked and was appointed with very pretty feet. Feet without tendon or bone, feet smooth as alabaster, the feet of the Mona Lisa should the framed portrait ever happen to grow legs.

What was her name? Nina. Mina. Maureen? She had also fed him the garlic paper. Said it deferred aging and was good for the heart and an aphrodisiac, too. Which it might have been, had he not met in conference with her father that very afternoon. M. Lafontaine of the Bank of Paris had not mentioned any accompanying daughter to Bobby Ayers, but he had apparently mentioned Bobby Ayers to his accompanying daughter: that rich American, unattached, and if you wish to ever go on a business trip with me again, *cheri*, steer clear of him.

Not Nina. Mona, maybe? Five-foot-nine and came to dine, bringing all the ingredients. Room service, she called it. They had met accidentally, although in retrospect not accidentally at all, that afternoon at 3 just as his meeting ended. She proposing to be his guide. First to the beach, barefoot. And then some shopping to do in the market, still barefoot. And then the surprise—the shopping was for him, Italian arrabbiata to be prepared by a Frenchwoman in Spain. "We are both hungry, yes?

And then, in his suite, the instruction in the peeling of garlic and the attributes of the paper. Those special attributes. She was wet from her traipse in the Biscayan surf, and he suggested his bathroom for drying off. Use the hair dryer. And now, during the proposition of the garlic, he noticed that beneath the hotel robe she wore nothing, a fact made manifest as she brought her toes up to his nose, so he could inhale their flavor.

"Nina-Mina—Mona (what was it? How unforgivable to forget), stop! You know my name, but I don't know yours." When she said it, a business card flashed in his mind. He remembered the name on every business card he had ever seen.

"Lafontaine? You're the daughter of M. Arnaud Lafontaine, perhaps?"

She pouted.

"Arnaud said he had a daughter, but not that she had come along. A 16-year-old daughter."

"My father will play cards all night. We have until at least midnight," she said, opening the top of the robe preparatory to dropping it to her knees. It took both hands to stop her.

"No, out."

"Excuse me, Bobby?"

"Wipe the garlic off your toes, put your wet pants back on and get going. Now."

"I won't." She stamped her naked foot.

It was so sixteenish it made him rest easy, and enjoy grinning at her. What had she called him then? *Un alésage.* A bore! And his life? *Une farce!* No tears, but instead full justified indignity at a situation in which two people were not to follow the course presented by accident, opportunity and compatibility! But back into her soggy slacks and out the door she went, insulted but intact.

The garlic trick did work, however, so Ayers adopted it thereafter, at least after a few glasses of wine, or whenever his company might be open to new adventures in food preparation. And the deal with Lafontaine's bank did go through, so the Bilbao trip was a success. Doors open. Sometimes success lies in not going through.

When the water had boiled for 11 minutes he removed a dozen quills of penne and laid them carefully in a bubbling sauce that was red and southern and a memory of Calabria, or Amalfi or was it Sorrento? A dusting of parmesan, two swipes from the hard block with the straight grater. The plate was lovely. At his feet the galley floor was still debauched by garlic papers.

What was her name, the flagrant, fragrant daughter of Lafontaine? And had he really been so gallant, or had the episode been revised in the retelling? You had to want to succeed, as he always had. You had to be enlivened by it. It had to be in you, and when you knew it was there it was easy. You succeeded for yourself. No audience was necessary. Others could watch but they weren't involved. Was it a way to hide? No, the game was one against one, always. One against one and one at a time. Well, Arnaud had made money too, there didn't always have to be a loser.

He was surprised to have no appetite, and to dump his full plate into the sink. There came a sort of fuzziness of the skin, an awareness of arms and legs and chest, as if he were hovering just outside himself. His singularity wandered off so that there were two of him, neither curious about the other. The disassociation was temporary, his rational mind could never sustain it for long.

Ayers pulled himself together and picked up the tenor saxophone from the salon bench. The reed was dry and when he blew, a hard wind issued. He blew again, groping to find the perfect form of the note which lived in the diatonic sky. All he had to do was bring one down to earth and then all the other tones would follow, and it would be music. But the forms were out of reach.

We must face the facts, Ayers, both of us.

Go fuck yourself.

You're losing the music.

No, certainly not.

Music is the first to go.

Everything you say is false.

Is it? Her name was Emma, Ayers. Emma! Not Nina-Mina-Miney-Moe, you derelict, you fuckest and fuckee and fucker-over of souls, of women and your better self, you non-thing, you pale memory of nothing much, you never-were, you circus of fleas.

Emma? Yes! I would've gotten it.

Too slow you fool, you dry turd, you rag on a stick.

You talk too much.

You don't talk enough, you never did know what to say, you fatherless motherless whore of the world, you darkness, you loveless corpse in a floating grave.

Ayers said nothing. He just stared himself down, and after a moment the fuzziness returned and he felt the involuntary recombination as an act of his own will.

He went to his stateroom and opened the lowest drawer. The plastic bag inside rattled with a thousand pills as he drew five out and filled a cup from the tap. He had been off them again for two weeks and now it was time to resume. Dr. Stein had said symptoms would come and go. But he liked to wait for evidence.

He lay back on the bed, imagining the chemicals entering his bloodstream. It usually took a few days for them to attain full effect, if in fact they had any effect at all. A lot of what doctors said was speculation. They were often wrong, and liked it that way.

CHAPTER EIGHT

Tax

Laura had been back from Seattle a week, and it had not been a very good week. Eleanor had sent 11 heavy boxes of her father's books, which now occluded passage through her small living room. In a supermarket a reporter from New York Magazine had tracked her down, describing to her his research into the emotional havoc wrought upon daughters by disappearing fathers. He had five powerful examples, he said, and she would make six. No, she wouldn't, and ran over his foot with her shopping cart. She was avoiding her mother, claiming press of her job search. But there was no job search, just avoidance of her mother. Maurice was coming over tonight, that was good. They could wait for the phone to ring together. It would be her father, home with a suntan and no longer the invisible man.

The phone rang. She answered it.

There was a knock on her door. She opened it to find a man replacing his phone to his pocket.

"Laura Ayers," the man said. It was a declaration, not a question. He had a topcoat and a briefcase. He was about

50, brown suit, no tie, Bass loafers. Took out his wallet, held out a card.

"I'm Revenue Officer Mark Scallone of the Internal Revenue Service. Is this a good time?"

"No, as a matter of fact," Laura said.

"No badge, no gun, just a card," he said. "We need to talk. This visit is required of me and it can't be done on the phone. So, is this a good time?

"No, it still isn't."

"I can come back in an hour, if that's better."

"You need to make an appointment, not just show up."

"We don't make appointments, Miss Ayers. But I can sit in my car and wait an hour, if you want some time." She noted his glance at her rumpled sweatsuit and stocking feet, and at the mess in her apartment. What look was that? Women needed to powder their nose before receiving callers? Or have time to hide the three unopened registered letters from the IRS that were lying in plain sight on the foyer table.

"Come in, then," she said.

"Are you satisfied with my identification?" Scallone asked before returning the plastic card to his wallet.

"OK."

"Can we sit down?"

"OK."

They sat down, boxes between them.

"So, how was Seattle?" he asked.

"Seattle was fine, Mr. Scallone. You know my movements, so get to the point, which is that obviously you're following me or something. I heard that you were here yesterday when I was out.

"It goes like this, Laura, if I can call you that," Scallone said. "The Internal Revenue Service has two branches. There's the agents, who figure out what people owe. And there's the collection branch. That's me. I'm called a revenue officer. So let's talk about Robert Ayers. He is your father, right?"

"Yes, he is."

"Any idea where he is right now?"

"He's sailing the world on his sailboat."

"Have you heard from him?"

"He's not big on checking in, with me or anybody else."

"And you're not looking for him."

"No, but if you find him, tell him to call me."

"You know why I'm here, right?"

"I do not."

"We sent letters, as I think you know. You haven't heard from Vivian Liu?

"If you're referring to my father's third wife, we don't exactly chat."

"But you're aware that there's a tax assessment against your father and Vivian Liu, which is why I looked her up. And Miss Liu said I should talk to you, since Miss Liu has no assets at this time, but your father does, and the assessment owed by both of them is substantial.

"What assessment?" Laura asked.

"Three point nine million dollars."

"You can stop acting like I know what you're talking about, because I don't," Laura said.

"Your father didn't pay his taxes. It's been three years, and you handle his accounts."

"I don't handle his accounts."

"You're the sole trustee of the Robert Ayers Living Trust, aren't you?"

"Yes, but my father is going to be back soon. You want to look in my bank account? You won't find $3.9 million there."

"That's not where we're looking. You say your dad went sailing. To my colleagues and me, that appears somewhat timely and convenient. To Vivian Liu, I can tell you, it seems like a criminal act, because she has no assets at all."

"I don't know anything about any of this."

"Ok, you don't know anything. Nobody ever knows anything. But you do now. My department did a jeopardy assessment of our claim against Robert Ayers and we've concluded that collection is in serious jeopardy. Your father fits every profile we have of claim skippers—he changes his address, he's incommunicado for long periods, he has the lifestyle. OK, you don't know any of that. But the next step here is Criminal Division. As sole trustee, if he doesn't show up you're holding the bag. And we will come after you."

"Me? "

"The Ayers Trust. You're it."

"What is it you want me to do, Mr. Scallone?" Laura said.

"Write a check for the tax due. You're the trustee."

"You make it sound like my father's never coming back. But he is, he'll walk in the door tomorrow."

"Tell me where he is, and I'll talk to him."

"I don't know where he is."

"I get it," Scallone said. "You think you're honoring your father. Well, I've got daughters, and I don't think your father is honoring you."

He got up, looked around, and glanced at the unopened IRS letters in their sterling dish. He'd seen them as soon as he came in, and Laura knew it.

"Read your mail, Laura. This isn't a game. People go to jail."

* * *

Maurice was more interested in the boxes of books than in the IRS. He said that the case was already in tax court and would run its course. He was even less interested in the matter of Inge-Lise Sorenson. She was obviously a love affair cooled. One side was always left without answers. One side always sought to know more, and how, and the cause. One side always called and then hung up. Breaking it off with someone wasn't science, he said, it was more like science fiction. Her father had extricated himself, that's all.

Maurice hadn't been there in Seattle and he analyzed emotions like a man, which is to say, clueless. But 'science fiction' did properly evoke the point of view of Phillip, the attentive young orthopedist with whom she had lived for nearly two years and then dumped in a week for Maurice. Tears, anger. Phillip's planet blown up, his world destroyed. But what could you say? There were no words for goodbye. There were no words for hello, either. She and Maurice had been seated together at a fundraiser auction. Then a week later his hands were on her waist in a summer parking lot. Then another week and she was packing up, Phillip trying to block the door, Phillip calling her an alien, demanding the human Laura back. What could you say about love? Maurice, who had pursued her, said of Phillip that "He doesn't know who you are." That meant Maurice thought he did.

"I'm anxious to see his books," he said, unaware of her thoughts.

"Great." Laura's tone was distant.

"No really, that one dinner we had together with your dad, I was impressed. He knew St. Augustine, he knew Miles Davis. It wasn't small talk, we got into things. He has curiosity."

"What you saw was yourself, Maurice. That's what he does."

"I know what I saw. Come on."

He led her to the boxes and dragged one to her and one to himself. He was a kid under a Christmas tree. He was the son of a scholar and born with a critical eye, education his sword and shield more than basketball ever had been.

"They're autobiographies," Laura said. "You know, Henry Ford, Thomas Edison, how to get rich."

Maurice read the spines as he pulled them out: "Frank Lloyd Wright. Salvador Dali. Andre Carnegie. Robert Mitchum, the actor." He laughed. "'It Sure Beats Working,' that's the title. This is really your father's stuff?"

"Albert Schweitzer," she read. "Who's he again?" Maurice told her to keep going. "James Joyce, 'Portrait of the Artist as a Young Man.' I had to read that, it's stupid. Listen: 'Once upon a time and a very good time it was there was a moocow coming down along the road and this moocow that was down along the road met a nicens little boy—.'"

"Joyce was remembering his moral education. He was searching, and he found something," Maurice said.

She threw the book at him, hard. He caught it.

"Look at the marginal notes he made," Maurice said. "Page 83: 'If a man stole a pound in his youth, then got rich and gave it back, should he pay interest?'" He laughed. "Your father says, yes!" He pulled out more books. "Ben Franklin. Tolstoy. Elie Wiesel, the Nazi hunter. The pages are loaded with his handwriting. Here's Liberace: 'I don't give concerts—I put on a show.' Who underlines Liberace?"

Maurice was pawing through the books now, tossing them into stacks, bits of cardboard floating down onto the rug between them. "Charles Darwin. David Hume, the philosopher. Hume says we think by instinct, we can't help it—"

"Stop," Laura said.

"Nobody reads Hume for the fun of it, your father was mining these guys. Winston Churchill, Malcolm X, P.T. Barnum, Nikola Tesla, 'Inside the Third Reich' by Albert Speer—"

When he didn't stop she got up and took a walk, the afternoon clear and cool. By dinner time, when she returned, Maurice was as he had been, hunched over. He looked like a medieval monk and she knew to approach with caution. There was a sharp edge to his study in contrast to her own long-standing impatience, even outright boredom, with classrooms. She had done fine without a need to know. He loved knowledge but distrusted it at the same time, especially ambition in the cloak of scholarship. At Yale he had prepared himself to have a real job among real people. Unlike his father.

Maurice's father lived in England now and they communicated only through others, as Laura had learned on their second date when a distinguished man named Derek took them to dinner in New Haven. He reported that Lionel Charles was teaching in Manchester, and said that it was a shame they were estranged and don't let it go on like that until he gets sick. He misses you.

Maurice had listened, noncommittal. Laura had liked Derek, and had seen his bond with Maurice. Only on the drive home did she learn that Derek Walcott had won the Nobel Prize in Literature. Only then had the door begun to open on Maurice's past, in which the family business was the business of books.

"Let's get some real dinner."

He didn't look up from reading.

"Maurice, put your shoes on. I made a reservation."

She craved a public place, bodies moving, glasses tinkling. She wanted space, time and a way forward, not the wisdom of ages. She wanted the future, not the past.

* * *

The Southport Inn was where her father had taken her many times. It spread across the waterfront cove like the hotel it once had been, glass fronting on moored boats and families strolling on the harbor walk. It was old-fashioned, and Maurice liked that. It was one of his quirks. Over the long bar with its colonial chairs and couples waiting for tables, NCAA basketball played on a flatscreen. At their table Maurice sat with his back to the TV. He had not played since college but he loved coming here, where she was Bobby Ayers' daughter. It had been her father's place. Now, to her surprise, it was their place.

She knew what was coming. For an hour, through half a bottle of wine, Maurice talked about nothing but her father, about how he had carved his own statue out of stone, about how he had seen the universe as a blank slate to be written upon. How that was the way to do it. How they could do it with the will to create themselves and the power to resist expectations. He wanted a house. He wanted children someday. He wanted success for both of them, with parity and obligation and steadiness. He wanted peace, a little utopia they would earn with their souls. These dreams she didn't fully understand. He said it was his intention not to live in the world, but to invent it.

Laura was salvaged from listening by a young, pale father who appeared with a skinny kid crowned with ringlets of golden hair. He approached cautiously, as if he knew how much Maurice did not like to be interrupted while speaking his serious words.

"Sir? Excuse me, I'm Jim Hollie, this is my son, Lawrence, he's on a league team for 8-10s." The boy stood uneasily in a basketball uniform of the Bridgeport Red Devils. "Mr. Charles, I watched you on ESPN all the way through college and into March madness that year, and you guys had such a great team, and I said to Lawrence here I would take a chance and see if we could get a selfie."

Laura saw the boy's mother, an elegant Somali woman, cringing where she had been left alone at her table: great, the man's having dinner, so come at him with a cell phone. But it wasn't one of those times Maurice didn't want to be interrupted. He pulled the boy onto his lap. He put up his left hand, and the boy's hand against it, displaying the size disparity. They grinned, cheek to cheek. The iPhone flash went off, and every head in the place turned toward the light.

"The doctors think he'll be tall," Jim Hollie said. "His mother and I are both tall, which they say indicates that."

"He already is," Maurice said.

Then Laura watched the boy rise, Maurice lifting him effortlessly with a smooth clean and jerk to hold him high in the air.

"Just tap it in," Maurice called up.

The boy swept his arm as if dunking a ball from 10 feet high, and as he did the iPhone flash went off again. And other phones flashed too. Maurice kept him up there a while, and by the time he brought him down the entire restaurant was applauding as father, son and Maurice smiled for the cameras.

Laura watched as the attention of the room slowly returned to dinner, its conversation animated by the shared moment. A waiter appeared with tiramisu, compliments of the house, and also shook Maurice's hand.

"What was that all about?" said Laura.

"I was just thinking, if we have a son, probably he'll look like that. Of course you're not as tall as her," he said, nodding at the Somali mother, who waved.

"That was nice what you did, Maurice."

He put down his fork and took her hand.

"No pressure," Maurice said.

CHAPTER NINE

Storm

Ayers was up to the 20-pound dumbbells now, and had been for two days. He had begun lifting weights a week before and knew from experience that months would pass before any visible change, but he already felt stronger. The constantly moving yacht could be relied upon to keep him limber, since every moment was an isometric exercise of balance. The dumbbells had come out in response to an unfamiliar looseness of his shirt sleeves. Well, he would get the biceps back. The cause of atrophy was electric winches, no cranking required. He smiled. Being rich made you weak, if you let it.

You, but not me.

The trapezoids of light cast by the cabin ports had moved to a new position on the varnish of the cabin floor. That meant a wind shift. He secured the weights to their rack and noticed the self-steering had turned to a new course of 160 degrees magnetic. No longer due south. He climbed to the cockpit and toweled off in the humid air. Overhead the white fulmar hovered. The day was as it should be:

cumulus columns against a tropic sky, scattered whitecaps all around. He urinated in a former Clorox bottle cut to receive his anatomy, then tossed the container into the sea. It jerked short on its restraining line, emptying and cleansing itself. The design was his own and made a trip to the head below unnecessary. The fulmar watched, pasted in the sky.

Beyond the bird was a haze of cirrus clouds frozen high in the troposphere. They had not been there before. His arms ached from the weights so he rested a moment, then slipped below to the galley. He drew a beaker of water and drained it. Thirty ounces a day were necessary to correct for perspiration. It was midday, and also prudent to eat something. But tonight he would make a stew with the Kobe beef already defrosting, and for desert ice cream with maple syrup. That would get the calories up. So instead of lunch he returned to the cockpit and the sky. Yes, cirrus: ice clouds that signaled an arriving front.

He had recognized them first in the North Atlantic, 10 years before. His hired captain, Campbell, made a story of all clouds, and the lesson of cirrus was that a gale would come, and that time it had. Campbell had been an accident. Sailboats had been an accident. The ocean had been an accident, if there were accidents in anyone's life.

He had needed to meet with a half-dozen Washington lobbyists for a day of government relations. It was recommended that he entertain them first, so he chartered a skipjack sailboat in nearby Annapolis, on the Chesapeake, with Captain Alexander Campbell in charge. That would loosen up his new friends prior to revealing his needs from them. The skipjack was a former oyster-dragger, broad and crude, with a steeply raked mast. The day had little wind, which his guests and their wives combatted with rum and tonic and oysters served by watermen in white aprons. The clumsy sails hung limp and the water was a brown soup of tentacled jellyfish. Ayers asked the taciturn Campbell if the business of sailing was always like this.

Campbell said yes, when sailing was business.

He discovered that year that he did not like government contracts, but he did like boats. He employed Captain Campbell to educate him. Campbell took him sailing on an International 14 dinghy in 20 knots, with Ayers on the trapeze. He introduced him to the Laser, a simple racing dinghy which he capsized half a dozen times, cracking a rib in the process. He was almost 50, at the height of his powers, and found himself transformed and redeemed. Sailing fulfilled a need for intimacy beyond people. Their concerns, and his, were swept away by the magic of his hand on a tiller, the wind in his face, and the power to align himself with universal forces. It put him at the helm of the world.

The next year he hired Campbell full time, and that winter they sailed in Newport, Charleston and Biscayne Bay on chartered yachts with pro crews whose brains he picked at his leisure. Ayers had never taken a vacation before, but that year he did almost no business at all. By spring he owned a Swann 40, a sleek Finnish sailboat. By fall, he and Campbell and two hired crew sailed her across the Atlantic from Newport, R.I., encountering two full gales. At Plymouth, England, minutes after the yacht was moored, Ayers shook hands all around, wrote a $5000 bonus check for Campbell, and called a taxi. Campbell never saw him again. The pupil had graduated.

Now he recalled the gales. He had been seasick for the first, violently, as they lay hove to for 50 hours. By the second storm he had begun to grasp the warning of isobars that bent close to one another, and under the tutelage of Campbell to understand the tactics and gear necessary to survive them. He became, that voyage, a student of weather. In Europe or China, wherever he was thereafter, he saw the signs, smelled the changes, felt the seasons as living things. The sky was the best business investment he'd ever made. It showed him the signs of the storms in himself, and to wait out the gales.

So: ice clouds meant an arriving front. In the North Atlantic it had been cold. Here the temperature was 82F and the wind only 18 knots, tropical and perfect. He ordered a shortwave weatherfax. It showed no storm in this sector. He retrieved the 10-day Grib wind predictions, which foresaw a pleasant 15-20 knots from the east. Perhaps it was not high cirrus he saw after all. He tapped the aneroid barometer and watched its pointer drop suddenly a quarter-inch. He got his reading glasses and looked again. That must be wrong. A barometer, Captain Campbell had said, is a simple instrument. It's just a needle glued to a copper box of air that expands and contracts with atmospheric pressure. But because a barometer is simple, it is never wrong. It leaves that to us.

By dusk a long swell was making up. The yacht jogged on across the remains of the afternoon. At the top of each swell the view expanded, as if the world became bigger, and in the troughs the world shrank. For dinner Ayers warmed a few slices of beef in the microwave. Not enough calories, but if he had eggs for breakfast that would make up for the deficit.

In the log he recorded the barometric pressure, wind speed and direction and then reclined on the curving divan of the main salon. The breeze entered the forward hatches, scoured the crew compartments, cleansed the two heads, wafted pleasantly through the guest cabin, fanned the salon and disappeared behind him into his own quarters. It made a breathy female whisper he could feel on his cheek. The wind was his only company. When he wanted more, they were in the letters of the plastic shoe box now in his lap.

Three were from Eleanor, his first wife, the ones which had reached him after he had fled to Spain. There was a photo of her sleigh-riding in a snowstorm. One mitten, waving. There were a half-dozen from Laura, the first in a child's hand, formally thanking him for their week on Cape Cod. Then as a teenager, complaining about her mother. Then, suddenly a young woman, apologetic about missing their dinner appointment. The letters from Julia, her mother, revealed handwriting as buoyant as she was, even in the fading ink of his own address. Of Vivian, his third wife, he had kept two letters. They were mature but erotic. The first was her note on hotel stationery accepting his transparent proposition. The second was her typed acceptance of his long-distance marriage proposal. It bore a fake notary stamp and a seductive Polaroid of her on a hotel bed in Singapore. All of Vivian was a weapon, sharp or funny. He had loved her. He still loved them all. Ayers had never responded to any of the letters, but knew why he had kept them. In them, all futures remained possible. In them, he could be someone else.

No saxophone tonight, the boat was moving around too much.

* * *

In rough sailing conditions like this Ayers slept sitting up, dozing on and off, revisiting the fog that for 40 years had interrupted plans and subjected him to profits lost, partners abandoned and periodic banishment.

Well, he couldn't explain to them how he periodically became a stranger to himself. The days and weeks of sitting in a chair. The months in which it was a dreary exercise to answer the door or to exist at all. The times of hiding lest he be found out and his weakness revealed and the useful mythology erased. He didn't feel the blackness now, nor did he any longer have to plan for its seasonable coming. No longer have to make every deal now, before incapacity came, to push and posture and persuade, to drive every day with a whip. No longer have to deceive his associates with the camouflage of eccentricity. He trusted himself now.

What had been his condition? Ayers had stopped asking after the winter of his 28th year. Newly millioned, he had traveled to Ottawa so Dr. Lang could save him or cure him or punish him or whatever shrinks were supposed to do. He had bought the distinguished psychiatrist's services for 30 days, an exclusive consultancy at the cost of $100,000 Canadian. Dr. Lang, of the tests and questions and curiosity and skepticism. Dr. Lang, eyes cold as his own, neither father nor lover, and who had said that since Bobby Ayers had no intent to harm himself, he should consider himself to be an artist. That is, different. That is, other. That is, of value beyond explanation.

There are chemicals we can try, Bobby, Lang had said. They may work for a time, or not at all, or forever. I could give you a diagnosis, Bobby, and then you would have a name for what you are. But you already have a name, Bobby. And, Bobby, you are a success in this life as few others are.

You may therefore think of yourself as the teacher of all the rest of us.

Why had he so valued their month together? Probably because his energy and spirits were already returning on schedule, as they always eventually did. And because Dr. Lang, at 88, was far from judgement or answers. They had been to the same nameless place, and both had come back, and Dr. Lang knew that this time he could not stay, and Bobby could.

Nothing like a dying shrink to tell it like it is. You can't get that from a live one.

At about 4 a.m. Ayers thought of tea, but the thought passed. He had no needs.

* * *

At dawn the swells were smooth blue hills. The wind and the course were the same but the sky different: it was red, and the cirrus had formed into grey altostratus that spread a halo around the sun. He had seen that in the Atlantic. It meant a warm front approaching, and with it a storm. He went below and found the barometer had dropped still further. Never seen it that low. He tested himself with deep knee bends. The strength was sufficient for what he had to do.

The storm trysail was in the sail locker aft and he intended to set it early, long before it was needed, because that's what all the books said to do. He found the 80-pound sack of heavy Dacron where it was supposed to be and wrestled it to the foot of the companionway stairs. There was no way he could lift it over his head and up to the cockpit. Therefore he ran a spare spinnaker halyard below, trussed the bag with a lifting strap, and used the electric winch to grind it in stages up through the cockpit hatchway.

On deck, he furled the mainsail into its boom. The trysail was designed to replace the big sail in stormy weather. It set on a separate track on the mast that extended almost 40 feet above the deck. Ayers realized for the first time that he could not reach even the foot of the track.

What's the matter?

I've never set a trysail before.

Find a way, then.

That's what I'm doing.

To extend his reach he rove a footrope around the joint of the boom and mast. It made a loop to stand in. He rigged the main halyard to the headboard of the trysail. From a drawer below he retrieved the power winch remote control. He balanced in the footrope and lashed himself to the mast by his tether. Using the remote control he could guide the sail into its track. The movement of the yacht made it difficult and the job took nearly an hour, but by noon the trysail was set, its skinny triangle replacing the lovely curvature of the mainsail. There was very little wind, but the light had changed.

Ayers returned to the navigation station but was unable to update his weatherfax or Grib predictions. That was the trouble with shortwave: just as the atmosphere got belligerent reception retired to a neutral corner. He thought to take more of Stein's pills, now, when he could. Or had he already taken them in the night? A shadow brought him back on deck.

Black nimbostratus clouds were bearing down, a ragged line advancing across what now seemed a dead calm. The yacht wallowed. Ayers quickly reduced the staysail by 50 percent. He felt over-prepared. The air here was sultry, nothing like the chill of an approaching front in the North

Atlantic. In this sector of the Pacific there were no major storms, which was why he was here, crossing tracks only with himself.

Scud approached, scraps of cloud pointing wispy fingers. On the dome of the sky the cirrus raced, propelled by upper level winds. He wondered why, with no jet stream to propel them. Now whitecaps turned the long swells snowy. He felt his hair blow back and his shirt begin to flap as what had been a rampart of cloud split vertically into harsh, down-driving lines of force that flayed the water beneath them: line squall arriving.

The trysail filled with a snap. Fat raindrops struck like pebbles. Ayers dropped down the companionway to yank on his weather gear and as he returned topside *Après Vous* entered a waterfall. He clung to the binnacle handholds as rain, astringent in its absence of salt, poured through his hair and down his back. The sea flattened to pewter, the yacht accelerating to 10 knots. It took an effort to look up to where the staysail spouted water in broad sheets that flew to leeward. Ayers heard a cry arise, a war whoop.

It was his own voice. Squalls were glorious. The yacht was built for them, and he was too. Under his feet he felt the vibration of the autopilot holding course. He disconnected it and took command of the wheel, bearing off two spokes south. Immediately the wheel centered, tractable again. The deluge continued but he steered easily. He carved "S" turns, just for the love of it. He turned upwind enough to feel where the wind was, and felt the boat heel obediently. He resumed course due south, braced at the helm, the decks drumming, the sails pulling, and seeing himself for what he was: a yellow smudge on a streaming watercolor of blacks and grays. Thirty minutes later, wet through and shivering, he set the automatic steering again and went below to shake himself like a dog.

But how grand this heavenly wash! How suddenly cleansed the salt-caked rigging, the stiff sails, the decks of their desiccated flying fish! He, too, felt clean. He wanted a towel and to dry his hands and to have the taste of chocolate in his mouth. Soon the squall would pass on, as they always did.

This one didn't.

In an hour, as he watched out the portlights, the long swells steepened, whipped by new gusts of 40 knots. On this beam reach, where the wind arrived directly from the side, even the storm sail lent unnecessary speed. They flew across the afternoon, the bow kicking spray 10 feet high. On the stereo speakers of the cabin the elegies of Rachmaninoff continued to play softly, but when Ayers stuck his head out of the hatch the wind was a roar.

He furled the staysail completely but they were still going too fast. The anemometer touched 50 knots, full gale force for a moment. He smiled at how the boat shrugged it off. Well, they had plenty of sea room—2,000 miles of it and no land to hit. He noticed the windmill electricity generator on the stern turning slowly, and tightened its brake. He checked the rigging—all systems good. The sky to the east was breaking up now.

The ship's clock said 1700 hours, 5 o'clock in the afternoon, and marked the beginning of fatigue. He had not slept well the night before. His arms hurt. One knee flexed involuntarily in the rat-tat-tat of a sewing machine. Without further thought Ayers laid himself on the nearest bunk. He forbad dreams to come, and by his own command entered the realm of sleep for a planned duration of one hour.

* * *

The crash of splitting wood woke him, or the recollection of it, as he flew through air, hands flailing for a grip, to land on his side in a shower of splinters. As he rose he fell again, the compartment floor dropping and tilting beneath him.

What?

The bunk board broke.

Get up, get up.

Something in my neck.

Pull it out. Get up.

I dreamed again of murder.

Get up, get up.

A machine-gun clattering shook the cabin as Ayers wiped blood from his neck. In his hand was a foot-long splinter of mahogany. The wound was insignificant, and he knew that at once. But the boat was being shaken apart, so he quickly clipped in the safety tether at the companionway. As he climbed the stairs tried to throw him off. On deck it was black night with walls of water on either side, and the shaking was unnaturally mechanical. He was blind, unable to sense the crest of seawater that burst in his face. He groped below to the electrical panel and switched on the spreader lamps. In an instant floodlights turned the world to day.

Now he could see the tower of the windmill generator whipping and the runaway propeller at its head. As he crawled to its base a scimitar blade spun by his head to slash into the sea. As he tightened the propeller brake the entire apparatus above him exploded in a shower of sparks and hurled itself into the wake.

Well, that solved itself.

He altered course downwind, and the long yacht responded with still more speed. He set the automatic pilot, switched off the blinding lights, and let the world return to windy darkness. He returned belowdecks, aware of himself as wet, nauseated, weak and also at peace. There was nothing now but to endure. He was good at that. He had a lifetime of practice.

* * *

At first light it was apparent that *Après Vous* was tripping over herself. In the bunk he could feel her slide down a wave, then sheer sharply. It felt like turning an ankle off a curbstone, but he knew what it must be. The keel of the boat was six feet deep. Inside the keel was a centerboard, a heavy knife blade which when extended gave a draft twice that for better directional control. That was not needed now, and was cutting her legs from under her. At the control panel he commanded the centerboard to retract. Motors whined as the plate withdrew, and when the next wave came, *Après Vous* was a different creature. Her heels free, she glided again, gracefully yielding to the confused seas. Never had he been more in tune with his boat. Never had he felt more kinship, or more sure of his command.

He slid into the navigation table to check the record of barometer readings. After sinking for hours the barometer now held steady. He tapped the glass and the pointer jumped. Ah, barometer rising. Wind speed now only 35 knots, in the lulls. So the storm was passing. He noted a sense of loss, almost an emptiness. All right, eat something. He put a teakettle of water to boil on the gimballed stove. The freezer was packed with elk from Wyoming, grass-fed buffalo steaks, gumbo prepared in New Orleans, frozen blocks of chutoro tuna at a thousand dollars each—sushi for his whim and the finest Japanese whisky to wash it down. It was dawn, but dawn was dinner time if he so declared, and many days he had. Time was his, here. He owned it.

No, ramen would do for now. He got most of the noodles down. Opening a cube of chocolate he found his fingers sore and knuckles swollen and numb. He nibbled standing, belted in at the galley stove, swaying with the crashing movement of the boat, until the clock said an hour had passed. Then he consulted the barometer again. It was still rising.

That should mean the warm front had passed. But in the North Atlantic it had not meant that. There, 20 years before in the westerly approaches to Plymouth, England, the rising barometer had been a cruel misdirection. It had meant in fact the sudden arrival of a cold front, a billion tons of frigid air falling to crash upon the sea and rebound in violent up-currents and schizoid gusts. Captain Campbell, his mentor and teacher, had seen it coming in the sky. What had been bleak Atlantic gray had split suddenly above them to reveal a brilliant azure sky flecked with colliding clouds. And then the worst of the gale descended. The seas had risen higher and begun to break. For 30 hours Ayers had been sick and cold to his marrow and lost in a private approximation of death. They had not died, but sailed into harbor triumphant only four days later. Ayers had never been seasick again. Every storm ended, as this one was ending now. He decided to wait another hour before opening the hatch to confirm, but could not. His strength was failing and he knew it. News now, whatever news it be.

He threw back the hatch and saw the sky torn across. Bright sun shone weirdly through the rent fabric of boiling clouds, painting the deck white against the shadows all around. The seascape was a cone of violence all around with the yacht at its core. They were in the trough of a wave, and as they rose on the next a violent gust from a new direction arrived. *Après Vous* fell on her side, shaking. The veer of the gust was 40 degrees, and set the trysail aback and hysterically thundering. Ayers crawled to the cockpit and took control of the wheel, turning the boat to starboard. She obeyed, but slowly. He knew he must guide her down the next wave, away from its breaking face. He bore off, surrounded by foam and spray as they surfed, steering with all his strength lest the yacht turn broadside, and broach. Then the next wave lifted them to be struck in the face from a new direction. The trysail turned inside out and the boat all but stopped dead as he fought to regain control. As they fell away a weird twanging came from above, the sound of metal bending. He lifted his eyes to see the entire trysail streaming like a pennant above him.

It had come off the mast.

The 40-foot stainless steel track that had held it was reshaped now to a shepherd's crook, curving free of its connection to the tall spar. It whipped and moaned like a bent guitar string. As the track swung it shed the sail one attachment at a time, flinging the slides into the air until it ballooned like laundry. The sight made no sense at all. The track was fixed to the mainmast every six inches with heavy machine screws. It could not possibly come loose. It could not possibly flail in the air like a whip. But it could, and he understood immediately why. Alfaro, the boatyard manager in Mexico, had warned that the installations were behind schedule. Alfaro, who had kept the secret of Ayers' premature departure, but uneasily, and in protest of his unreadiness. The yard crew had put in the machine screws as high as they could reach. The rest of the track installation would require a ladder. But no ladder had been used, and the missing screws were not visible from the deck. Well, he couldn't blame Alfaro for that. It was the cost of haste, and payment had now become due.

With a clang! of rending metal the upper track restraint broke and he watched the entire trysail depart into the sea. The yacht wallowed, its driving force lost. They lay helpless, sideways to the breaking seas. Ayers was knocked down as a wavetop burst aboard, filling the cockpit with water. Take action. Any action. Take it now, before we are swept again.

He reached for the fish knife Velcroed inside the companionway. The trysail halyard was half-inch Dyneema line, stronger than steel, but would cut with a knife. And once cut, the halyard would run wildly through its blocks and the trysail would be lost. It was, as with a loud report the line ran smoking to the top of the 90-foot mast. In an instant a new wave hurled the yacht sideways and as Ayers watched, *Après Vous* overran her own lost sail.

He retracted the centerboard too late. The lifting motors whirred, but stopped. He kept his finger on the toggle switch until he smelled smoke from the motor. The sail had fouled in the keel. The yacht went sluggish, as if it had run aground. New seas advanced from the east, steepening. He could see through stinging spray parallel lines of spume that marked them like roads to the summit.

The anemometer read 60 knots. That was as high as it went. *Après Vous* lay vulnerable. The seas were three stories high. Ayers knew the boat must point into them, or be overcome. He started the engine, opened the throttle, and turned the wheel. A strong prop wash erupted under the stern and he felt the rudder respond. The big diesel faltered, seemed to recover, and then with a shudder jerked to a complete halt. The propeller had caught the trysail lines, wound them around the spinning shaft, and strangled itself. They lay now without steerageway.

You're frightened.

No, but my mouth is dry.

This boat is too big for one man, you knew that.

No, this is why we came.

He watched himself like a movie, and what he saw was a lone man, skinny and ragged, in a flooded cockpit far from land. It was true that he felt no particular fear, or any emotion at all except a dull impulse to get on with it and see what happened.

He had prepared for gales with a Jordan series drogue. It was 350 feet of line festooned with 165 fabric cones and 50 pounds of chain as a weight on the end. It was to be streamed behind the boat in a storm. The drogue, each of its cones acting as an individual drag, would keep the boat's stern to wind and breaking waves. That was necessary because even without sail up, *Après Vous* could hurtle out of control down the face of a monster wave to trip and be rolled and torn apart. The drogue would prevent that, or so it was said. Ayers had never deployed a drogue before. It would be heavy and awkward for one man to set. The forces upon it were huge, and rehearsal in storm conditions was not practical.

The drogue was stored in the dinghy locker in two heavy bags. Only one of his arms now obeyed Ayers' commands. After two more hours the maze of cones and lines filled the cockpit. As he untangled their coils, arriving seas flooded the cockpit to tangle them again. The heavy loops of the bridle he placed over the yacht's stern cleats. He tried to think through what would happen when he deployed this rig. The heavy chain-weight would drop first, to unspool the drogue and its cones as if pulled by a harpooned whale. If caught in its coils Ayers would go overboard too. The drogue would stream aft in the wake behind them. They would then run before the storm, guided and steadied by this long kite-tail. The Jordan drogue had saved many a short-handed crew. If launched successfully, nothing else had to be done. You went below, dogged down the hatches, and waited for the gale to blow itself out.

But if he screwed up the deployment the drogue could pull the rudder off. It could pull the whole stern right off the boat. If it pulled Ayers off, he would gasp and flail and then sink two miles to the ocean floor below. Right now he could hardly move. Muscular response was slow and even the involuntary action of breathing seemed ineffective. Clarity remained, however.

It was hard to look into the wind, but when he did he saw a wave larger than the rest. It stood above them all. It gathered itself, steering toward the target of *Après Vous*.

To set the drogue he needed to head downwind, at least for a moment. He could use the bow thruster. It was a separate propeller in the front of the hull, useful in docking. To turn it on took only a finger on a switch. He heard the motor whine and saw the bow begin to turn. A sea burst aboard, knocking him down again. He got his finger back on the switch and the turning continued.

There was time to study the mountain of water bearing down from behind. It was a rogue wave, all right. He had read about them. In any field of waves it was statistically inevitable that one three times the height of average would periodically appear. That made this one six stories high. It stood like a master of its kind, foam-capped, towering, shouldering aside the lesser brethren in its path.

That one has our name on it, Ayers.

Your name, maybe, not mine.

With his hand on the bow-thruster control, the boat still sluggishly turning downwind, he had never been more willfully alive. The black dog that had trotted by his side all his life was left behind. The emptiness was gone, and the present world was brimming full. The body that contained him was a ruin, starved, aching, but awaiting commands. It would do what it was told. The sight of the world exploding all around, the feel of the gale on his skin, the roar in his ears, the salt in his eyes, was him, its creator, the beginning and the end of everything. He had no safety tether on and stood balanced awkwardly on the snake pit of rope and drogue that filled the cockpit. If the rogue wave washed him away he would be lost without hope of rescue. He observed it begin to break along its face, 200 yards away, on target.

If I die, so will you, wave.

When I end, so does all this.

There was no time to wait, so as quickly as he could Ayers crawled over the lumpy pile to the chain-weight at its end. It took all his strength to lift that to the fantail, and as he did his feet sank deeper in the clinging coils. With useless arms he embraced the chain against his chest. His legs were numb. He could not hurry and so he didn't. He concentrated on the work and didn't look up until he felt the stern rise like an elevator.

The time was now. He pushed the 50 pounds of chain over the transom. As the first links fell they drew the others behind them, link by link, grinding the elegant taffrail. The rate of deployment accelerated, rattling, until the drogue itself followed, its cones grasping at his legs. The first of them did nothing to slow the boat. But as more followed, 10 cones, then 20, they gripped the wake in handfuls, accelerating in their departure. The whipping cones were like a rug being pulled out from under him. He dove away to cling to the handhold of the binnacle guard as the hundreds of feet of line now poured into the sea, leaping and twisting in a violent blur as the stern of *Après Vous* rose suddenly toward the sky. He looked up.

Directly above him was a wall of ocean, its face impossibly steep. Bits of seaweed hung as if nailed there. Its vertical streaks of foam were ladders to the clouds. At its peak, surf was forming. From it a cloak of white spray blew horizontally like the anvil head of a thunderstorm. The wave was transparent, and within it Ayers could plainly see the long line of the drogue and its cones, suspended.

The yacht seemed pointed straight down, and began to fall head first into the valley below. Ayers felt the world tilt, his own bare feet sliding. He watched the top of the mountain collapse and the avalanche begin, his boat running down the slope in flight. When she hit the bottom of the trough her bow would dig in, she would veer and broach, and there, belly up and helpless, the rogue would devour her.

But as she fled down the face of the wave the drogue found purchase. Its long length had penetrated not one wave, but also the wave to come. No single one of its cones could resist, but all together they formed a mighty drag, an irresistible slowing force. Ayers could see them hanging in the blue precipice and watch the miracle unfold.

Après Vous, racing toward disaster down the breaking face, stopped suddenly like a dog reaching the end of its leash. Her broaching turn snapped straight and for a moment she hung suspended. The avalanche caught them then. Ayers watched it fall from the sky. It swept the deck five feet deep and plucked him from his handholds.

He swam floating in the airy foam, borne somewhere he could not see and conscious of the instant that the universe disappeared.

CHAPTER TEN

Drive

The afternoon was gray. Laura was due at a baby shower at 5 p.m. Her car headed north into the drizzle of Interstate 95 toward Guilford, where her college girlfriend Holly was giving birth soon for the third time. The wipers swished rhythmically. She kept to her box of traffic in one wet, hissing lane. She navigated unconsciously, houses and hills passing, Long Island Sound appearing occasionally in the mist.

Wiper wiper wiper.

She resisted confronting her mother with the new will. It put something between them. She chose not to know her father as others knew him, and the Living Trust changed that. Her stepfather Ed and her mother Julia were the home fires burning. Bobby Ayers had been something beyond, something interesting in her she kept for herself. She felt sometimes like a village girl in a storybook whose father is a vagabond king who appears in the dead of night to sweep her away on his white horse but always bring her back by morning. Now it was more like he had sent her out to bring him back.

She felt the wheel in her hands and her tongue in her mouth. It was the only evidence she had of herself, the one they called Laura, the competent one, the one with the crazy, rich dad.

The exit for her father's divorce house was one mile ahead. The turn-off always jolted her back. He had only lived there only a few years, when Laura was nine, but she remembered the entry into leafy streets, and her stepfather Ed parking in the crescent driveway and Bobby Ayers, coming out to open her backseat door. It always seemed to be summer, and she always seemed to be happy. She liked that her father and stepfather shook hands warmly, and seemed to be friends. That hadn't been weird until later.

Her father took her on the train to New York, which she liked, and to Radio City Music Hall and to hotels where she had her own huge bed with a chocolate on the pillow. Sometimes he had meetings, but most of the time it was just a succession of taxicabs together to places she no longer remembered. He had been the master of the declarative sentence. He would say, "Tonight we're going to the theater." He would say, "Let's go down and have some breakfast." He would say, "The reason the sound on the TV won't get any louder is that the hotel doesn't want our TV to bother other people." He often began sentences with "The reason," as in, "the reason we're going to this Broadway play is that you've never been to one before." She waited for him to say, "The reason your mother and I got a divorce..." but he never did. You could relax around him. There was a sort of mutual trust. He didn't inquire, he seemed content just that she was there. Whereas her mother drilled questions into your brain.

She would have been nine that first train ride to New York. Where was it he first bought her ice cream? Rumplemyers. The cone upsidedown, like a clown hat. There had been a girl her age at a nearby table. Their eyes had met. "This is my real father," their eyes had said. It was a secret, haughty, heady thing, and they both had felt it instantly. Can a girl see her father objectively? Sure, if he's not around much. You can see how women look at him and smile. You can know he was handsome.

Is handsome.

The exit for Guilford and the baby shower appeared out of the rain and Laura went by it at 60 miles an hour.

Wiper wiper wiper.

Wait, that was the exit, wasn't it? She looked for the next off-ramp, trying to get over through the trucks. She was already half an hour late. Selma, her old roommate, would be there, who had met her father at Penn. They'd had dinner together, the three of them, and Selma afterwards had called him a 'rascal.' Hands off, Selma, you don't say that. You don't act *interested*. The sky was low and darkening and headlights gleamed from the opposing lanes. The next exit to take her back was Durham Road. She went by Durham Road without even slowing down.

Of age nine Laura remembered only school and friends. Also, their two Labradors and a general anticipation of things to come. Being nine was temporary. Everybody moved up right on schedule, you just had to wait and in the meantime they told you everything to do. Teams. Clubs. Sleepovers. Parents.

She called Maurice, who answered instantly.

"Hi, what's up?"

"Nothing, just driving in the rain."

"OK," Maurice said, "I can talk you through it but give me a minute to finish up this last meeting."

"Talk me through what?"

"Talk to you, that's all," Maurice said in his even, patient tone. She could hear voices around him, phones ringing, his office busy and alive.

"You finish up, I'll call you tonight, love you, 'bye."

She ended the call and the hiss of the roadway returned. She exploited him and he indulged her. He would talk away her miles on the telephone speaker better than any radio. He would talk about her, them, his childhood, the news. He would dredge his well-informed mind for stuff to fill the air, he would marvel for her at the Chinese economy or microbes on Mars or just how things were made, curtain rods to pharmaceuticals, in a seamless modulated baritone solely intended to pass her time on the highway, and be with her. He was interested in her, when in fact she had no clear idea what he did all day, or what the insurance business, or specifically the re-insurance business, was all about. Yet he contended that they were alike, the two of them. She didn't see how. She was an uncompleted project and he knew it and accepted it. He was always talking about the natural intention of things to complete themselves. That was Aristotle, right? So let it.

Wiper wiper wiper.

Thirty-two years old and driving nowhere. What to do with her life? Well, the art business had not worked out. That was still hard to admit, and maybe wasn't even true. No, it was true. She had bailed out of the master's degree program in art history after two weeks. She couldn't face being guided by the academy from cave paintings to graffiti just for a degree. She wasn't an artist. She liked artists, or at least had until she met too many of them. She had worked in galleries. She had become the right-hand person of Pamela Bishop Fontaine in Chelsea, whose stable of needy humorless psychopaths drove her, after 18 months of very hard work and keeping her mouth shut, out of the business forever. She did not fit. She did not fit, either, she had discovered, as a museum curator in training, nor an importer of artifacts, nor an interior decorator for women who knew her mother.

A three-toned blast from the horn of an 18-wheeler meant she had drifted out of her lane. The driver peered down from his high cab, wagging a finger in fatherly warning. She gave him the finger and fell back behind the spray of his wheels.

On the other hand, Maurice did know who he was. Here's a brilliant guy, handsome, black in that Caribbean way that crosses all boundaries, almost could've played in the NBA (Ed said), who wore suits and expensive shoes and chose insurance as a career and was determined to live with minimal turmoil or rage. Had as his goal to do that, and be married to her. She kept looking for the part of him that was nuts and couldn't find it. Whatever Maurice had been through, he had been all the way through it and out the other side. She hadn't been through anything.

Wiper wiper wiper.

Maybe she was alone too much in her head. Maybe a person can't exist independent of other people, crowds of them, with all the yammering and arguing. Maybe you were somebody only if there was somebody to notice it. Like Maurice did, Maurice, who would give her his soul if she asked.

The signs said "Salem" ahead, which meant she was in Massachusetts and already north of Boston. It was dark and the rain had stopped and without noticing it she had driven 180 miles. Her butt was sore and her eyes strained, so she exited to splash into a McDonald's parking lot with puddles. The place was atom-bomb bright, with yellow plastic that made her feel like a visiting germ. At the counter was "Penny," about Laura's age. Thick glasses. A cross at the neck of her uniform. Laura ordered a Big Mac and fries and coffee, paid, and stood there.

"That's OK, I'll bring it to the table."

Penny's smile followed Laura to her table like a spotlight. Penny said something to the fries cook, who said something to the manager, who was squeegeeing a window. Penny had a name tag and a role in life. It wasn't much of a role but it was better than nothing—you could see that in the way she drew the coffee from the machine. No irony or comment. Efficient and at peace with the God around her neck. At 11 p.m. Penny would go home to her dog and her boyfriend and, what? Clean a shotgun? Make cookies? Just collapse exhausted?

"Here you go. Three ketchups enough?"

Laura wondered what it would be like to be her. Take the orders, guess the ketchups. The new MacDonald's uniforms were charcoal and black, with a nice cut to the ball cap. Could she wear that?

"Ma'am?" asked Penny.

"Yes, three is fine, thanks."

She decided not to eat any of the fries, and then ate them all. Then, noticing Penny with a pail and mop, and no longer able to imagine being her, she washed up and returned to the road to nowhere.

Driving was good if she were driving alone. The hum of the road, etc. The fake sense of movement toward a goal, and so on. The time to reassess, ha. She was mostly just fleeing blind north, and it was nearly midnight when she turned off at random for Kennebunkport, just over the Maine border. The GPS led her to a bed and breakfast called Apple Tree Farm, where on the phone Mrs. Johnson said yes, we have a room, do come.

She woke up in a room with a slanting floor illuminated by ocean light behind thin curtains. In the shower the water was not very hot. She dried her damp clothes with a hair dryer, put them back on, and brushed her teeth with her finger. Downstairs, she was the only one for breakfast.

"Hi, I'm Janine, my mother said you came in late." Janine had a pot of coffee. She was about Laura's age. Slender, sort of pretty. Sort of dreamy, which was where the comparison ended. Nobody called Laura dreamy.

"It's Laura, right?"

Janine was poised with carafe in hand, waiting.

"Yes," Laura said, snapping out of it.

"Well, would you like some coffee?".

"Yes. And just some toast."

"The full breakfast is completely included."

"Thanks, but I have to get back. Just bring the bill with the toast, if that's OK."

"Where to?" Said Janine, who was tired but trying not to show it. Tired, with a tattoo of a wedding band on her finger.

"Fairfield," said Laura. "In Connecticut."

"Oh, we used to live in Bridgeport." Her eyes went to a guy who had just come in from the front porch. His hair was jet black and swirled theatrically in the humidity. Laura had seen him smoking outside as she came down from her room. Nervous energy. Old-style duck shoes, which were hip again, sort of.

"So, Janine, is running a bed and breakfast really like you see on those romantic movies on TV?" Laura said.

"Well, Laird and I got this place two years ago. People appreciate it better than those Air B&B things, that's what they say. Is your room OK?"

"Yes, fine. And bring the bill with the toast, please."

"I guess you really do have to get back." Janine poured more coffee. Her fingernails were dirty. "Well, it's only $120 off season, oh —and there's 10 percent off if you'd rather pay cash, which is sort of a little easier for us."

"That's fine," said Laura. She put two bills on the table, a hundred and a twenty, which Janine stuck in her pocket.

Laird had been watching. Janine went over to refill his coffee. Then Laird went back out and drove off in his car and Janine went back to the kitchen. Laura got out her cell phone but decided not to check her text messages or email. Instead, she watched a video about wolves as pets. Not a good idea, it turned out. Wolves are not dogs. Laura could hear urgent tones from the kitchen. Too urgent for toast. Out of the kitchen came Mrs. Johnson, Janine's mother.

"Thanks for taking me in out of the cold last night," Laura said.

"Did she ask for cash?" Mrs. Johnson said.

"Who, Janine?"

"Yes. Did she ask you to pay in cash?"

"Not really asked, but it's just as easy."

"We don't accept cash here," said Mrs. Johnson. "Credit cards only. I'll get it back for you."

"OK."

Mrs. Johnson went back into the kitchen, and then came back out and walked out on the porch, where Laird no longer was. Then Mrs. Johnson returned to the kitchen, where yelling occurred. A moment later, Mrs. Johnson reappeared with a plate of cold toast and placed it in front of Laura.

"Visa OK?" said Laura.

Mrs. Johnson took the card and returned to the kitchen. Janine appeared from the kitchen with a cigarette and went out onto the porch. Mrs. Johnson returned with the Visa form. Laura signed. Mrs. Johnson counted out four Twenties, two Tens and four Five-Dollar bills. Her hands was shaking.

"You want more coffee?" said Mrs. Johnson.

"No, I'm good," said Laura. "Is everything OK?"

"You just come back when you can stay longer," Mrs. Johnson said.

Laura put the money in her purse, took a mandatory bite of the toast, and having no bag to retrieve went on out the porch toward her car. The sun was shining thinly through the sea mist. Janine was smoking, holding her own arms with both hands, and waiting for Laird to return. She didn't meet Laura's eyes or seem to recognize her presence. Laura crossed the driveway, got her seat belt on, and drove slowly onto the gravel service road, not looking back.

Immediately she encountered Laird returning up the gravel. He had both hands on the wheel, did not turn his head toward her as they passed, and already seemed to be nodding off.

Laura was glad to get out of there. What was it the comedian said? Wherever you go, there you are. Escape to where? Not to a bed and breakfast with speedy heroin delivery. Not to a MacDonald's, however sanitary. What she was looking for she didn't know. She was already the competent one, the good daughter, the loyal wife to be.

Who would want to escape from that?

CHAPTER ELEVEN

Red Boat

Ayers regained consciousness on the floor of the cabin. His arms ached, but he was able to roll on his side and then, after a while, to his knees. He remembered the seawater sloshing on the cabin floor and the hum of the bilge pumps removing it. Now he opened his eyes. Seven feet above the companionway hatch lay open to the sky. He had been thrown through it and was lucky to be uninjured. The yacht rode easily. The tropical sun revealed itself from behind a cloud, dazzling the varnish around him. He was lying in a mess of wet cushions and soggy books. A galley drawer had overcome its sea-latch and exploded, flinging cutlery everywhere. The thermometer at the chart table read 96 degrees Fahrenheit, which was why he could hardly breathe. All the other hatches were dogged closed and there was steam in the air. Gripping the companionway ladder with his claws he climbed toward the light of the day.

The sea spread around the yacht in undulations of low amplitude and long periods. *Après Vous* rose and fell with them as if in a comfortable hammock. The drogue he had labored to deploy was simply gone. The stout stern cleats to which he had attached it had ripped away, leaving ragged eruptions in the stern counter where their steel backing plates had been torn through the skin of the deck. He remembered that, vaguely. How the yacht had come to the end of her leash. How he had been sent flying through the air. He didn't remember hitting the cabin floor, only the rogue wave engulfing. The drogue had saved the boat.

All that remained of the windmill electricity generator on the stern was a twisted tube of steel. The mainmast still stood tall, but from it extended a high crook of twisted metal: the storm trysail track. The deck was girdled by random trysail control sheets, boom preventer, genoa lines, all fouled now under the boat. He could see the trysail underwater, snagged on the hull and waving like a Jules Verne sea monster. Otherwise, it was all blue sky with cumulus making castles in the air.

He went below, a long journey one step at a time. He was dizzy, empty, blank. He took one each of five pills and marked them in the log. He drank all the water he could hold, which was three cups. In the galley, ignoring his own revulsion, he defrosted and cooked two eggs. He ate chocolate. He opened a bottle of Corona beer and took half of it down in one continuous hydration. It foamed in his mouth. He succeeded in eating one of the eggs. He felt the return of color all around. He belched, a long honk that reverberated through the silent ship. And laughed.

As expected, the circuit breakers labeled "Swing Keel" had popped. Theirs were the only two red service lights not illuminated on the hundred switches of the instrument panel. When he moved the toggle to retract the keel it was dead under his hand. He remembered that the trysail was wrapped around it and would have to be cleared. The track on the mast would have to be dealt with, too, which might mean climbing it. He checked the bilges and confirmed that the automatic pumps had done their job. He had now merely to solve certain problems for which a boatyard would be handy and a crew of six nice to have, and solve them singlehanded. Well, it gave him something to do. First, he must pee in the ocean. He must show the Pacific how a man works his will.

In the engine-room tool boxes were every sort of cutter available, from diamond grinding wheels to delicate Dremels, draw knives, chisels and bolt cutters. He considered which would be best underwater and none seemed right. He selected a small air bottle and SCUBA regulator. He would need to be weighted to work nine feet down, and for that he could use a short length of chain around his waist. He tied a light line at each end, for quick release. For cutting he decided on the Yanagiba, his sashimi knife. White steel, perfectly balanced. He taped a short line to it, then hauled himself on deck.

Wind light. The boat, tangled in her underwater sail, jogged sideways at two knots. He lowered the swim platform and pulled on the small tank and chain weight. He rigged a safety line to suspend him nine feet down. He spit in his mask, rinsed it, chomped the regulator and looked down. Through the transparent water the storm sail beckoned. The propeller was fouled with rope, so clear that, too.

Ayers let go and fell like a stone, jerked to a stop with the keel in his hands. The hull drifted away, and he kicked to seize hold again. He was making too many bubbles and stopped to quiet his breathing. The wicked knife in his hand went to work, slicing the lines and sailcloth jammed in the centerboard. As he cut, his body gyrated absurdly behind him. He could apply no more force than a butterfly. Soon he was surrounded by fragments of cloth and rope yarns rotating as if in a kaleidoscope. Steel sail slides, freed, sank like glimmering fish lures. Soon, or not so soon, for he had lost track of time or space or up or down in this snow-globe of debris, the sail was no longer fouled. A 40-foot section of white Dacron drifted away, waving like the wings of a manta ray.

Job done.

Not yet.

He pulled himself up his safety line to the propeller, and sawed away. The knife was duller now, and the Gordian knot there resisted. He kept on, watching his right hand as it moved back and forth. Action, not thought. Endurance, not speed. The propeller was free just as the air in his tank ran out. He gagged. He let go of the knife. He swam for the surface and the shimmering clouds above it. He made no progress. Free the chain weight around his waist. He could not. The knot had jammed. He kicked harder. His lungs screamed. Ah, the safety line. Find it, climb it. Don't need to find it, it was suspending him. Pull up. Pull up, pull to the air.

His head struck the bottom of the hull, hard. The barnacles there cut him cruelly. He hauled harder on his line, keel-hauling himself toward the stern, blood in the water around him. Regulator and air bottle off, let them go. He pulled to the rungs of the boarding ladder. The yacht rose and fell in the easy seaway. It yanked the rungs out of his hands once, twice. He had nothing left. The chain at his waist weighed him down. He would sink only to the end of his tether, but that was enough. He would dangle, drowned. When the boarding later came in reach again he grabbed it with both hands and pulled himself up, one rung at a time, arm over arm, until he lay on deck in the hot air, breathing it.

Twenty minutes later he crawled below to the main electrical panel. When he closed the keel circuit breakers their in-service lights blinked on. The keel retracted with its confident hum, freed of the jam. He ate two chocolates, drank the remaining half-bottle of beer, and sat on the galley floor in his ragged shorts, thinking of nothing. In a moment he tipped sideways, and slept.

* * *

At three o'clock in the afternoon what was left of Bobby Ayers, and it wasn't much, came on deck again. Smears of blood from his barnacle cuts had clotted. The same blood had dried in his hair and on the decks. The sea was flat, the air torpid. No sails set. From the mast, the Bo-Peep shepherd's crook of the ruined trysail track extended, wobbling, held only by the lowest of its attachments. Ayers smiled. He understood completely. The 40-foot track had been only partly installed since Mexico. Well, that made it easy to take off. With an impact wrench from the tool bay he had it free in 10 minutes, and tossed over the side. He found himself shaking, but the jobs were done. So much for a storm. He would tidy up later. The world would wait. He gave it no choice.

There was a speck of white on the far horizon.

He looked away, and then back.

Still there.

He reached for the binoculars.
The speck was white sails, hanging limp in the dead calm.
And under them, a red sailboat.

CHAPTER TWELVE

Marika

Ayers looked through the binoculars a long time. When he lowered the glasses to his chest the picture was clear: a small yacht with a red hull, main and jib sails set, becalmed. They could see him better than he could see them, because *Après Vous* was a much larger vessel. Ayers did not like sharing his nowhere.

He went to the VHF radio. No doubt the other vessel would be hailing him, but all he received was static. He listened for 10 minutes, then went topside for another look. No change. Both boats lay still, miles apart. He waited for two full hours, until only an hour of light remained. At this latitude darkness fell suddenly. In darkness, he could make his escape. A few hours of motoring should do it. The smaller boat had no radar dome, and so once out of visual range it would be as if he were never there, and any memory of having seen him an hallucination. His only need was invisibility.

In the fading light he recalled the violence of the storm. How would it have been for the other boat? The giant seas that tore his drogue away would have wreaked havoc on her. But even if her radio were disabled, there would be someone on deck by now. Life makes its signs, and he saw none. Well, good. Not his affair. He started the engine and *Après Vous* crept away toward the disappearing horizon, an illusion departing. Yet he could not but imagine what he was leaving behind. A young cruising family, with children. Perhaps an elderly couple, dreams of retirement ruined by the gale. Perhaps a singlehander, like himself.

He turned back for a closer inspection pass. As the faster yacht, he could always escape at will.

It took half an hour before the other boat became real. Yes, the hull was faded red. Wind vane self-steering was installed on her stern. Sails bleached, hanging limp. The whole boat was whitened by long exposure, and along her waterline a garland of weed clung. Yet nothing seemed obviously amiss. Just a typical small passagemaker, 30 feet long, hatches closed, cockpit empty. He passed silently at 500 yards, and then circled again, close this time. No sign of life. He cut speed to idle, and lingered. He saw solar panels on the dodger. He saw a rainwater collection bag hanging from the mainsail. He saw clothespins on the lifelines of the cockpit, a dish towel drying. In the binoculars it was not a dish towel. It was a swimsuit. A bikini.

Twilight arrived around him. The sea was flat, both boats motionless upon it. Ayers turned on the loud-hailer. His first words were a hoarse cough, unintelligible even to him. He tried again:

"Hello red sloop abeam. Do you require assistance?"

The amplified words hung in the air. He waited for a response, feeling dizzy. Then, again:

"Is there anyone aboard the red boat?"

In one portlight he saw a light turn silently on, then off. It startled him. He turned involuntarily to sweep the horizon, as if discovered and ruined. The sun was low and the sky cinnamon.

"Do you require assistance?" Ayers said again, his tone more carefully modulated.

He waited.

"If so, show me the light again."

Après Vous drifted a few degrees and the light winked again, as if reflecting a glint of water. Perhaps that was what he saw. Not a light, a reflection.

"Last chance," Ayers said in his own voice.

The boats were 10 feet apart now and amplification unnecessary. He could not see into the other vessel, its companionway closed by two of three hatch boards. Ayers began to mutter under his breath. It felt like a dream and he knew it wasn't.

"God damn it! Is anyone there?" he shouted at the other boat.

When no reply came he commenced to rig fenders along his own starboard side and dig deep into the dinghy locker to find the dock lines he had stowed in Mexico. It took half an hour, accompanying by much clunking and heavy footfalls to further announce his presence. A burst of throttle brought Après Vous close, and with a quick reverse and a blast of bow thruster the yachts came together with a gentle thump. The topsides of the red boat were much lower than his. He dropped down upon her, dock line in hand, feeling his knees nearly buckle, and lashed the boats tight together. In anything but this calm that would be difficult or impossible, yet now they lay side by side, rafted up a thousand miles from any land. He should have brought a firearm.

In an act of will, not knowing what he would see, Ayers thrust his head into the small companionway to be overwhelmed by a putrid, enervating smell. He saw a mess of blankets and scattered cassette tapes. On the small stove was a soup pot of mold, luxuriant in golds and greens. On one cabin bunk was a hand, and as he descended the ladder an arm, and as he knelt to it he found the shape of a woman, hair matted, neck swollen.

He saw no wounds. Her eyes were closed, and she seemed unaware of his presence. From under the twisted blanket a foot emerged, unmoving. He placed his knuckles upon her forehead and found it dry and hot. She should be sweating in this reeking, miasmic sepulcher, like he was. Condensation ran in rivulets down the bulkheads.

'Are you alone?" Ayers said.

The body breathed, but erratically, and not in response to him.

He stood, self-conscious and hyperalert. It was a time for strength, but he had none. Above him was her cabin hatch. He released the dogs and thrust it up like the lid of a coffin. Venus appeared in the sky overhead. He raised his chin to breathe the air. He pushed forward in the tiny boat, opening the door to the single head compartment. The toilet lid was open, the bowl caked in vomitus. The V-berth forward was shelved for food and spares, no place for crew. She was alone, intentionally so, a long-distance solo like himself. The boat rocked like a dinghy as he moved inside it. He found a case of spring water and brought a bottle to her, kneeling by her side. He touched the open bottle to her lips, which reacted not at all. When he poured, the water ran down her cheek. He confirmed again she was breathing, and she was, barely and without rhythm. In the sink behind him, dirty dishes lay piled. He checked the bilge under his feet, which showed only a few inches of greasy water. She was not dead, and not sinking. He would know what to do about either. He did not know what to do about this.

He pulled himself back up into her cockpit, gasping. *Après Vous* lay next to him, massive and obedient. He needed to get back aboard. He needed to wash the stench of vomit and sweat off himself but the dizziness and tremors had returned and he wasn't sure he could do it. It took his last strength to grasp his lifelines and climb up.

"I'll be back," he called down to the red boat below.

Aboard *Après Vous* he found the engine still idling, and turned it off. He slipped below and ate a Mallomar cookie.

Find the medical books.

In a moment.

Do it now.

I am weak.

He was hyperventilating, so he held a plastic bag over his mouth until the concentration of carbon dioxide eased the dizziness. The medical library was four thick books and he didn't know where to start. He needed guidance for smell, shit, vomit and rot. He scanned without retention. Ayers was no doctor, had no skills of compassion for strangers, knew nothing of any illness but his own and for which his treatment was to ignore it or damn it or power through and leave its wreckage behind.

Against his will a shade came down. There was the taste of the Mallomar still in his mouth and the pages of the medical books before his eyes as he tipped toward the settee and fell upon it, helpless.

* * *

Ayers awoke in the *madrugada,* that hour before dawn when he had first found himself in the paralysis of profound depression. It had been in Madrid, after his flight from Philadelphia, and the fear of recurrence and disability was forever associated with this time of darkness before the light. He climbed on deck. The red boat had not been an apparition, it still lay clinging alongside. His head was clearer.

When he boarded the red boat again its occupant still lay as she had been, breathing and stinking. This time he spread her lips with his fingers, pried open her teeth, and poured water in. She choked, and when he elevated her head it came up like a dirty pillow. It was light now, and he could see the film of mildew everywhere. In the moldering sink lay glass mason jars of preserved food, each labeled in ink by a youthful hand. He thought of this debased creature provisioning her boat on a budget, dreaming of foreign lands where the anchorage was free.

"It stinks down here, do you know that?"

She didn't answer.

Ayers saw her trash bag, hung under the ladder. It was rimmed with wriggling maggots. He returned to the sink, where a red jar foamed red. The label said, "Beefeater," with a handwritten date from the summer before. Tomatoes, canned by her. A chill swept over him and he backed away. His books had warned of botulism. It was listed under "Poisoning at Sea." The crawling plates in the sink were alive with mold. Botulism toxins were borne by food, tomatoes specifically. What had the book said—that it was extremely dangerous. That the slightest transfer of the toxin to an open wound meant instant infection. He recoiled from the sink. He recoiled from the flesh under the blanket. He had touched her. He had spread her lips.

He studied her as she lay. Her face was expressionless, as if paralyzed. Her neck and face were swollen, although it was hard to tell how she might have looked before. Her vomitus was all around, and her shit on the bunk and floor, and her breath came halting and uneven and spewing poison. The whole boat was poison, and he stood in it. He looked at his own hands, which were flecked with sores and cuts. His bare feet seemed to absorb from the dirty floorboards under them the radiation of invisible infection.

He fled, scrambling back to the spacious familiarity of *Après Vous.* His attention was acute. He reviewed his medical books again and confirmed the diagnosis. He decided to cast the red boat off immediately and power away, and was immediately revolted by his own cowardice, or logic. He stopped thinking and lost himself in action, the first of which was to retrieve from his laundry locker a gallon of bleach, and the second to draw a bucket of water from his sink, and the third to obtain from the engine room his respirator mask and a box of nitrile rubber gloves, and the fourth to wonder what the hell he was doing.

But he knew what it was: something. He had to do something.

In his cockpit he stripped naked, throwing overboard his contaminated shirt and stained shorts. He observed his own frail body, the broken fingernails, the unhealed barnacle nicks on his head and back and his own stiff hair. He doused himself with bleach water from the bucket, feeling it burn, until he stank like an overchlorinated hot tub. The book said bleach would kill Clostridium botulinum, but not its spores. They lived on in the air, odorless and tasteless. His yacht lay moored to a garden of botulism tended by a living corpse.

He put on shorts and boat shoes and the rubber gloves and climbed back aboard the red boat. He groped below and threw the bag of maggots overboard. The book said a mere touch could kill, and the plastic bag had been full of disease. Probably she was, too, along with her boat and plates and spoons and clothes and now, himself. The task of decontamination seemed hopeless, and started with her. The boat had begun to rise and fall, which meant a breeze was springing up, and with it the first small waves of the day.

Not knowing how else to start, he sluiced the chlorine water over the cabin floor, watching small, foamy waves expand around his feet. A powerful chemical reek rose, and he saw her hand rise to her face as she gasped. He arrested the hand with his glove, and with a paper towel swabbed it with chlorine. His eyes burned and so must hers. His skin burned, especially the wounds under his hair. This was absurd. This was poison against poison, burning against burning, insanity against insanity.

He paused, alternatives flashing. He had always been good at sorting them. He had always weighed risk and loss. He had always known what to do, and to do it in time: List the options and choose one.

The options were:

1. Call Coast Guard Honolulu, 1800 miles east. They would divert a commercial ship. His location and identity would be revealed.

2. Abandon her. She might recover and have no recollection of him.

3. Take her with him. His position would remain unknown.
Ayers chose Number 3.

He dumped the rest of the Clorox into the bilge and returned to his own boat. This would not be easy and had to be fast, before the wind came up. He was not strong, so he would be smart. To lift her he could use his man-overboard sling. The contamination must be controlled so his own yacht was not compromised. He must not make the situation worse.

It took two hours to rig the transfer sling, during which the morning breeze rose and the two yachts began to sail slowly in circles like conjoined twins. The power winch would enable him to guide her up through her narrow companionway. But then she would hang like a doll for the transfer to his own boat. He would deal with that as it happened. If it didn't work, start over. And try not to touch her skin.

In rigging her to the hoist he discovered her naked beneath the blankets in her own filth. He wore two set of rubber gloves. He splashed Clorox on the lifting straps, on her, and on himself. She was limp as a coil of rope. When her thin arms slipped through the lifting straps, he duct-taped them to her sides. Her head lolled as he winched her up and her shape deformed like a sack of apples. The body weighed no more than 90 pounds, and the halyard flew it like a kite.

The rising of the innocent form was complicated by the new rolling of Ayers' boat, which swung her port and starboard as he held her toes in one hand and the remote control in the other. As he lowered her through his main hatch she collided unavoidably with the companionway sides until finally the boneless body unfolded in slow motion upon the varnished floorboards of the *Après Vous* salon. He climbed down to find her inert and exposed, a small thing on its back, hip bones pressing through skin. Somebody's daughter this was. Somebody's Laura. He covered her gently.

The breeze and seas were building, and by afternoon the competing motions of the raft would turn violent. He knew what to do. He put on new gloves and re-boarded her boat, intending to fetch for her what he could. In her cabin the knowledge of botulism in the air was impossible to put from his mind. Spores inhaled required immediate hospitalization and radical antibiotic therapy. Everything here was tainted. Everything here was death. He ought to sink this plague boat, now.

He opened the tiny head compartment, its toilet crowned with vomit. A seacock would be there, if he knelt to find it. If opened it would flood the boat. To reach it all he had to do was lie in the pools of her excretion, groping for the hose with his face in the toilet. No. The duty was to survive, for both of them. Just get away. Far away. Leave this death ship to sunlight and time. Do it now.

As he retreated he saw on the compartment door a postcard of a grinning dog. In its mouth was a Frisbee, caught in mid-air. One eye winked and the other was open wide as if to say, what joy the world is! It was framed with blue painter's tape. Across it was written, in French, a single line: "Marika! This is the dog you must have! Love, Claire."

So she had a name.

Ayers cast the infection off, sending his own contaminated dock lines with it, and watched the abandoned boat dwindle to a smudge on the western horizon as *Après Vous* gained speed ever south. He looked neither back nor ahead but at his cargo below where it lay on his floor, shivering slightly. With new gloves he pulled her into his own shower, where she lay fetal on her side. With the handheld showerhead he painted her with water until her soil had washed away. He sluiced Clorox everywhere. He anointed her with dish detergent as if she were a heap of dirty plates. With a washcloth he gently scrubbed, ignoring his distaste. He washed her hair with his gloves, and her small hands, with their line of callouses. Of course: she was a singlehander like himself. He cleaned the fingernails with his own toothbrush, scrubbing carefully, and then threw the brush over the side. She lay in the shower pan, mute and breathing.

"Marika?" he said.

No response. He covered her in a Turkish towel and carried her to the guest-cabin berth. He accepted the thing "Marika" not as a woman, but as cargo received and now stored. Under her dripping hair he placed a pillow, pulled off his rubber gloves, and fetched a bottle of spring water.

"Try," he said, holding it to her lips.

Her lips resisted, then out of instinct seemed to respond. The face remained passive. He counted the swallows as three, and went to the navigation station to note them in the logbook.

There, pencil in hand, Ayers became conscious of a whelming pride. Her breathing was lousy and her body inert, but her mouth had drunk from his hand. That was something, wasn't it? He was thirsty himself, and almost sipped from the same bottle. Now he carried the bottle to the deck and threw it as far overboard as he could. That motion used the last of his aching body. He went below dizzy and trembling, almost as pitiable a figure as she.

Almost, but not quite.

CHAPTER THIRTEEN

Sullivan

Maurice had doubts about Laura's stratagem to put off telling her mother about the new will. He thought she should show her cards. His advocacy was Socratic rather than declaratory, and advanced through colloquy. Ah, Maurice. If he were a book he would be leather-bound and heavy with footnotes. An open book, unlike the book of Laura. At the moment they were both naked, lying in twisted sheets, and the topic at hand was blowing off a baby shower just because you felt like it.

In Maurice's analysis that was defensible on many grounds. Nothing wrong with not going. Nothing wrong, even, with deciding not to go at the last minute. But, *note bene*: it is wrong to deny knowing what you already know you will do, and hiding it from yourself and others. Because: that encourages in other people later assessments that misinterpret prior intentions.

She was sipping tea with her head against his chest, admiring the smooth expanse of his bronze forearm as it lay over the skin of her breasts.

"My mother can wait," Laura said.

"Who's talking about your mother?"

"You are. And I'll tell you why she can wait, Maurice, since I know how it bugs you. My father could walk in tomorrow and tell us himself about his girlfriends and his unfinished business and deal with mom and Vivian and Eleanor. So why doesn't he?"

"Don't get mad."

"Because he can't face it. That's why he made me the detective in this case, the one who has to go around finding people, investigating his past, uncovering the family secrets. The problem is I don't want to know about anybody's life but mine and yours. We're complicated enough. That's what I was thinking about on that drive, who am I? Who am I supposed to be?"

"Laura, if you thought it through and you need to get out of this trusteeship, we can do it. We'll make it happen, starting today."

"You didn't understand a word I'm saying."

"OK."

"I have to do this thing. I know now I can't back out. Daddy left a mess and I'm supposed to clean it up. I'm the only one on the outside, because that's where I always was, the protected one, the one who didn't know anything. He wants me to know who he really is, now, before it's too late. He wants you to know. He wants us all to know."

She wiggled out of the sheets to stretch in the dim light of his big bedroom. How Maurice admired the hidden strength in that tall, strong form so luxurious in its contradictions.

"What now, then?"

"Tomorrow I'm going to see one of my father's business partners. He owes him money. I finally found out where he lives, it's in New Jersey."

"I'll drive you," Maurice said.

"No, it should be just me."

Maurice expected no further explanation. He wouldn't get it anyhow.

* * *

The Living Trust documents had listed Thomas A. Sullivan at a business address in Cherry Hill, N.J., which no longer existed and hadn't for years. Laura was to hand Mr. Sullivan repayment for a personal loan to Robert Ayers of $10,000, 40 years before. Her own $29 background check revealed Mr. Sullivan to be 86 years old and currently living at 12 Sailfish Lane, Forked River, New Jersey. Google Earth showed a small tract house on a lagoon, with dock and fishing boat. Eleanor had mentioned him as her father's first boss.

She drove to New Jersey as Officer Laura of the Robert Allington Ayers Living Trust. To pass the time on the Garden State Parkway she searched for the emotion to feel if her father were lost at sea. It didn't come. You couldn't know what to feel about the dead while they were still alive. She tried it out on her mother, and Ed, and on her Aunt Sarah. OK, the phone rings and they're dead. And—nothing came. Apparently you could fear somebody's death, or dread it, or maybe even in some cases root for it to put them out of their misery, but you couldn't know how to mourn while they were still out there walking around somewhere. Being alive was a shield against the final assessment. Being alive left people incomplete.

Being dead explained everything.

* * *

The tiny house had a yard paved in crushed rock that glared in the afternoon sun. She could see a figure behind the screen door, watching. As she approached with her briefcase the door was opened from within by a large man in red trousers and enormous hands.

"Mr. Sullivan? I'm Laura Ayers."

"Say that again?"

"Laura Ayers, sir. I called on the phone."

"I remember," he said. "Come in."

She followed to encounter a young man in a Mohawk haircut who took her briefcase and bowed.

"This is Ray, he's my gay wife," said Mr. Sullivan.

"Not exactly," Ray said.

"He's right, I've got two other wives. Fat Sharon comes at 4 o'clock, then at 10 clock the night shift is Pearl, when it's dark. I have Alzheimer's disease. Right, Ray?"

"Right," said Ray.

"I have to remind him," said Mr. Sullivan. "Excuse me."

He turned toward a bathroom, Ray following close.

"I can hold my own self," Mr. Sullivan said. "Dream on."

"You're not what I dream about," said Ray.

"Don't lie to her," Mr. Sullivan said, closing the door behind himself.

"How's he doing?" Laura asked.

"He's fine. I told him what you said on the phone about your dad, but I don't know if he really caught it. He likes visitors, though. He's better on the old days than he is about yesterday." Laura had her briefcase open and was pulling out newspaper clippings. "Yeah, pictures are good," Ray said.

Mr. Sullivan barged out, pushing Ray aside.

"Did he molest you?"

"Watch out for him, not me," Ray said to Laura.

"How about some cold cuts?" Mr. Sullivan said. "Ray brings them from Hoboken every week."

"Maybe in a minute," Laura said. "Sir, I don't know if Ray explained it, but I have a check for you. It's a repayment of an old loan. My dad is Bobby Ayers, who used to work for you when you had Sullivan Construction down in Cherry Hill. He borrowed some money and wants to pay it back. This was 1981, a long time ago. There's no strings attached or anything, it's part of his living trust and I'm the trustee giving out his disbursements according to his wishes."

Mr. Sullivan stared at her. Laura continued:

"My dad thought highly of you, sir, and he wanted to make sure it was done personally, so I drove down from Connecticut."

She took out a cashier's check and put it on a battered coffee table next to a tray of salami. Mr. Sullivan didn't look at it.

"Connecticut," he said.

"You're sharp today," Ray said.

"I don't know if you remember him," said Laura. "He was married at the time to Eleanor, who I recently met, and who remembered you. She said you and my dad were pretty close, back when you had your construction company, and as you probably know my dad went on to have a lot of companies himself, in this country and overseas, and to follow in your footsteps, I guess."

"You don't look like him," Mr. Sullivan said.

"Everybody else thinks I do," Laura said with a laugh.

"Does she look like Bobby?"

"How should I know?" said Ray. "I wasn't born yet."

"So do you like Ray's tattoos?" Mr. Sullivan said. "I don't understand who wants a comic book on their arms. It used to be just criminals. Now they've all got them, even the girls." To Laura: "You have tattoos?"

"Sir, I think you ought to just look at the check I brought."

"I don't need a check."

"Yes, we do," said Ray.

"As I said, it's a repayment from my dad, Robert Ayers, who used to work for you."

"Bobby."

"Yes."

"You're his daughter."

"Yes."

Ray was showing him the folder of clippings Laura had brought. Mr. Sullivan lingered on the photographs. Ray read headlines over his shoulder. "Vandals Strike Sullivan Again."

"Vandals, nope," Mr. Sullivan said.

Laura passed him an 8x10 glossy photograph of a storage yard on fire. She passed him clippings of himself, age 50, with Bobby Ayers, age 24. Laura had retrieved articles and file photos from archives in Philadelphia and from a South Jersey newspaper called the Camden Courier-Post. They told a story of a construction war, of burning trucks and bulldozers in a time when newspapers were black and white and files had date stamps. Mr. Sullivan looked at them all briefly, as if none were news at all.

"So how come Bobby didn't come?"

"My dad is currently on his yacht in the South Pacific, which is why he asked me."

"He's got a yacht?" Mr. Sullivan said.

"You've got a rowboat," Ray said.

"Be quiet, you didn't even know him."

"You talk about him enough that I do," said Ray.

"Actually," Laura said, "I don't know him very well either."

Mr. Sullivan looked at her and shrugged. "I can't tell you anything more than the cops did."

"I haven't talked to the cops. I came to bring you a check from my father."

Mr. Sullivan had dropped into his chair and was picking through cold cuts with his reading glasses on.

"Tommy told me a lot of stories about your dad," Ray said. "Let's give him a minute."

"A lot of stories," Mr. Sullivan said.

Ray lowered his voice. "He talks and talks, up to a point, then he loses the track. His sister says he remembers better than her, but she won't talk about it. That's who's paying for this house, his sister, and believe me anything your dad can contribute will help because they don't have a lot of money and three of us caretakers is a big expense."

"What're you telling her over there, Ray?"

"What a problem you are, Tommy."

"Mr. Sullivan," Laura said, "you and my dad were close and anything you can tell me about him I'd like to know. Anything at all you can remember."

"He saved my life, Ray tell you that?"

"No sir, how did he save your life?"

"Wouldn't you like to know. She's pretty, Ray. Couldn't you go for that?"

"She wants to hear about her father."

"From what I've read it was a difficult time for you," Laura said.

"Not really," Mr. Sullivan said. And to Ray, "Did you offer her some ice water?"

"What're you doing, Tommy?" Ray said. "Jesus, she came all this way to see you. Tell her about the Mafia and how all your equipment was getting blown up and how you almost got killed and all that stuff I have to listen to, show some respect to the daughter of the guy who was supposed to be like a son to you."

"Mafia, there was no Mafia."

"A guy named Eddie 'Small Peas' Leseur blew up your Town Car with you almost in it," Ray said. "I heard these stories a million times from you."

"Not Mafia. Bobby checked him out with Angelo Bruno's people. They said they didn't know him, go ahead and do whatever you want."

"Do whatever you want?" said Laura.

"Just excuse me a minute," said Ray, who disappeared into a bedroom. Mr. Sullivan leaned close to Laura.

"Do you know where my car keys are?"

"No, but I can look around," Laura said. "Where did you leave them?"

Ray came back with a glossy police photograph of a large automobile with its roof blown off and windows shattered.

"This was Tommy's car," Ray said.

"Lincoln Town Car. Better than a Cadillac," Mr. Sullivan said.

"And it was a warning they were going to kill you like they were killing your business, and it's why your whole family had to go to Ohio for a month during this Mafia war, and they couldn't come back until—tell her what happened, Tommy."

"Eddie Small Peas blew up," the old man said.

"And who did it?"

"It wasn't me. The kid was a firebug, he blew himself up. Ask the cops if you want to."

"Yeah, right," said Ray.

"Bobby Ayers was your father?" Mr. Sullivan said to Laura.

"He still is, Mr. Sullivan."

"Now you do look like him. Bobby was just a kid, but he was more than a kid, he could weld, he could manage people. He was just good at business. The construction business is a naturally competitive industry, you bid for contracts, you protect your reputation, it's a lot more than moving dirt. People are always trying for advantage."

"So how did my father save your life?"

"What?" said Mr. Sullivan.

"You heard what she said," Ray said.

"He was a lifesaver, like the candy. He was very sweet, like you. He saved me, I saved him."

"Bullshit, Tommy, you never tell the story twice the same way."

"I have Alzheimer's Disease," said Mr. Sullivan. "And Ray and my sister hid my car keys, don't think I don't know that, and what Ray don't know is every night when he goes off shift I got Fat Sharon and Pearl down on their knees looking for them until they find them."

"Whatever," said Ray.

Laura said: "According to the news reports the body of Edward Leseur was found in the remains of a garage that had burned down, possibly as the result of illegal storage of construction explosives, and that police were investigating. But there was never any ultimate disposition I could find."

"Eddie Small Peas? That kid was an open and shut case. He opened it, and then somebody shut it on him." Mr. Sullivan's burst of laughter was loud and abrupt. "Nobody missed him, believe me. Yes, we had some visits by the state troopers, they had a bomb squad with ATF support so they kept coming around to talk to us. Bobby had to take off, he had a lot of personal stuff going on at the time, but I'll talk to anybody just like I'm talking now. It was basically just a normal business environment at the time."

Ray seemed annoyed. "You call Hoboken a shithole, but if you ask me, South Jersey in those days was 10 times worse."

"Who wants a nurse with personal opinions?" Mr. Sullivan said.

"What do you mean, my father 'took off'?" said Laura.

"He went on vacation."

"Was he under investigation?"

"Nah, just questions."

Laura looked at her files. "Mr. Sullivan, the last time you saw my father, was that possibly Sept. 23, 1981?"

"Sweetheart, half the time I can't remember if I had breakfast."

"Because that's the date of the loan you made to him of $10,000, which this check I brought is paying back."

Laura handed the check to Ray.

"Holy crap," Ray said, "this is a quarter of a million dollars."

"Edward Leseur died on Sept. 21 of that year," Laura said, consulting her notes. "So my father left on vacation two days after Mr. Leseur was killed?"

Mr. Sullivan said, "I don't need a check, we're all good here."

"No, we're not good here, Tommy! This is a fortune! It's $245,239. What is that, 10K with interest over what, 40 years? Holy shit, that's unbelievable!"

"Be nice, Ray."

"It's what he computed he owed, sir, at 8 percent," Laura said.

"If Bobby says that's what he owes, it's what he owes. And don't worry, he's good for it."

"This money is for you, you dope!" said Ray.

But Mr. Sullivan's concentration had lagged, and Laura could see him drifting away.

"How do you like that," Ray said. "I'll call his sister, she'll come and sign for it. And don't worry about Tommy, he just needs a nap. Tomorrow I don't know, maybe you were never here, but like I said, the old days he remembers. When Pearl comes she puts him in bed, I usually just let him lay back in his chair like he is now.

Laura bent and took his hand.

"Mr. Sullivan. My father wanted to thank you. I want to thank you too, for knowing him and helping him."

"Kiss me," the old man said.

Laura leaned over and kissed his forehead.

"Tell Bobby I said hello," he said as his eyes closed.

Ray led her into the linoleum foyer and the brightness of the gravel through the glass storm door.

"Who knows what really happened back then. It's like he relives his life when somebody comes by, but it doesn't last. Anyway, the check will keep me and the others on the payroll. His sister will probably have a heart attack. Listen, your dad, is he OK?"

"Yes, he's just taking care of the loose ends while everybody's still around."

"Good name for us, 'loose ends.' For what it's worth, I always thought Tommy killed that guy Eddie Small Peas. Sometimes he says he did, sometimes he says he didn't. All we know is that somebody did. It was all a long time ago, before the dinosaurs."

They shook hands.

"He likes you, Ray. You're doing a good job."

"He's losing his life one day at a time," Ray said. "You brought a day back. Drive careful, Miss Ayers."

CHAPTER FOURTEEN

Voice

During their first days together Marika and Ayers sailed as unconnected selves on the same course. He needed to heal as much as she did. His habit of waking automatically every few hours had yielded to exhaustion, and now he stirred in his cabin only when the light changed. Then, startled by memory, he would pad quietly to Marika's stateroom to confirm her breathing. He would lift the water bottle to her lips and count his success. On logbook Day 101, 10 swallows. On Day 103, "one bottle, part of two."

This evening, after his pills and the night reef, he noticed his head wounds no longer stung to the touch and the inflammation had gone down. He was tired of nibbling chocolate and wished never to never taste it again. He had not defecated for how long? Well, that was the chocolate. His belly was cramped and sunken. He discovered his eyeglasses, looped by a length of Spectra line around his neck, to be opaque with hardened glop. Cleaning them brought the world back in focus. How easily the yacht rode steadfastly south, asking no questions. The breeze was hardly more than a zephyr as they approached the equator, yet *Après Vous* made a steady three knots across the sultry ocean. But if the yacht had no questions, Ayers did.

Why had he taken her aboard? Well, because she was sick. Not really a choice. But of course there was a choice. Anyone else would have immediately called Honolulu on the satellite phone and declared a medical emergency. The advice would be to rendezvous with some commercial ship to whisk her to a hospital far away, and also to pin Bobby Ayers like a butterfly for dissection, deposition and suits in courts of law. Her salvation, his complication.

His choice left all options open, and the husbanding of options was his personal gift. Options were why he signed hundred-page contracts without reading them, which drove his lawyers nuts. They were how he made a hundred decisions a day by phone or with a handshake or when cornered. Options bent time. They could make it run backwards, undo the done, fix the broken, and save the day. Options allowed uncertainty, and uncertainty was the natural order of things. If you could endure that, it made others abandon the field and besiege themselves behind protective walls. Of every hundred decisions Bobby Ayers made, most turned out to be wrong, or based on information later revealed as incorrect. When a decision was wrong he got out of it. But you had to be in before you could be out and so he was always in, and in first. Most people avoided being wrong by making no decisions at all. He made them all and kept the ones that were right. It had made him rich.

Marika, this present flotsam of fellow humanity, was an option. If she recovered, he had choices. If she worsened, he could pick up the satphone at any time. There was no right or wrong, only actions taken. He smiled, feeling himself return to function. The days of rest had oiled his joints and he was no longer Tin Man squeaking. He yawned and noticed that the boat was a mess. He set about picking things up, wiping down the light mildew on the cabin bulkheads. The toilets of the two head compartments were appalling, and so he set upon them with a bottle of cleaner and a toothbrush. The ammonia of the spray was like smelling salts. He counted inventory, checking jars and tins against their lists. He lost track of time, lulled by the bow wave thrumming on the other side of the hull. He was rearranging cases of wine when a cramp ran crosswise across his abdomen. When he stood to relax the sensation came again. He noticed his hand trembling and breathed deep, imagining invisible spores of botulism growing inside him. No, probably not. Probably, he was hungry. Yes, he had inadvertently run himself nearly out of fuel. It was inexcusable. Of all the checklists on board he had never made one for himself.

The first beer, a St. Pauli Girl, went down easily. He finished it while chopping leeks and mushrooms for a one-egg omelet which he ate standing at the sink. It proved insufficient. He found a slab of fatback, sliced off a long inch, and laid it in the hot omelet pan. As it rendered he dripped bread in the swimming fat. Still insufficient. With a dish towel he seized the sizzling block of pork belly, gnawing it, burning his lips on the tough pigskin. The grease settled him and then disgusted him. He climbed the ladder to the cockpit and retched over the stern, spewing into the quiet wake. It felt good.

Above, a white fulmar hovered, pacing the yacht. Go ahead, bird, observe the trait of regurgitation our species share. But he felt no kinship. There was a cookie in one of his hands, so he ate it.

After a few moments he went below to quietly enter the compartment where Marika lay in her bunk. One small foot was extended, so he pulled the sheet over it. She had not moved in an hour and did not move now. He withdrew to his books and the notes he had made.

The symptoms of botulism were nerve paralysis, slurred speech, nausea, tachycardia and breathing issues. But his thickest volume, a British publication called "Ship Captain's Medical Guide," lent responsibility beyond diagnosis. He must take care to inspect all vomited matter, its color, consistency, odor and approximate amount. In cases of poisoning, which this surely was, it should be labelled and secured in a cool place. Traces of blood might indicate gastric ulcer or growth in the stomach, but on the other hand could just result from violent ejection. Does the blood in the vomit have the consistency of coffee grounds? Then likely it had been retained for some time. Discharge from the mouth containing fecal matter suggested reverse flow of the intestines, or maybe not. Regarding sputum, he was supposed to record whether thick, or yellow, or green. Frothy spit was characteristic of pulmonary edema, and if bright red, of a lung injury. Or maybe just bleeding gums. Obviously he had not ought to have thrown her puke away. Or her shit. Too late now.

He opened another beer and read on past making the patient comfortable, past minimizing the injury, past symptoms of venereal disease and burns from superheated steam, past intubation and catheterization and pregnancy and madness, which "in a crew member may be a danger to other crew," and on to Signs of Death. "No pulse will be felt and no heart sounds will be heard. Put your ear on the left side of the chest near the nipple and listen carefully.

If you are not sure what to listen for, listen to the left chest of a living person first." He could feel his own heart beating without doing that. "To test that circulation has stopped, tie a piece of string tightly around a finger. In life the finger becomes bluish, but in death it remains white." Ayers wrapped a USB cable around his own finger as tightly as he could, and waited. His finger turned red, not blue.

He kept on, preparing his options. The body should be preserved, if possible, for examination by a pathologist in port. If burial at sea was required, the subject was to be sewn into a shroud. "There should be three or four slits or openings in the shroud to allow the gases of decomposition to escape and prevent flotation due to trapped air." Be sure to enter the exact time and position of sea burial in the ship's log.

He finished the beer and moved to where he could observe the guest cabin without being seen. She remained still, just lumps in a blanket. He heard himself breathing, but not her. The full water bottle he had left by her side was untouched. He felt surprisingly strong but uneasy about it, as if his vitality were at the expense of someone else. After five minutes and no change he entered her compartment.

"Are you all right?" Ayers said.

When there was no answer he reached out to touch the thin shoulder and leaped back instantly as the form spun toward him. Its eyes were wide, the face frozen, the lips contorted in a silent "O." The body under the sheet remained stiff as the plank of mahogany bunk board between them.

So, not dead! He ignored her shudders and backed away, feeling lively. In the galley he made soup. As the chicken stock reduced, he chopped a stump of carrot and dropped in a rind of parmesan, and then, for more fat, a remaining

177

slab of pork belly. And salt, she needed salt. Soup would be hard to administer with a spoon, so he chose a plastic squeeze bottle, and filled it.

"Coming in, bringing you something," he called.

She lay as before.

He knelt. "This is soup." Without pause he stuck the bottle between her lips and squeezed. She gagged, but he kept at it, holding her lips closed. It was thin stuff and ran down her cheek onto the pillow. She got half of it down before the choking stopped him. She could swallow, all right. He licked his dripping hand. It was good soup, salty and warm.

"You did fine. Stand by."

Ayers poached four eggs in a pot, ate three, and carried the last in a ramekin to the guest cabin. Her eyes followed as he knelt beside her.

"Ready?"

He held out the egg, quivering on its spoon. Her head lay on the stained pillow, mouth closed and vertical. The spoon, however, required horizontal orientation. He put his hand behind the mass of her matted hair and lifted her head on its fragile neck. He waited for her mouth to open. When it didn't he jacked open the teeth and mashed the egg between them. When the yolk ran down her chin he caulked her mouth with his thumb. She gagged.

"Swallow."

He waited, thumb in her mouth, her head in his hand. When it was time he removed his thumb like a cork from a bottle and the egg stayed in. He hid his satisfaction, which she didn't seem to share.

"I'll change the pillowcase," said Ayers.

* * *

By the fourth day he was no longer a singlehander, and knew it. Marika had become crew aboard the yacht and in his head. He was consumed every moment with her temperature and fluids. She was inert, he was movement. She was mute, he had the gift of speech. Working the boat was no longer enough, he was obliged to work her, too, to bring her fully to life, to see her reconstituted. Ayers had never felt, on this long voyage alone, an absence of people. Now, in the presence of one helpless passenger with only a single name, he accepted the universal obligation of hospitality.

What music might she like? In his 100 gigabytes of recordings there was no Justin Bieber or Taylor Swift or whatever they called it, hippity-hop? So he tried Glenn Miller and "Moonlight Serenade," setting the volume in her cabin speakers low while the Miller horn section blended its easy swing time. Watching her impassive face he felt himself borne away to the Meadowbrook dance hall in 1943 and its eddying, tuxedoed dancers.

Nothing.

He tried Bach, but a fugue was all wrong and rattled the whole boat. Jazz was next, for which he chose Django Reinhardt's "See you in My Dreams," its time so upbeat his own foot automatically tapped. She lay unmoving. He thought he saw a small attempt to smile, an acknowledgement of his intention but failure of achievement. No resurrection. Four days unable to move and no significant change. He feared she would evaporate before his eyes like steam and leave behind only the wrinkled sheets.

He tried pictures from his sailing library, holding up for her glossy photos of women voyagers proudly at the helm and of Francis Chichester applauded by Queen Elizabeth. He turned for her the pages of Nigel Calder's "Mechanical and Electrical Manual," on the off chance that engine diagrams might light up her eyes. They didn't. Her eyes stayed on him.

He tried reading to her, as his mother had read to him during the delirium of his own childhood fevers. He chose William F. Buckley's sailing memoirs, which he remembered as funny, but after two pages was tongue-tied in polysyllabic convolutions. He declaimed from the autobiography of Miles Davis until the great trumpet man revealed himself a monster, braggart and pimp, and he had to stop and explain that genius sometimes came in a garbage bag. He read aloud from Albert Schweitzer on music. The book had fascinated him as a young man with its fervid argument against machine-driven bellows as the ruination of the old church organs around which cathedrals were built. The great Schweitzer put her to sleep. Ayers could not find his way to her, wherever she was, and gave up. He turned off the music, stacked away his books, and returned to her side in defeat.

"I feel bad I can't do something," Ayers said, sitting beside her. "I think you're getting better but I don't know why you can't move. I remember being crazy inside and trapped like you can't get out. I remember how the silence seemed to echo, and my mother putting cold washcloths on my head. If that's where you are, I've been there, and all you have right now is me talking about myself."

He saw her blink, and the small chin move. That was good.

"How about another egg?"

The eyes abruptly closed. He waited.

"So, what then?"

Her eyes snapped open.

He laughed. "I'm supposed to be alone, you know," Ayers said. "If you weren't here I'd being going nowhere exactly according to plan, watching every day go from long to short and then the night come, quiet or with squalls. You know about night squalls because you're a singlehander, too. I like them. They remind me of thunderstorms back in Pittsburgh, running to get the laundry off the clothes poles before it rained. When I'm putting in a reef I think of that, I don't know why."

Her eyes were locked on his.

"Maybe I need somebody to talk to, too. If you weren't here I'd have my saxophone as company." He pulled a reed out of the pocket of his shirt. "This little sliver of wood makes the sound. I'll play for you sometime, maybe tomorrow, if you're better. I was a good player in high school, and then in Philadelphia later on I played in the jazz clubs, but only if somebody else didn't show up. They called me Toadstool, the white kid always waiting at the bar. "Hey Toadstool, come on up." I could play in all the scales, I practiced every day, but in the clubs the guys would transpose keys as they were going along and lose me. They never looked back, I was just faking to keep up and they thought it was funny."

He laughed. "Who I wanted to be was Charlie Parker. You don't know who that is, but he played the saxophone fast so I played fast, too. One old guy told me, 'Bobby, slow down till you know where you're going.' He was right, because fast is just a trick if it's somebody else's riff you're playing, if you just have it memorized and you're waiting for a place to put it in, and that's what I was doing and they knew it. But I had a pretty mellow tone when I wasn't showing off. It was a good tone for dances, people liked it. Believe me, if I played like that for you you'd just hop up and start gliding around the cabin, you wouldn't be able to stop."

Something happened around her mouth, a tiny contraction that despite the dead cheeks was the first element of a smile. He felt embarrassment and shut the moment down. He had not talked for so long in many months, and to talk about himself felt dishonorable.

"Rest now. You did good with the egg."

He slipped out without looking back to see if her eyes were still open. He drank a cup of protein powder in almond milk, and then in the engine compartment he resumed his regimen of weightlifting. The last workout recorded was many days before, but he felt strong and so he just picked up where he had been then.

* * *

That evening the passenger ate one-half piece of toast, one cup of tea and a few ounces of granola in almond milk. He celebrated with Hendrick's on ice. Her jaws now moved and she swallowed successfully. Her neck remained weak but the arms and legs occasionally stirred. He noted that when he was present she appeared alert, but when he departed she resumed an immobile state. She appeared to rally at the sound of a voice. He tried playing his library of TED talks but her eyes glazed.

It was only when Ayers ventured into the story of himself, no matter how off-handed or tangential the reference, that interest showed in her eyes. It was intimate, female and disconcerting, because Ayers had always had only one witness to who he was, and that was himself. Now this skeleton girl listened like judge and jury. Should he reveal himself to her? This he pondered while carrying a second Hendrick's gin into the guest cabin.

The answer was, no. Or maybe, yes. In fact, it had to be yes. Otherwise, subsequent events might cast him as kidnapper or pervert or lunatic, which would complicate matters as much as if he had given away his location. If the story of Bobby Ayers was required, he could give her one. She would find out later that everyone's story is a lie, that everything we know about anyone is a lie, and that the secret of life is to lie to yourself and lie to the world and smile when the world lies back. But give her a story. Drive it into her heart like a stake for all to see if she's called upon for testimony.

Marika's eyes were wide. He remembered that her face was paralyzed but his wasn't, and that his face could scare people.

"Marika," Ayers said with a big smile, "I think I have done you a disservice. Here you lie, uncomfortable, over-coming a severe debilitation, and some guy is standing over you like a shadow and for all you know he's a cannibal and you're dinner."

He looked for a trace of smile but got only eyes.

"It's OK, I'm not a cannibal, I'm Robert Allington Ayers, "Bobby" to you. And so we get to know each other better, I'm going to tell you things I never told anybody before, and you know why? Because you finished your toast, that's why."

He was weak on small talk and knew it. Light stuff came out heavy and heavy stuff came out so light that people said, 'really?' It was why he had perfected his stare, so they would talk and he could listen. Now, with a sip of gin and an uneasy sensation, Ayers plunged headlong into his own autobiography.

"My dad was a roofer and we lived outside of Pittsburgh. I was in college when he died, and if your father's a roofer and he dies, everybody says, did he fall off a roof?"

She was listening, all right. He wondered how to proceed, and then remembered he could always lie.

"But he didn't fall off a roof. It was a massive heart attack. I dropped out of school right away. I got a job, I got married. I think probably that's because my mother had died just three years before, and then he did, and it felt like there was nobody left but me. Yeah, married. I don't know why, I was 23 years old and she was only 20. Eleanor, really smart and funny. One of her school friends introduced me to his uncle, Mr. Sullivan, who had a construction company, and he hired me as a truck driver. They had about half a dozen backhoes and forklifts and a couple of trucks, small outfit. I'd been around equipment all my life so I could fill in for everybody right away, the drivers, the operators, the foremen. When you're a young guy you don't know how good you are, but pretty fast I did. I was a natural manager. We had all our tools stolen by our mechanic, who was a drunk, and Mr. Sullivan didn't like firing people so he let me do it. Then I found a new mechanic, so it paid off. I filled in for the bookkeeper, too. I had two accounting courses in school so I knew our ledgers were terrible. I bought three of the first computers and put the whole business on floppies. In a year I was vice president, and Tommy and me, that's Mr. Sullivan, we bought up two other construction outfits that were going bankrupt and suddenly we had a whole yard full of equipment and no more renting everything. I was working 15 hours a day and running home at night to Eleanor. Half the time I didn't even see her because she only got computer time in the middle of the night. She did math and statistics and stuff, she's a full professor now, Eleanor is. I guess I would say we were definitely in love."

He was surprised to hear himself volunteer that, and stopped to see if Marika had heard. He saw only eyes and lurched quickly on.

"The point is, growing a business was what I was born to do and I knew it. I was out selling Tommy and us and meeting everybody. You know what that felt like? It felt like a man. I had a wife, I was making money, I discovered I didn't have certain limitations that other people had. I had more energy, and I knew it. I was good with people, too. The construction culture in those days was friends helping friends. This is not understood well, but if you want to succeed it means people working together, not fighting each other. I'm talking about the foremen, the crews, the inspectors, the zoning guys, the firemen and policemen, the deputy mayors, everybody. One good contract means a profit for you, but that should be shared, because the more pieces that go out the more pieces come in. Sullivan Construction at the time was not a big outfit, payroll about 20K a month with a few months in reserve and too many accounts receivable, but we did well. I think Tommy already knew I was burying bad personal stuff, but he let me alone."

Ayers abruptly broke off and held the water bottle to her lips. As she steadied it he felt her hand on his. It was like an infant's hand. He brushed it carefully away and continued with her talking cure.

"Actually, the problem was that I didn't know who I was yet, I had just discovered some aptitude. I had a wife, I had a boss, I had a sports car. You think you're on the way. But then we had a D9 Caterpillar disappear from our yard in Pennsauken. A 100,000-pound bulldozer that suddenly nobody can find, right? Then our other yard got wiped clean of three front-loaders and an excavator. Then stuff started blowing up, literally. Sure, we all had dynamite lying around and there were accidents, but this wasn't accidents, this was messages. Tommy said lay back, let it sort itself out. Fine, but he wasn't out there like I was, having dinner, playing cards, developing my lines of information. I knew there was this guy from Atlantic City, Eddie Leseur was his name, they called him Eddie Small Peas, who was buying up companies under stress. They were under stress because he was cutting through their fences and blowing their stuff up. I went to see him to buy back some of our missing equipment. I knew he stole it, but Tommy said let's pay a little ransom, it's easier. Eddie Small Peas was this red-headed peanut in a swivel chair that he wiggled back and forth. He advised me that Sullivan was growing too fast, and we should slow down. I disagreed, especially coming from this obvious cokehead. Cocaine was prevalent then, and take it from me it is not good for business. But I'm cordial. You have to listen and show respect if you want to get anywhere.

However, after the meeting I go to the parking lot and there's a note on the windshield of my sports car that says, 'Babombe." So I took it off, thinking what is this, somebody's name? Or maybe it's Italian, I'll have to ask somebody what it means. So I'm halfway back to the office, looking at this paper in my hand, when I realize that what it means is, 'baboom!' Like, they're going to blow my car up. 'Baboom!' OK, these guys weren't in the front row in school, but still, if you're threatening to kill somebody don't spell it wrong. That's just stupid. And the mood I was in, it didn't sit well.

"The fact is, looking back, I had no idea what was going on with me. I was doing well but I wasn't that happy. I was having some bad ideations, and my wife, Eleanor, said I should rest, take it easy. I couldn't, because I needed to be doing something all the time just not to being doing nothing. The nervous agitation is difficult to describe. I have to say, though, that I had it under control until Tommy's Lincoln Town Car blew up in his driveway. He wasn't in it, but it scared his wife so much he sent her out of town on vacation. I knew exactly who did it and so did Sullivan and who was next. Tommy had a lot of cop friends and he said they would handle it, he took me to dinner and made a long speech about forbearance, and all the time I was thinking, this particular adversary you can't forebear, because he's a nut case. He's not a businessman, he's a delusionary personality and it could come to a bad end for everybody. Because as I said, construction is a family and it was the only one I had. I was in a bad mood more and more. I stopped going out, I stopped going home. I didn't know what was happening to me, but even in that condition I knew what to do, so I went over the bridge to Philadelphia to see Angelo Bruno's people. Mr. Bruno was sort of a deputy mayor over there, and I put in a complaint about this business with Eddie Leseur from Atlantic City. Was Mr. Bruno a friend of his? Could they talk to him and maybe work something out for us? Or was it OK to talk to him myself? My father had always said to me, get permission, it's polite.

Three days later the word came back that Mr. Bruno didn't know the guy, and right then I knew the problem was going to solve itself. And I was right, because what happened was that Eddie Small Peas accidentally blew himself up in his own garage from playing with matches. They had to scrape him off the ceiling, according to what I heard. And Tommy was back in business like nothing happened and everybody was happy again.

Naturally the police stepped in, they talked to Tommy, they talked to Eleanor, but she didn't even know where I was because to tell you the truth, neither did I. I was sick, and it was the first time but I didn't know that yet. I was as paralyzed as you, Marika, from the darkness that came down. At first I hid out in a motel room because I couldn't go home, which was Eleanor's student apartment. After a week, I went to Mr. Sullivan and told him I had a duodenal ulcer or something like that and I needed an operation. He didn't ask any questions. I'd been sleeping in my suit for a week, he could see that, and all he did was nod and write me a check for $10,000, and he said, "Yeah, you better go."

"'You better go', those were his words. So I did. No goodbyes, not even to my wife. There was no Bobby Ayers left to do it, it was like I died. But I didn't. I went to Madrid, just because it was far and nobody knew me there. I was in a dark room in Madrid for three months. I thought it would never end, but it did, and then when it did I couldn't go back. I knew I had to start over, and in my life I have started over a lot of times, but that was the first, and the hardest, being so blindsided, seeing the sun just go out. Afterwards I was afraid to look back in case it happened again. I needed to move forward, stay on the bright side, because if I had a gun in Madrid I would've probably used it. And hey, if I'd used it then I wouldn't be here now, and neither would you. So it works out, right?"

He tried to smile. He decided not to look at her face and went to the galley for some water, and when he returned her eyes followed him as he entered and sat down. Well, enough of that, so he started in on the foreign sports car from the James Bond movie, and how he bought it because it set him apart even though he got kidded at construction sites, and then on to his theories about the elements of successful investment, and the real problem with tariffs on steel, droning on intentionally for too long until when he looked up her eyes were closed and he could turn the overhead lamp from white to red, the night vision setting which made everything soft and warm.

To see her peacefully asleep gave him something very like joy. He went up the stairs to the big cockpit to feel the yacht running easily across the night. He looked at his hands, which were steady, and at the fingerprints that identified him as one of a kind, for better or worse. He had been talking for hours, listening to himself with interest to see what he would say. It had been like reading his own autobiography. The night reef was already in and there was nothing more to do. The breeze was light and warm and the sky was a billion stars in a glass dome. He slept on the deep comfort of the cockpit cushions, and woke when dawn did.

The first thing he did was check on his guest, and when he entered her cabin he noticed the change immediately.

Marika was wearing his pajamas.

CHAPTER FIFTEEN

Fayetteville

"Nobody has a complete understanding of their father," said Maurice at the third mile of their jog around the reservoir. "I don't, you don't. Nobody does."

"Ours were absent," Laura said.

"Because they were absent we probably know more about them than if they stuck around. There were more witnesses and testimony and more people rolling their eyes. More stuff you eventually hear, like it or not."

"You're going somewhere with this, aren't you."

"Nope."

They flopped onto a wood bench, his long legs straight, hers across them to trap him there. She took a long draft from the water bottle on his hip. A song sparrow sang in a tree, early sign of spring.

"Compared to everybody else's father, mine was easy," she said.

"You think you understand him?"

"No, but I don't understand you, either. I don't want to. You're like a piece of art, Maurice. I don't know much but I know what I like."

"You don't want to understand me? Interesting."

Laura recognized her own defensive banter when she heard it, and with him it didn't work. He was more sensitive to her moods than any man she had ever been with.

"OK," Laura said, "to explain: I would be disappointed to think that you understand me, because that means there is no mystery and nothing left to learn and it would get boring. Therefore, I don't want to understand you. If you want me to really figure you out, say the word. It would take about five minutes."

"I'm talking about your father."

"Yes, you think I should understand him and I don't. I never had to. Whatever gossip there was, was lost on me. That's what I mean by 'easy.' I had Ed and mom, I was in a bubble. And I thought my real dad was cool and that was enough. The rest of it was for somebody else."

"Not anymore," he said.

"I think the father stuff is more a wound for you than me."

As soon as she said it she wished she hadn't, because Maurice seemed visibly to relax. That was what he did when tension rose, or push approached shove, or a cop pulled him over for being black in a Mercedes. It was some sort of reverse fight-or-flight response accompanied by a smile and loosening of the musculature. It was what happened when the basketball came to his hands and a three-pointer loomed and he seemed to stop while everyone else was moving and then the ball was arcing up from his arms. Maurice, more than anyone she had ever met, knew what he wanted of himself. It was not a good idea to be in the way.

"Not a wound," he said easily. "In my case, more a malfeasance of disclosure, as in too much of it too late."

"Hey, I didn't mean anything," Laura said, taking his hand.

"My father, I was told, was a virtuoso. He was a brilliant scholar, a Renaissance man, the 'Pericles of the Podium' one student newspaper called him. I wanted to be him. Hell, by the eighth grade I thought I was him, and as I've explained to you before, so you'll understand where I'm coming from if it ever becomes necessary for you to understand me—"

"Stop," she said.

"As I've told you before, he was at that time fucking his way through the student body to the eventual offense of a faculty wife he was also fucking at the same time, and who got him fired and sent us off to some new leafy shithole college where the same thing happened again. Four colleges, Laura, from Georgia to New Hampshire, four sudden departures in the night, because nobody sent word ahead to the next stop to say, look out for distinguished professor Lionel Charles, the West Indian wordsmith and crowd pleaser, hide your daughters because he is not what he seems. I didn't bother to understand him, you're right. I just watched my mother make dinner for the undergraduates he brought home to discuss Voltaire around our dinner table, no bras, them hanging on his every word while my mother served black cake Christmas pudding. I didn't understand it because I didn't ask. I don't know how much my mother actually knew, probably some but not all, probably she didn't want to. Other people knew, eventually I knew, but everybody just sat back and let her swing in the wind. Until I told her."

Laura had heard the story before, and always delivered in the same even, conversational tones. Maurice, as a high school senior, had intervened, forced a divorce, produced a non-disclosure agreement and overseen a generous settlement that stipulated his own father was never to return to the United States again. His mother had died three years later, and in England the career of his father now flourished. Maurice forgot nothing. He was like a tree riven by lightning that had survived to grow tall but still retained its fiery scar.

"You think my mother is swinging in the wind?"

"Please talk to Julia. Don't cut her out. You've seen his first wife, you've met his last girlfriend, you spent the day with his old boss. People don't like being the last to know, and the financial implications are huge."

"I'm not ready," Laura said.

* * *

The Laura problem, Laura believed, was Laura. She was not lonely or abandoned or needful. That was her secret in a world that presumed continuous intimate interactions, dependencies and mutual goals. That was the lesson of every schoolroom, team, sorority and social network. It was the church and state and history in which all must hang together or surely we'll hang apart. That Ben Franklin quip had won her an eight-grade essay contest, even though Ben Franklin was in fact not like anybody else at all.

They said she was distant, or held herself apart, but it wasn't true. She was present. The present was a state of grace and the state of nature. Alone was freedom and definition. Alone was Laura, and only alone could she love. Love Maurice, as a separate thing. Love Julia for what she was and Ed, too, in their specifics. You couldn't love people in general, the way you could love dogs. Only an individual had identity. Only alone could you know who you are. To deny that, to hide from it, made you nobody.

Such were her thoughts on the trip to Fayetteville, N.C., the home of Vivian Liu Ayers, for four years a temporary stepmother and whom she had never met. The plane landed in Charlotte. The car she rented had crank windows.

Vivian had not returned Laura's three telephone calls made over the course of a week. The fourth she had answered with a single word: "Yes?" When Laura introduced herself, the phone went dead. Laura then sent a long text message saying she had financial information to deliver under the terms of the Robert Allington Ayers Living Trust, that a meeting was in Vivian's self-interest and her signature required, and that she would appear at Vivian's home address of 117B Ponderosa Court this day at 4 p.m.

Vivian's reply changed the address to that of a donut shop in a mini-mall.

Laura arrived at exactly 4 o'clock, already irritated. The donut shop had a counter but no chairs or stools. Vivian was waiting outside, wrapped in a black raincoat and wearing a 99-cent-store sun visor. High heels brought her up to Laura's chin. Large black sunglasses obscured her eyes. Of the woman behind them there was nothing to see.

"You must be Vivian," Laura said in her best voice.

"Some identification, please."

"OK." She dug out her Connecticut driver's license. The other woman peered at it and handed it back. No words.

"Well, then I'd better see some ID, too," said Laura, flashing the smile that almost always worked.

"I don't drive," said Vivian.

"Fair enough," said Laura, making a show of examining her from several angles. "I've seen your pictures, and you match."

"What is the purpose of your visit."

"Vivian, can we at least sit down?"

"You said this would not take long."

"It will take longer standing up in the street."

Vivian led her to a laundromat a few stores down. Washers were churning. A guy stood in his underwear, filling a dryer. They sat at a plywood folding table where Laura opened her briefcase as slowly as possible, hoping the mood would soften. Vivian sat rigid across from her, watching.

"As the trustee of my father's living will," Laura began, "it's his desire that I inform you of the disbursements that will occur at the time of his death. He thinks it's better all around if folks know what he intends."

"Where is Robert?"

"I'm the designated trustee, Vivian. He asked me to do this."

"You're his daughter, you're not him. Where is he?"

"My father is currently on vacation."

"Ha. Not true."

"Why?" Laura leaned quickly forward. "Have you heard from him?"

"No vacations, ever."

The hope of information faded. It was obvious that Vivian wasn't any more up to date than she was. Angrier, though.

"So you come to give me money?" Vivian said into the space between them.

"Well, yes, basically, to inform you of his desires. There's an acknowledgement to sign saying that I actually met with you, and I have a couple of personal questions I hope you can help me with."

"You brought $3.9 million in your briefcase?"

"No, Vivian, I don't have $3.9 million in my briefcase."

"Then we're finished. Goodbye, nice to meet you."

She stood up.

"Sit down," Laura said.

Vivian gestured to a taxicab waiting in the parking lot. It cruised over and stopped outside the laundromat door.

"Vivian! I flew four hours to get here, so don't blow me off. And if you want to know your share of the loot when my father dies, I advise you to listen up, because I'm the one handling it."

"I'll talk to Robert."

"No, you won't talk to 'Robert' because nobody's talked to him in months. Nobody knows where he is, don't you get it? Please, help me with this. When did you hear from him last?"

Vivian stared at her. She wasn't much more than five feet tall, lips firmly together. No purse. Wind could blow her over. And the cheap visor? She was supposed to be a gold-digging femme fatal from across the world, seducer of the ever-unreliable Bobby Ayers and last known inhabitant of his world. Rich, like him. A full partner in his most recent ventures. An international sophisticate. Yet she looked like a raincoat on a hanger.

"Sit down or I'm leaving," Laura said without inflection. "I don't need this, I can just check you off as 'declined,' it makes no difference to me." She dug into her briefcase for a folder and a pen.

"I'm not signing anything," Vivian said. "I want my money he stole."

"Are you talking about the case in tax court?"

"Do you have my check?"

"There are no checks for anybody yet. If you let me, I'll go over with you the percentage he wishes you to eventually receive, and the conditions."

"Then since you won't pay, you and Robert will be in court and there my lawyers will dig it out of you and your crook family with a sharp stick! I am not going to jail! I will fight you, you don't know me!"

The small body didn't move as she spoke. The words came like bullets.

"Sit down for five minutes, five minutes only, and talk to me," Laura said.

"Ha!" Vivian started for the taxi.

"Stop! This is ridiculous. You and my father made a lot of money together, and you were his wife. Vivian, I have a million questions, so why are we here in this laundromat? I happen to know that you're a sophisticated woman, just talk to me. I don't know anything, my father asked me to do this, it wasn't my idea. Why does he owe you money for his taxes?"

"Tell Robert to call me. Nobody else."

"I don't know where he is."

"Ha!"

"It's the truth."

"He knows where he is. If you don't, you are same as me."

To Laura's astonishment the small figure stepped into the waiting cab and closed the door without looking back. The taxi cruised out of the mini-mall, bounced over a speed bump and miniaturized away down Martin Luther Highway.

The documents remained open before Laura. Vivian was to get 20 percent of Robert Ayers' estate according to a complex formula that did not have a dollar value because nobody yet knew the scope of the Ayers holdings. The idea was that people would be remembered. What they would remember was the question.

"Tell Robert to call me." Yeah, dad. That would help.

Her flight home was the last of the day, which gave five hours to kill before returning to the airport. She plugged 117B Ponderosa Court into Waze, suction-cupped her iPhone to the dashboard of the rental car, and headed there.

Vivian's residence was a tired brick duplex with a side yard behind a steel security fence. She rang the buzzer and waited. She knocked and said loudly who she was, that she was not going away, and that she genuinely needed to get some things straight that they both had in common, and that if they had gotten off to a bad start perhaps it was her fault. All this to a closed door, when in fact the bad start was sure not her fault. No answer. She heard an interior door open and close.

Laura walked to the side yard, where through a fence she saw Vivian standing on a porch, smoking a cigarette and looking at her.

"I flew down from Connecticut just to talk to you," Laura said, raising her voice just enough to be heard. "My father has been off on his sailboat since December and we don't know where he is. Everybody's worried, Vivian. He has me going around talking about his will and explaining what everybody gets. You get a lot. I'm supposed to tell you the details, and you sign saying you understand, and you can have your lawyer look at it. It's my duty as the sole trustee, but also, please, I'm his only daughter and you and I never even met."

Laura's heels were sinking into the soft loam of the grass, tipping her backwards so that she had to hold onto the steel palisades of the fence to remain upright and casually engage the stick figure 30 feet away.

"Please, we're in each other's lives, like it or not. We deserve to give each other a chance. We deserve to hear what we have to say, don't you think?"

Vivian slowly approached across the porch. Her walk, even under the shabby raincoat, was light as a dancer's. The sunglasses were too much, sort of Jackie-Onassis-on-Capri, but the shoes were Louboutins, she could see the red soles flash.

"All I know about you is that you were a translator, and there are three companies with your maiden name on them—Liu Ayers Associates, right? Dad never did partnerships with anybody, so I know that means he trusted you a lot. Vivian, I'm standing here talking through a fence, come have a cup of coffee with me someplace before I have to catch my plane back."

The stream of hose water looked at first like birds in flight rising into the sunlight between them. It landed short, 10 feet from the fence. As Vivian moved forward, dragging behind her an unfurling reel, it splashed closer. When the range was accurately gauged the cold jet struck Laura square, spraying her with rubber-smelling water and up-splashing mud. Retreat was inhibited by her heels, which were impaled in sod. She felt the stream paint her neck and blouse as she stumbled backwards, guarding her face with her purse, losing a shoe.

"Why are you spraying me with a hose!" Laura called out.

"Go back to your bad mother and get the money!" Vivian cried, zeroing in.

"Stop it! Laura said, reaching down for her shoe. "This is ridiculous."

"Get my money, thief daughter!" Vivian cried at close range, the hose stream snaking.

"They told me you were nuts!" Laura shouted over her shoulder.

"Family of betrayers!" Vivian cried.

"What?" cried Laura, stopping, dodging.

"I will not be cheated like your mother cheated him!"

"You're crazy, Vivian, and everybody knows it!"

That was all Laura could get out before she was obliged to run for the protection the building, shake herself in fury, hobble soaking to her crappy rental car and then floor it for the airport where she drank three Jack Daniels in the lounge, ate an entire pepperoni pizza and eventually got home at midnight, still damp and slit-eyed with fury.

CHAPTER SIXTEEN

Vivian

After 10 days Ayers' passenger had achieved the status of crew. Marika had been in turn a sighting, then a potential contagion, then a mechanical challenge (her transfer aboard by halyard sling) and then a puddle in the berth of his guest cabin. On the fourth day she had first raised a spoon. By Day 10 she had put on twelve pounds and now prowled the yacht like its master, beating Ayers to the galley to prepare meals, dressing herself in his amended clothes and sunning herself naked just out of reach of his gaze. She still couldn't speak, her throat immobilized by the toxins. She still wasn't strong, which was why she lay in her bunk each evening listening to him talk about himself, which was all she seemed to want to hear, as if his life were proof of her own.

From time to time he called her 'Vivian,' caught himself, and apologized. The resemblance was not mysterious. They shared the same light frame and guarded sensuality. Mute as a stone Marika might be, but in Ayers' mind she had Vivian's voice, too: the occasional plural insufficiently vocalized, random words pitched outside the monochrome of native English speakers, the lack of labial vibration by which 'boom vang' came out 'boom sang.' She would sound, if she could speak, just like Vivian Liu. And then there were the eyes. He found it difficult to look at Marika's eyes because when he did her face lit up, and he had to cast his own eyes down. In certain lights he even detected an epicanthic fold. Some Europeans had it, you didn't have to be Chinese. At dusk the effect was strongest, when she brought his pills, when the slender hands administered to his lips. Especially then. The smell was the same. Smell of Vivian.

Vivian Liu had been his interpreter in Shanghai at the end of a bad business year. It was the year that Ayers had been fired as CEO from his own development company after successfully covering half the hills of San Diego with red-tile-roofed luxury homes. He called that disaster the Rebellion of the Scions. The scions were three sons of the original Orange County landowners, three skinny-leg empty suits with recently swallowed MBAs who had managed, behind closed doors, to convince their fathers and grandfathers to spit Ayers out. Services no longer required. New blood to be injected, theirs.

Just business, Bobby, his board of directors had said. You've been distracted lately, Bobby, those old farmers had said. Everybody sees it except you, Bobby, the sons had said. They had used against him a brief depression, a mere month or two of inattention to timetables and hand-holding and the constant reassurance of worrisome bankers. He was Churchill, kicked out after winning the war. Forced into leisure, Ayers had joined a county trade mission to Shanghai. He came home three weeks later with a protégé, then soon a partner, then soon Wife Number Three.

Vivian Liu had been eager, but not eager to please. She was barbed, guarded, beautiful and crazy. He qualified for her attention, she explained, because he did not display an expectation of submission on the part of an Asian female. Well, that was not likely in her case. Vivian said neither 'please' nor 'thank you.' Her eyes drew a bead like a hunter sighting, and if you were in the sights, look out. He had made himself willingly a target. Their romance had been a revelation to both, and she had pursued it with the zeal of a Jesuit. Ayers, struggling back from the depths of his black hole, found her smarter and quicker and more determined than anyone he'd ever known. Had he lost a step by then, at age 55? Maybe so. Ouster from his own company had been no fun at all, and cost him all his play money.

Vivian talked nonstop while listening at the same time. She devoured details. She read the contracts Ayers had never bothered to. She studied the complications of tax codes that Ayers dismissed as citizen abuse. She had no money and wanted some. She had no material needs in the usual form of cars or horses or gold-plated mansions. The material she needed was him. And to have him, she saved him.

Marika arrived, bringing Ayers' lunch to his bunk. She kissed his cheek and sprung away like a released rubber band. Same goddamn moves as Vivian. He called for her to come back so he could check the folds of her eyes, but she laughed at him from the cockpit above, where she had taken manual control of the helm just to feel the yacht in her hands. On his tray, the five pills.

Vivian had two sons in China whom he had never met. She sent them money—hers, not his. When the money stopped, she plotted war against the landowner sons.

Ayers, not yet recovered, wasn't up for it. He proposed instead that they return to Shanghai and start over there. Vivian said no. Ayers suggested a lucrative Mexico City partnership, an open offer he had resisted for years. She said no. While he drifted in darkness she walked in light, and spun a web of personal informers that made her better informed than the rump sons or the doddering board of directors. It was what Churchill had done when out of power. Vivian told him to shut up about Churchill and stay out of her way.

He did.

So it came to pass that the sons of the landowners tired of getting their hands dirty in tract-house construction, with its rough foremen and under-table bribes and specifically with a vengeful Chinese woman who stopped the project dead with an injunction on behalf of a fringe-toed lizard (*Uma inornata,* Threat to the Habitat of, Friends of the Sierra Club vs. SoCal Ayers Partners). Under her enfilading fire they retreated to the surer thing of a venture-cap start-up, ho ho, and in two quarters lost their shirts and jock straps and nearly their fathers' fortunes too.

It was Vivian who ran the campaign to return Bobby Ayers' to power. She made the case, set the meetings, commandeered the focus, dissolved the memory of the sons in acid sarcasm and singlehandedly restored the myth of Bobby Ayers. She was an exotic in stiletto heels and the directors were squinty old farmers, but they liked being rich and now they were in a drought. She could bring back the rain, and the rainmaker was Robert Allington Ayers.

It would cost them $10 million cash.

Ayers watched from the sidelines. His role, Vivian specified, was to be offended, distant and unavailable. It was a new role, and as the darkness passed he more and more enjoyed it.

After two months the directors agreed in principle to Ayers' return but balked at the massive initial payout. Another month passed with no houses being built. The landowners and investors became agitated. The bankers reassessed. Vivian herself stopped sleeping, worked her backchannels, and fell into doubt. Ayers waited. He liked things to fall apart. He let them fall apart. When they had, he played his card.

Ayers owned a $10 million annuity. He would sell it to his directors for face value. He would take no other compensation for three years, so it was really a signing bonus with him as collateral. The directors were the beneficiaries. If Bobby Ayers fell off a roof on his head, they got their money back. The old boys liked that part and bourbon flowed to celebrate the deal. Everybody knew that Vivian Liu had made it happen.

The $10 million had arrived as a paper cashier's check. Vivian held it in a trembling hand, dazzled by the zeros. But Ayers had saved the best for last: The money, as the sale of an existing annuity, had no taxes due. Five million clear for her, five million clear for him.

In their suite that night at the San Diego Astoria they drank champagne. He was proud of her and of himself, too. He had never had a partner he had come to love, not one he so respected, not one so much like himself. Their balcony faced west, and together they watched the lower limb of a burning sun set the blue Pacific on fire. The big Jacuzzi off their bedroom was bubbling. Vivian was bubbling too as she stepped out of her clothes. Ayers had never seen a woman so mission-complete, so grateful for his love and so happy to be rich at last.

On an impulse, naked, he picked up the check and with a formal bow of respect tore it in two and handed Vivian her $5 million-dollar half. They had done it!

She screamed as the paper tore. It was as if she herself had been ripped in half. She pummeled him in fury. She raged at his disrespect, his stupidity, his ruination of their hopes, his insult to her and her children and of the gods of good luck and specifically of his chances of getting her into that Jacuzzi, idiot check-ripper! Stupid moron fool! Undeserving jackass! Did he not know anything about the world? Did he not see the violation? Had he never been poor? Was he blind to this insult to fate and chance?

Ayers apologized. Just paper, wasn't it? He did miss social cues sometimes.

It took days and days to get the check redrawn. The rough old boys who had hired him back didn't get the joke, they thought this stunt was some new Bobby-Ayers fastball of unknown meaning or mockery. They demanded from Vivian a full explanation in writing of how come the reinstalled CEO tore their check in half, what kind of nonsense was that, is that some message we're too dim to understand? You tell Bobby he can stick our check up his own wiseass.

No, no, sirs, it was not Mr. Bobby. It was the action of Miss Vivian. It was, she had explained, a venerable Chinese custom always to tear such checks in half. It signified that all parties would double their success. (Or something like that, Ayers had not been there to hear.) But the old boys bought it, and even asked forgiveness for their parochialism.

But when it came to developing land Ayers did know what he was doing, and the hills east of Mission Viejo grew new tile roofs again.

Vivian sent her $5 million, all of it, to China and her two sons. She had done her work, she was now a dutiful wife. Her marriage to Robert was warm with mutual respect. He had never enjoyed success more, for the joy it brought her in the completion of her goal. She beamed, she hung on his arm, a warrior at peace. He loved her without explanation. He watched the smile she wore while sleeping and felt himself its architect. They were sun and moon, linked in orbit and facing always as they revolved. They were different and the same, they were, against all odds and appearances, one.

Then, two years later, the IRS had presented a tax bill of $3.9 million.

Après Vous heeled suddenly, and by the rush of water under the hull Ayers felt the boat accelerate in a squall. Rain pattered the deck along with the sound of footfalls and gear clattering. In a moment a shadow appeared in the main salon, shaking off a foul-weather gear jacket.

"Vivian?"

The shadow laid a wet washcloth across his forehead.

"Don't pay them a dime," he said.

She had put in a reef and the yacht was already riding better. It was Marika, bringing him tea and his pills. Vivian he had lost again.

* * *

The next day at lunch Marika approached him with his iPhone in her hand. She used its selfie camera to brush her hair, since there were no mirrors aboard the yacht. Ayers had read the autobiography of a blind writer who believed that mirrors and copulation were abominable because both increased the numbers of men. His name was Borges, or something like that, an Argentine poet. Ayers wasn't much for poetry, but the phrase made him smile, so he had had all the mirrors on the boat removed in Mexico. A singlehander doesn't need mirrors, that's pretty much the opposite of the whole idea.

The iPhone flash dazzled as Marika took his picture, then turned the screen toward him.

It showed an apparition in a fright wig. From the scalp clots of dried blood clung on thin twists of tangled hair-strings. A mangy beard hung from the face, nose hairs protruding, both ears black with bilge grease. The upper forehead was scored as if a bear claw had drawn across it, leaving red welts of infection in its wake. The photo captured also a hand on which claw-like nails protruded, one split and bleeding. The hand was blurred by its shaking. The monster on the screen was him. Ayers fumbled inexpertly at the glass controls, accidentally enlarging the portrait before he found "delete."

Marika was impassive, the wall that held the mirror.

"I didn't know," Ayers croaked, newly self-aware. "I'll take care of it."

But Marika had brought scissors. It took her a long time to trim his hair and disinfect his wounds and to snip away the fungal toenails and close the suppurations on his back and legs before leading him to the shower and helping him into its stall. Ayers watched like a child as the water around his feet ran brown with his own filth. He clung to the handholds of the stall, his back to her so she could not see the tears that mingled with the water streaming from his eyes.

Afterwards he slept for hours. Not restless, not remembering, just weightless and sweet-smelling in his bunk and vaguely conscious of Marika beside him and the press of her hip against his. When he awoke her hands were in his, pulling.

"Let go," Ayers said.

She didn't. He rose with her, groggy. She led him up the companionway ladder to the afternoon, which was bereft of wind. The sails hung lifeless. The yacht sat lodged as if aground on an ocean 8,000 feet deep. The swim platform was deployed and extended like a dock over a still pond. She drew him there. He was without clothes and the flat ocean reflected his ribs and the sticks that were his legs. On the surface before him tiny lines appeared that he had never seen before, the wakes of ocean insects gliding on the surface tension. Mirror clouds lay painted on the water. The air was the equal of his body temperature and he did not feel his skin as separate, but part of it. So too, the salt water at his feet. Tracers of sunlight shot straight down into the sea around him, penetrating beyond his sight.

There came a plunging from behind him. In a moment a frothy envelope of bubbles rose and from it a spray of steam from Marika's snorkel. She passed him a mask. When he put it on she pulled him in.

Underwater, Ayers was mute, too, the task of speech no longer necessary. He saw below him the dark form of the keel, sharp against a background of nothing at all. The hull of *Après Vous* was enormous, her bottom like a whale's back upside-down. There was no language, but he could hear the world speak in a faint crackling. In harbor there was always a clicking of shrimp and sea urchins and the grunts of fish communicating. Here it was the yacht's own barnacles talking, the conversation of crustaceans waving feathery tendrils. A flash of stripes near the keel caught his eye. So his three pilot fish were loyal still. They had been with him since Mexico, as if the boat were a big fish soon to have a meal and send scraps streaming. Even in disappointment they stayed true. He lay still, floating in the bosom of the universe. How beautiful it is to be what we are, no more, no less.

Marika went by like a mermaid showing off. A few kicks and she was directly below him, T-shirt billowing. He watched her blow out the air in her lungs, the silvery bubbles rising. Now she lay on her back, buoyancy neutral, curling a siren-finger to lure him. He grinned around his snorkel bit, tasting sea water enter. She lay there longer than he thought possible without air, and then launched back up toward the light. She was stronger than he was now, he realized with approval. He also realized that he had drifted away from the yacht. It seemed a great effort to swim, and when he tried his legs seemed powerless to move him. When he raised his head the boat was no longer in sight. Urgency rose, and with it the first sign of panic and of doubt.

Then her arms went around his back and in a few strokes he was back at the boarding platform. He found the ladder with his feet and remembered how to climb it. He was limp and that seemed all right, it seemed at least his authentic condition, and so he lay on the platform and let the sunlight do its work and in a moment he was Ayers again, and could stand up and resume the world. Overhead the white fulmar dove for a closer look and Ayers instinctively covered himself with his hands. He shook his fist and the bird banked away. He still had the power.

* * *

That evening at the navigation station Marika watched silently as Ayers plotted the new course. It was the 180-degree turn he performed every 300 miles. It was the course back to where they had been. It was the course that for three months had kept *Après Vous* on the International Date Line, sailing north and then south along the reciprocal, maintaining position off all shipping lanes or yacht tracks or observation of any kind, as far from anywhere else on earth it was possible to be, in a pattern than went nowhere at all.

If she wondered why, she made no sign of it. Instead, when he wrote the new course in the log, she sprang without sign or gesture onto the deck, tacked the yacht, retrimmed the sails, and reset the autopilot in confirmation of his will.

Dinner was linguini alfredo, of defrosted cream and a chianti he had been saving. They dined in silence. He noticed her color had returned, and that when he looked away, she studied him. He did not wish to know what she saw. He could not see it himself, because he had thrown the iPhone overboard.

CHAPTER SEVENTEEN

Mom

They spoke little on the ride up Greenfield Hill to the crunch of the driveway above which the big house glowed. Laura had set out a bottle of pinot noir to bring, but forgotten it. Maurice said nothing as they walked to the house. It was sometimes a good idea to say nothing.

Ed was salting steaks at the big stove. Come in, come in. Laura went straight for her mother, who was coming down the stairs.

"Mom," she said, nodding at the French doors and the patio beyond.

"Why, dear?" said Julia.

"So you can smoke," Laura said.

"Martini?", Ed said to Maurice.

At Ed Newman's house, everybody got the cocktail they wanted. That was the way it should be, and would be in Maurice's house, too. It was inconvenient for the host, but Ed never seemed inconvenienced by anything. He was in his early 70s, still easily mobile and with a flat stomach. He was long since retired, having sold his company before duties on

Chinese steel had wrecked the heavy equipment business. He still played college-team tennis, which was better than Maurice's self-taught game, and both had 20 handicaps at his tough country-club golf course. Despite the age difference Maurice found him a better companion than any colleague or former classmate. Ed was particularly good on people under stress, and more than once Maurice had called him from a meeting for advice in crisis management. Ed had been a "Wild Weasel" pilot in Vietnam. They flew F105s out of Thailand to Hanoi as bait for ground-to-air missiles, a job as dangerous as it sounded. Many were shot down, and Ed's best friend had been a prisoner of war six years. This Maurice only knew from research, because Ed never talked about his war. Ed never asked about Yale, either, or basketball, or the NCAA playoff game the papers said Maurice had lost for the team by his errant free-throws. Laura took Ed for granted, a high compliment from a stepdaughter. Maurice did not. Ed Newman, despite being actuarially near the end of his assigned lifespan, still looked forward. All the world lay there, and every moment started again from here. Ed got it.

Maurice was tasting the first icy lap of martini on his tongue when Ed dropped into the big chair beside him and asked quietly, "So, Maurice, are you two engaged, or what?"

"Are we engaged? You know we are."

Ed touched his wedding band.

"Oh." Maurice said, "the ring you and Julia offered us is perfect. We're incredibly pleased at the generosity and the only reason it isn't on her finger is that we haven't gotten around to the formalities, setting the date and so on."

"It's Julia's ring. It was the engagement ring Bobby gave her."

"Laura loves it, Ed, and I do, too." He glanced at the patio where dark shapes and the glow of a cigarette moved. "Do you know what they're talking about out there?"

"None of my beeswax. How are things, really?"

"Things are good," Maurice said, his guard up.

"I'm not her father but I love her and I know her."

"Come on, Ed. You don't think I can handle this?"

"Not what I meant. Laura has to handle you, and you're kind of a prize, you know. She can drift. She can disappear, like her father. It's in them, and I don't judge it. They need to get cornered once in a while, and it takes us to do it. It takes a leap of faith to figure out what they want and how to give it to them and then how to get home from that afterwards. That can be the hardest part of the mission, getting home after."

"What's 'drift' mean. There's somebody else?"

"No, you're it, pal. What I'm saying is, Laura's not a simple case. She never has been. So, put the ring on the finger. Close the deal."

Maurice said nothing.

Ed drained his Manhattan and refilled from the amber pitcher at his side.

"You know, you're at the same time the most patient and impatient man I ever met. So quit fucking around, put her over your shoulder and drag her to the cave."

Maurice heard the eight-foot-tall hall clock sonorously begin all four stanzas of Westminster Chimes, and waited while it announced the hour of 9 p.m. with nine deliberate, clanging strokes.

"That goes on all day and night?" Maurice said when it ended.

"We don't even hear it," Ed said.

The twin French doors from the patio flew open and Julia and Laura clipped in on their heels, rubbing their hands.

"Manhattan?" said Ed.

"I told mother that my father has changed his last will and testament and instead of being the sole beneficiary she's going to be sharing his assets with five other people, and you're all right with that, right, mom?"

"Well, no," Julia said, sitting down in front of Maurice. "How are you?" she asked him.

"I'm good, Julia."

"What're you talking about, mom? You just said you didn't care, you always knew there would be changes."

"Oh, sit down and take a load off," Julia said. "My daughter's concerned about money for the first time in her life. That's a good sign for you, Maurice. And since we're going to be family, there's a few more things I think we should air in the light of day. Right, Ed?"

"Good a time as any," Ed said.

"Now Laura, I didn't say this outside because you had to talk, and I listened, and now here's a little more. On this new will thing, Eleanor Szabo called me the day after you went to see her. So it's not like I didn't know. Eleanor and I have talked every year for 30 years now, dear, and mostly about you. And I understand Vivian Liu went nuts on you, and I'm not surprised because Vivian has called me and Ed five times in the last month. Vivian may be nuts but your father's nuts too, and we deal with it."

Julia liked to move while she spoke. She was an actress in community theater and knew to keep her head still and project without effort. Laura knew who the old-time movie star Bette Davis was by the third grade. It was her mother.

"You two are going to have children, right? Well, you are, and so you're going to have to make decisions, like Ed and me, and you're going to have to defend every one of them because you never know how things are going to turn out. I've got to say, though, two months is a long time to not tell your mother something. My god, Laura, it's only money. Anyway, Ed and I were right: you turned out great."

"Damned proud," Ed said.

Maurice sipped his second martini, knees drawn up. It was like sitting on the bench during a game, watching the score change.

"What're you talking about?" Laura said.

"So you found Bobby's original will in my closet? That's just what I would've done, if I'd bothered. Because really, there has never been a second wife who doesn't figure the third wife will cut her out. For example, Ed changed his will when he married me. Poor Frances, his first wife, got almost nothing."

"Frances died," Ed said.

"After," Julia said.

"Frances had cervical cancer," Ed said to Maurice. "But if she'd lived Julia and I would have taken good care of her."

"Mom! What are you talking about!" Laura yelled.

"Look at you two, you're perfect. And for that Ed and I get a little credit. And in large measure we have completed our task now that Laura is 32, which is hard to believe."

"Julia was 32 when we got married," Ed said.

"And you were just a baby, Laura. It was seamless."

"Seamless?" Laura said.

"We tried to make it be. And it worked. Right, Ed?"

"Yes, and I'm glad Maurice is here for this."

"For what?" asked Laura.

"Ed will start," said Julia, "I'll get the medical records. Maurice can have them to keep."

The Bobby Ayers "project," as Ed Newman called it, had always been a shared responsibility of his friends, wives, doctors and banks. Bobby suffered from highs and lows, and therefore so did everyone around him. That was the family understatement for periodic unpredictable descents into the bleakest of depressions followed by brilliant recoveries and protean energies. Ed believed history to be populated with such personalities, magnetic but also pathological, so that your time with them was a gift and also a commitment. All time with Bobby Ayers had to be shared. Bobby and Julia and Ed and Frances, as couples and friends, had shared everything, at least until Bobby was institutionalized shortly before Laura was born.

Laura launched to her feet at that, but Ed took her hand. He asked her to listen. He asked her not to judge. He looked at Maurice, who sat frozen. He waited for Laura to sit down.

In that season, Ed went on, Bobby had suffered a series of the business setbacks which usually accompanied his depressions. He had signed himself into a psychiatric rehabilitation facility in Massachusetts and would remain there on and off for nearly a year, from before Laura's birth to after it. He was mute, refused to communicate, and had absolved himself from the world around him. Ed visited him every few weeks. Julia too, as long as her pregnancy allowed. Bobby, Ed recounted, had lost interest in life or his ability to contribute to anyone but himself. During the same period, Frances, Ed's estranged wife, entered the last stages of her fatal illness. Julia and Ed, thrown together by fate, had found comfort in each other. There is a need in human experience, he said, for family. It is a powerful predisposition that supersedes all else. And so, out of the ashes of loss and despite a good deal of understandable confusion, emerged the union of Julia and Ed, and their bond with infant Laura, and now, many years later, with Maurice Charles.

As Julia returned with a thick accordion folder of Robert Ayers' hospital records, Laura said:

"And you two didn't tell me this my whole life, that my father was in an insane asylum when I was born and that I have a genetic proclivity for fucking clinical depression? And now when you say it, it's in front of Maurice, so now he knows I'm nuts too?"

"You're not nuts," Maurice said.

"No? Well, they are!" she said, pointing to her mother and stepfather.

"Don't be silly, dear," Julia said. "We watched you very carefully. Any sign of unusual behaviors and the best therapists in the world would have stepped in."

"But," Ed said, "there was no need."

"Maurice, are you hearing all this?"

Maurice was holding his knees.

"That's not the father I know," Laura said.

"Hey, I was married to him," Julia said. "I loved him, too. He was a persuasive guy and you were a love-child, baby girl. You carry in you both me and him, his genius or whatever you call it, I see him in your eyes right now. We all loved him, and it was hard. Ed loved him, didn't you Ed."

"I do, yes."

"Oh come on, Mother! My father goes into the hospital and 10 minutes later you get married to somebody else?"

"Not somebody, Ed."

"I'm going to be sick," Laura said. And to Ed: "You're his best friend, you marry his wife, how's that work?"

"He'll tell you," Julia said.

"I will tell you," Ed said slowly. "Your father had a long fall. I watched him close down over the months. He exited everything, door by door. He switched off his past, light by light, because he preferred the darkness. He asked for nothing. He still knew me, he still knew everybody, he just went cold, like we were dead and buried. It wasn't his fault, it was just the way it went for him. Some self-preservation thing, I guess. It wasn't so hot for us, believe me. It was pretty confusing and hard not to bear a grudge, because he seemed to know what he was doing. It was just, goodbye. Just, so long. To him, we were no longer there."

"But I was there," said Julia. "And you were, Laura. And thank God Ed was."

"Your dad asked to see me just after he was discharged," Ed said as Julia stood next to him. "He told me he was filing for divorce. He asked me to take care of you, Laura, and of Julia, and to let him off the hook. That's how he put it, get him off the hook. He had his suit on again and he looked like Bobby again but none of the Bobby I knew was there. He said he was going to Europe and not coming back. I believed him. He said to me, that he was inside-out. That was the phrase. He didn't expect to be Bobby Ayers ever again."

"But he was," Julia said, "because you really can't believe anything Bobby says, ever."

"Why the hell didn't either of you ever tell me any of this?" Laura said.

"Because when you were nine he came back in a Jaguar and said, hi, I'm your father! We have reservations at the Plaza! And that was in a conspiracy with my sister that I didn't even know about and neither did Ed! You knew he was back before I did!"

"And you don't undermine somebody's father," Ed said.

"Who isn't here to tell his side of the story," said Laura.

"Honey, his side of the story is the only side there ever is. And it has to be difficult and marvelous, it has to be mysterious, everybody else has to be the audience. The only exception is you, and you know why? Because he thinks you're him."

"That's a compliment," Ed said.

Julia said, "I'm not so sure of that."

"Maurice? Nothing to say?" said Laura.

Maurice felt her face upon him. It was almost impassive, unscored by identifiable emotion. It was a picture from one of her art books, a painting of a woman, peasant or princess, whose expression had meaning only according to title or to an academy caption that told students what to think. On Laura there was never a caption. To Julia, he said:

"I think Laura was concerned about the Ayers Trust and the new division of assets. I'm glad that part doesn't seem to be a problem, at least."

"The money?" Julia said. "Seriously?"

"A little clearing of the air about money is useful for everybody," Maurice said, standing his ground. "I think that was probably Laura's father's intention in all of this."

"Really? The money?" said Julia. "OK, I met her father in a sand pit on Cape Cod. He had big plans and he was broke, and my father liked him and backed him. Really, how did you think Bobby got started again? We set him up. His office then was in two bedrooms of our beach house on the Cape, which had eight of them, by the way. Money? Yes, he knew how to make it. He would make it and lose it and then make it again, up and down like a roller coaster and proud of it. My family never even talked about money, it was just there, it was quiet. If you were actually interested, Laura, all you had to do was ask. You didn't, that's fine, you were in your own cloud. Really, you were oblivious. But I just can't believe you think Ed and I care about our share of your father's assets."

"I knew we were rich, mom, I just never thought it was something to be proud of," Laura said.

"We are who we are, dear. You are too."

"For what it's worth," Ed said, "I think Bobby is doing the right thing, asking you to go around and check off his life and straighten things out."

"A life we were lucky to survive," Julia added.

Ed proposed moving to the dinner table.

"Are you kidding, Ed, you think I can eat?" That was Laura, standing up.

"We can perform the ritual."

"Jesus Christ, I'm not having dinner with a box of my father's nuthouse records under the table. Maurice, come on."

"That's him, not you," Julia said. "But OK. Can you still hug me?"

"Of course I can hug you, mom. I just can't put a napkin on my lap right now and sit down and chat like none of this ever happened, how hard is that to understand?"

"We probably should take a rain check," Maurice said.

The women hugged, the men shook hands. As Laura went through the big doors into the night the hall clock went off again, and Maurice was aware that as an outsider, which he knew himself always to be, he was the only one who heard it.

* * *

The drive back to Hartford was long and mostly silent and weighted by the psychiatric records in the back seat.

Laura said, "Am I really like him?"

"You're you," Maurice said.

"And you're OK with that?"

"I love you and they love you too, and so does your dad. I'd say, this night, you are very possibly the most loved person in the world."

She slept after that. Maurice drove the speed limit, recalling his only dinner with Robert Ayers, and the likeness of father and daughter.

CHAPTER EIGHTEEN

Julia

At first, when the responsibility for Marika lay heavy, Ayers had tried to rebuild his own strength to make up for her lack of it. He had taken his meds on time, remembered to eat again, and redoubled commitment to the checklists and routines of a solo sailor at sea. But as he had worked and worried, day by day her lot improved. He willed it and so did she. Soon all he had to do was watch. What had been pale skin and boney angles, as the days passed, became flesh again. He found himself less necessary. He found himself hardly necessary at all.

Now he lay in the master cabin listening to her footsteps on the deck above. She was reeving new staysail lines, to judge by the swish of rope. Any other crew would make a racket to show off their work, boat shoes thumping. She went barefoot on his behalf. In the portlight over his head he saw an ankle pass, a flash of skin. He thought he heard her laugh, but that might be the cry of a shearwater or the squeak of a sheave in a block. He should swab the decks. No, she would have already done that. So he lay on his back. After a while she appeared in his doorway.

"I'm getting up," Ayers said.

She stuck her head in and smiled. Almost all her face worked now, but the effect was still oddly crooked. The pills she brought went down with a full glass of water. He watched her carry pancakes to the salon table, which was set for two. Her back was tanned and smooth. She had done something funny to her hair: twin pigtails, like Pippy Longstocking. She had gained what, 15 pounds? The canvas shorts had been his, now cut down and reworked with his sewing awl. His droopy T-shirt was now scarf-like bands of cotton that passed around her neck, crossed over breasts, and surrounded her waist to tie in front. When she turned toward him, it was Laura. It was Eleanor and Julia and Vivian and Inge-Lise. It was every woman he had known at the moment when youth ended and womanhood began.

He joined her at the table, willing himself there. She said that the dawn squalls were clearing, or at least he thought she did. Her voice was hardly audible. Words had become possible only a few days before, and she tended to turn away as she spoke. He wasn't hungry, but Marika ate like a boy, twin tufts of auburn hair bobbing.

When she took the plates away he began his morning saxophone practice, each day a new scale. Today it was E mixolydian, patterns in the mode. His intonation was more certain and the tones warmer. More of him, less of his many teachers. The scales were repetitive, but she never complained. It occurred to him that she might be deaf, which would explain a lot.

After he packed the saxophone away she helped him up on deck to lie in the sun. She drew buckets over the side, pouring them over him, painting him with blue ocean, cooling his back and the hot teak of the cockpit. She drenched herself, too. Ayers could look only for a moment. He was too aware of the French curve of her lower back where it met the orbit of her waist, and of the thighs and ankles unblemished by the crust and vein-breaks of his own. He knew that when she turned toward him he would look away. And when she did, he did.

Ayers lay on his stomach, feeling the salt of the sea bath drying, and felt a finger prodding the small of his own back.

"Go away," he said good naturedly. "Find something to do."

The finger continued, stabbing and tracing. He reached back and seized her hand.

"Just a tattoo," he said.

The tattoo read, "Three Things." The words bridged his lower back a foot across and three inches high. The font was Admirable Cursive, an unnecessarily flowery script he would not choose today. It had been proposed by a young woman in an antiseptic parlor one cold morning in Philadelphia in 1981. His first experience of the blackness had just begun, and he was therefore unfamiliar with its meaning or duration. He had abandoned Eleanor a week before and was living in a Motel 6 with cinderblock walls. He had lost all sense of goals or meanings. There was no future or past or even a present. He felt neither regret nor despair. No particle of self remained, no compassion or need or spark of fire. He was a void, a hole in the universe, and for all he knew tomorrow would be the same. Grasping for a remnant of his former self he had scribbled on the lid of a pizza box all he could remember: "Three Things."

1. Marry a woman you really love.
2. Make a million dollars.
3. Kill a man who truly deserves to die.

Marika's hand pressed his back. "You never tell anybody what the three things are, everybody has their own," Ayers said.

Her fingers dug harder.

"And I'm not going to start now."

The little fists began pounding his spine with increasing force, as if he were an engine that wouldn't start. Thump! Thump! Thump!

"Too much sun for you," said Ayers, rolling over. "Come on, let's wash the salt off."

He lowered himself painfully down the companionway but Marika remained on deck. She had found a flaw in the set of the mainsail and paused to crank in a few more pounds of mainsheet tension. She was doing it manually, with a winch handle, instead of the electric motor. Well, let her do it her way.

* * *

All afternoon he lay in his berth, breeze wafting through the open ports. He was reading Dizzy Gillespie's memoir again, mostly for the Charlie Parker stuff—how the greatest sax player of them all actually did it. How Parker and Gillespie had invented bebop, the lightning fast jazz form that succeeded the big bands and made pop stars like Sinatra and Crosby seem lame and lazy. He had studied the book for years and its margins were full of his notations on technique and fingerings. Some of the page corners had been folded down, which he never did. So Marika had been reading it, too.

His arms flailed, as they sometimes did, set off by the paroxysm of his legs and body. No, that was Marika holding his hands. Her face was close, peering. He was too tired to talk, but knew he must. She lay next to him. The intimacy was like a fever dream over which he had no control.

Ayers had met Julia Ford at the town dump outside Sandwich, Mass., on Cape Cod, with no intimation that she would soon become his second wife. He wasn't looking and neither was she. The dump was a family outing in those days before municipal trash pickups. The residents and summer people drove their junk to a backwoods lot entered by a sandy trail. Every Sunday morning a caravan of cars arrived with families greeting each other and kids disgorging on treasure hunts. Yankees left nothing to waste, so cast-off copies of National Geographic were deposited neatly stacked for the next reader. In the sun lay ranks of old snow shovels, busted fishing reels, iceboxes bleaching in the sun, Elvis Presley records—all awaiting adoption. Ayers found Julia pumping the cast-iron foot treadle of an old console sewing machine and stopped to watch. It was from the turn of the century, she said over her shoulder, and might be fun to restore. He examined the cast-iron frame, and declared it structurally sound. She had come with a friend in a tiny MGB. He offered transport of the sewing machine in his station wagon, since hiring a truck to haul trash out of a dump seemed backwards, didn't it? She accepted.

I'm Bobby.

I'm Julia.

She was about 30, hair in a bandana, with one of those overbites people had before braces removed their personal face. Her dusty flip-flops looked like they came from the dump, too. Ayers had been in a period of success, and the mall he had built in Milwaukee was returning a small fortune every month. He was 35 and about to be rich, Forbes Magazine predicted. But that day Bobby Ayers was just a guy in a Phillies cap offering a broke girl a ride home because he could, and who could also, if he chose, pay for the restoration of her rusty Singer. And pay for dinner, too.

Delivering the sewing machine to Julia's home was a longer ride than expected. The directions she provided, turn by turn, took them not back to the humble town of Sandwich, but to the old Cape bastion of Osterville, and over the bridge to Grand Island, and up the curving driveway of her parents' seaside summer house, and to dinner with her father and mother, and by Christmas to his second marriage.

Julia's energy matched his own. She was restless, inquisitive, determined and certain. He had to talk hardly at all because she talked all the time. He followed her on walks, where it was no use trying to lead. He gave up trying to swim with her because she never got tired. She could catch lobsters in Cape Cod Bay with one hand. She couldn't cook them, or anything else, so he did. Her father, Ralph, wrote Ayers a check for 100K the second week he knew him, and in two years Bobby doubled his money. Ralph Ford was the first wealthy man Ayers ever met who had not done a lick of actual work his entire life, and who lived in Boston in winter and Osterville in summer and had a historical gaff-rigged catboat on which Julia taught him to sail. Ralph Ford's world was of family charities, salt marshes saved and anonymous plaques on new university buildings. He always answered the phone, because it was always for him. His voice low, his pipe smoking, he quietly conferred, and when he hung up lives on the other end changed.

Often, in summer, they would all squeeze into Ralph's battered Chevy wagon, quarter panels rusted out and muffler dangling, to dine at fabulous restaurants where the valets knew his name. After recognizing the effect of the jalopy, Ayers made a quiet phone call to cancel his recent order for a flashy new Jaguar. Julia's family was an education in the subtleties of stature.

So was Julia. She played bridge like an axe murderer and took her dummy turn with body signals that were illegal and immoral. She hated anything new, and when they set up housekeeping in Fairfield filled their stone house on Greenfield Hill with battered old furniture. Their marriage bed cost $200, an old walnut sleigh design Ayers liked as soon as he saw it. He got to sleep in it $5,000 later, after the "restoration." If he grunted at such projects Julia's eyes flashed and she whipped out the checkbook of her personal account. So he accommodated himself to a household in which every chair, lamp or fork had a provenance, even if he didn't.

You don't know who you are until you're married, Ayers came to believe. You're straight, no chaser, like the jazz tune. Combination makes the cocktail. With his first wife, Eleanor, he had been a tough kid strung out by work. With Julia, he was older and wiser, but he had to keep up. She accused him of insufficient spontaneity. Of the error of personal urgency. Of cloudiness. She was impatient with his need for options, or as she put it, always for a better price. The prior Ayers had been seen as reckless, dangerous, even beyond the law. She told him he was boring. And in fact he was, if boring was the need for control. Sometimes, among the Fords of Boston and Osterville, he felt himself to be a runaway horse restrained only by the reins in his own hands. He watched himself, spurred himself, then had to clamp down on the bit in his mouth. Maybe it was the sense of the blackness waiting beyond the light. He knew he was going somewhere, but the people around him were already there.

Marika lay next to him in the bunk. Her thigh touched his and he knew her scent well. He could sense her moving in her clothes. He lay constrained, accountable to the Three Things. Unconstrained were her breasts under the shirt and the round curves of her shorts and her breath against his arm, listening. His hands had minds of their own, they reached for her and pulled her to him. But the mind in his head constrained them. That made him better than himself. Better than he ever had been. He hovered like a fulmar over Marika.

Yes, Julia had been a delicate balance to keep. He was travelling, of course, but now there was a place to return to: The house in Fairfield, up a long, green hill from the town. In a taxicab it would feel like coming home, and when the driver opened the trunk for his luggage from Europe or Bombay or wherever the job was, he knew where he was. Thanks to Julia, they had friends. They got one dog, then another, Labradors who bumped his legs in passing. He was faithful and attentive. He listened. She said he tired her out by saying nothing. But what could he say? That he was the happiest ever in his life? He came and went, making money. Absence left gaps in his understanding. He returned from Buenos Aires to find her bent over her writing table, sobbing. He left for New York with her off to her doctor again. When he was home she was ebullient, or pale, or desperate, until finally she confessed that she was sterile and he may as well know it. He held her as she wept. It seemed so unfair, this punishment for 10 years of immoral birth control pills and now such a terrible deferred price to pay.

Then, one rainy day when he had returned late from a conference in New Jersey, a plastic wand the size of a matchstick turned blue and the streets rained confetti. Julia was no longer barren, flowers filled the house, she picked up the telephone and never got off and all Ayers had to do was nod to be the most wonderful man in the world. And he was, for a while.

The story of his downfall was not the Percodan. It was not the sudden reversal of fortune caused by the desertion of his partners and the double-cross by the legislature of the State of New Jersey. It was not any loss of concern for Julia, or his home, or the child she bore inside her. There are two worlds, Marika.

What worlds are they? she whispered.

There is World One, in which you and I lie side by side, and through which the yacht sails, and in which the glasses clink in their cabinets and the water flows under the hull. It's what we see, feel, hear, and what appears in movies and books and newspapers, Marika.

Tell me, Bobby.

And there is World Two, he explained: a parallel world of the same causes with different effects. In World One, as now, my hands lie by my sides. In World Two, they embrace you rashly. In World One, you lie listening. In World Two, we are lovers, we invade each other and fulfill our desires.

World Two sounds nice, she said. He could feel the vibration of her lips at his ear.

He had fought against the loss of World One with every available means, and not just the Percodan, its oxycodone a brief salvation when crushed or snorted or shot in his arms, but also with Adderall and Ritalin and Coke and gin and whatever else he could get his hands on, as around him life went on without noticing as he fell to pieces. The discretion of his colleagues and friends and even his family had been admirable, and nearly fatal, as when he rolled his Mercedes into a ditch. He remembered being suspended upside-down. He remembered the faces in the hospital, all World One as he watched their pantomime from World Two. The rehabilitation center had been Ed Newman's idea. It put him out of sight. Nobody had to talk about it, and nobody did. That was their way. It was nobody's business, please, and proper people knew not to ask. He bore Ed no grudge, or Julia. They were on the other side. Her child was on the other side. There was no self-pity, only the slow rise from the pit, cleansed of himself.

You want to spare them, Ayers explained. Either that, or to die.

Marika seemed far away, though he knew she was close. What was left of him did not always respond to his commands. His chest was heavy and breaths did not come easy. He felt his former self balancing Julia over his head, strongman style, to the applause of a beach crowd. He recalled his mother, and her wash-lines, and the thunderstorms. His father, dead in the walnut steel coffin. Inge-Lise, who made no excuses nor required them. Eleanor, pulling off his shirt in the yellow car with the urgency of youth. Vivian, coming down a hotel staircase in Kuala Lumpur, all the heads turning. There was no need to move, they moved for him in memory, lively and companionable. He wished for a large room and all of the witnesses together, everyone drinking champagne. No one ever heard the whole story and no one could ever tell it. The tremors started in his toes and rushed up his legs like short-circuits in a panel, breakers tripping, warning light flashing.

He recalled the current project, and it gave him satisfaction. He recalled his destination with anticipation.

What is there more? Marika asked.

It was good to have Marika near. She had tricks up her sleeve. He had rescued her, and now she would rescue him.

You can hear it in the ocean if you listen.

Yes, Bobby.

We are blameless when the worlds change.

Yes, Bobby.

We make each other in the image of ourselves.

Yes, Bobby.

We only live to be known.

Was she still there? He waited a long time, and then saw she had slipped away and left a tray by his side. There were his pills and a saxophone reed.

Ayers took some pills, not counting. Then took them again, to be sure he had, and put the reed in his mouth. Tonight his tone would be perfect. Marika deserved that, for all she had done. He lay alone with his eyes open, waiting for darkness and music.

* * *

It was around midnight when Ayers first heard the commotion in the main salon. Heavy low voices, thick shapes in the amber of the night lamps. Marika entered his cabin, pigtails gone and her hair swirled and backlit like a cabaret singer. Where'd she get that dress? It was one of his black T-shirts, shrunk to her waist. She seized his useless arms and heaved, hoisting him like a sail until he stood unsteadily erect. She should more cautiously enter the master's cabin—a knock perhaps, that was the naval courtesy. She handed him his saxophone.

In the salon Dizzy Gillespie was leaning back on the seat of the big settee, goateed and grinning. He rose as Ayers approached and shook his hand. The cabin was full of men in dark suits and skinny neckties. They looked bored or restless, not at ease in the rolling yacht. The noises he had heard were their rumblings. Gillespie gave a sweep of his arm to quiet them.

"Listen up, I've known this cat a long time, and you all have too. So say something nice to Mr. Bobby Ayers."

"Can't you stop it movin'?" said a man with drumsticks.

"No, he can't, Roach, because it's a boat you're in, and that's the boat you're in!" He seemed delighted with his own joke. And to Ayers:

"Bobby, you know Max Roach, he's on drums tonight— or whatever." The drummer was standing in the galley behind a pile of copper pots, shaking his head. "This here's Charles Mingus on bass, and that fella sitting like a lump at your little tiny piano is Mr. Thelonious Monk, or as his wife calls him Mr. Melodious Thunk, and who do we have right here on this bench? I think you know him, Bobby."

Ayers' hero, Charlie Parker, the greatest bop saxophone player of all time, didn't look up. He was slumped and seemed to be already nodding off. They called him Bird, or Yardbird, and he had shown Ayers the light at age 15, and the darkness, too.

"Can we get a drink!" Max Roach yelled at nobody.

Marika appeared from behind him with a bottle of whisky. Roach upended it.

"Not too much of that shit," said Gillespie, but Roach just passed the bottle on to Mingus. "Give me that, mothafucka," Thelonious Monk said, pulling it his way.

"How you like the ensemble?" Gillespie said. "Just like we had back on 52ⁿᵈ Street, huh?"

All Ayers could muster was a nod, but Gillespie had his arm around him, proud. Hugged him like a brother or an old friend. Pulled him in close, private:

"I know it's not perfect, Bobby. Too many bandleaders. What you want is cats that can keep up, not coming down right off their own billboard. Look at Mingus, he's pissed off already. Monk and him, they're always on different pages, but they'll be cool. We're lucky to have Bird—good for you he didn't come late, or then it'd be all on you!" That gave Ayers a chill of pure terror. "So, you ready?" Gillespie raised his horn. Ayers discovered his saxophone hanging around his neck.

"Mr. Gillespie—"

"Diz, that's me. Now don't worry, you know these tunes. But of course you gotta listen, because Monk there, he's not gonna be playing your regular chords, but you can guess the tonic. And Mingus is gonna be Mingus, and Roach, don't let him trip you, 'cause he will. But it's cool, they know they can jam out here where there's no musicians union representative going to turn us in for playing for free. We're doing this for you, Bobby."

When Marika brought the whisky bottle to Charlie Parker he perked up. He had his hand on her thigh and she was kneeling in front of him, leaning in to hear whatever he was saying. Ayers felt a surge of discomfort. Bird's hand were all over her, and Gillespie leaned close.

"Never mind Charlie, that cat been married four, five times, and she ain't what he loves, what he loves is the music and that shit he puts in his veins." Bird took Marika's hand and put it on his alto sax, showing her how to finger it.

"You want to say something before we start?" Diz asked.

Ayers was floating. The tenor sax felt weightless around his neck. For once he did have a voice, and words to spill: How as a boy these men had taken him by the hand beyond the big bands, beyond Sinatra or Elvis or the Beatles, to a bebop world with its own language, a language that if it spoke to you, you suddenly understood everything, the whole epistemological puzzle. It had happened to him, with a rented instrument hung next to his roofing hammer, and all these heroes had been there as sure as they were here now. He would tell them what they couldn't know, him being white and rich on his own yacht—which was that it didn't matter, boy or girl or any color, drunk or sober, Alabama or LA, choirboy or sinner, mothafucka Einstein or dumbass hillbilly fiddleneck, if it spoke to you, you were changed, you saw, you heard, you were resurrected and transformed. Bop could do that, bop was the true savior. He looked eagerly face to face, and even though they looked back blank and surly that was all right, because for the first time in his life he knew what to say, he knew how to tell these rough beasts who he was, and how he had always loved them.

"I do want to say something," Ayers began, but stopped as from the galley a clattering began, hollow and low. It was Max Roach on the pots and pans, and it went on a couple of bars. The time signature, the pattern of emphasis, was entirely obscure.

"Uhnnn," Monk grunted from his keyboard, recognizing it.

Mingus came in, fat man and bass stringing a line in an odd modality. Gillespie raised his bent horn and as Ayers watched his cheeks inflated. Not just his cheeks, but his whole face, and not just the face but also the skin behind the ears, all of it blowing up medically impossible and weird to see, until the tune came out of the upturned bell and filled the cabin pure and unmistakable. It was "A Night in Tunisia," Gillespie's own tune.

Just as Ayers smiled Monk dropped a chord bomb, his big hands falling on the keyboard with no warning at all. The whack invention shouldn't have fit, but somehow it did. Then another chord, percussive and inside out, its inversions provoking the next Gillespie phrase, tempo slowly building.

Marika grinned from across the salon. She heard it too, Ayers wasn't alone. Diz was playing smooth, his tone the best Ayers had ever heard it, and the others knew it too so they laid back, letting him roll easy, savoring the gift of mood, yielding to the master. Charlie Parker looked down at the floorboards, waiting.

Ayers knew that you waited for the solo break, that's how it worked. Each man had his time, each man got his due. But Bird was up before the break came, spun toward Dizzy and blew right over his line. Gillespie's eyes flashed as Parker just ran him over, and in the next few bars it was like Bird played at a speed beyond the speed of light, more notes in a single phrase than Ayers had played in his whole life, all of it spilling out like the plume of a steam geyser from the bowels of mother earth.

Diz took him on, answering with a virtuosic run into the scream-register, and then they just kept going, the two of them blowing and dueling, attacking and retreating until neither could go on anymore, their jubilant argument run out and left as tendrils hanging in the air.

Ayers saw Thelonious come in, criss–crossing, tonking and plinking in his own language while accompanying himself with moans and grunts until Mingus had had enough of that, spat on the floorboards, and in one of Monk's weird interludes, before he'd even finished the phrase, the huge bass fiddle interrupted.

"Mothafucka!" cried Monk, outraged.

But everybody else just jumped in and off they all went again, nobody leading now, all of them running and jumping key to key in a way that left Ayers helplessly far behind.

"He cut Monk's solo," said Gillespie, grinning, loving it.

You couldn't dance to it, nobody ever could. But Marika swayed in her black torch skirt. Marika got it, and it got Marika. The jam went on for an hour, the players at ease now. Those Parker solos—where that speed and certainty came from nobody knew, and much less Ayers. He was sweating and sick and felt a target on his forehead. Ayers desired to be ignored, or better yet, invisible, and tried to stop his fingers following on the keys lest the clicking draw attention. He kept his mouthpiece far from his face. He sensed his hips flexing and stopped them so as not to draw attention. He wished he did not have his shiny instrument hanging so conspicuously around his neck. Max Roach was finishing a marvelous drum solo on the crockery when Ayers felt Gillespie poke him in the ribs. Ayers shook his head 'no." Gillespie punched him in the arm, hard.

"Now. Quick!"

The solo break was coming and Charlie Parker was about to rise to play. But Diz held Parker down with one hand and physically lifted Ayers up with the other. Ayers closed his eyes and felt for the last key still lingering in the air. They had gone back to that, and so he took the deepest breath of his life and grabbed the nearest note, didn't even know what it was called, and sent it out high and long and held it there. He held it and held it just because it made sense, because he knew it fit in, and it wasn't even his choice it was way beyond him, it was the universal harmony speaking through the instrument called him. It wailed and sang, that one note, one essential, one tone that stood for them all.

Monk muttered something and Ayers heard it. It was, "yeah."

Charlie Parker took his note and ran off with it like a thief. Diz caught him four bars later and then they were all back at it and it was "A Night in Tunisia" again, yet another new world on the old chords. Ayers could hear what it was and they could too. It wasn't mist or fog or any kind of words at all, just bop or bebop or rebob or bip bop, whatever name you want to call it and at a speed like the wind, no rests, and when it ended, no ending at all, the music just—stopped.

They played for hours, finishing the expensive Japanese Scotch and Marika breaking out the 40-year-old Glenmorangie. The smell of sweat was strong and Ayers couldn't keep up, but sometimes they let him in to take a phrase or join the bridge. They did it because they knew it was only at times like this, crazy times, not times scheduled in some cold studio at 10 in the morning or in Carnegie Hall with a sea of neckties or in some club in Europe as performing seals for royalty and whores, that the music really came. Every cat knew this shit only happened when it happened, and almost never when some mothafucka behind a glass wall said "Ok, any time." The music was always there, but the musicians weren't. To make a living you had to show up, but the music didn't have to. Tonight it had, and they all knew it.

They played the whole fakebook and Ayers knew it all. He took a solo on "Round Midnight," which Monk liked to play slow. When it was done Monk nodded, a trophy Ayers could keep forever. They were all drunk and Parker tried to dance with Marika but then nodded off. Light was seeping through the portlights, thin the way false dawn always was. It was 04:45 hours and Mingus was wrapped around his double bass, doodling, and that was all the sound there was except the swishing slow passage of the ocean past the hull. Memories hung, each to his own. Sense of endings. Sense of where they were, and who.

"I miss Lester about now," Mingus grunted.

In the galley Roach was drunk but not disorderly, and Monk had his head in his hands and even Gillespie, buoyant and irrepressible, bowed to the moment. Ayers knew what Charlie Mingus had written about the saxophonist Lester Young, protector of Billie Holiday, sojourner among them all. It was called "Goodbye Pork Pie Hat," and it was the saddest tune in the library of the lost and unexplained. It began with a sax solo, usually, but Bird skipped that and picked up on the first bars of heartbreak.

"Shit, Yardbird!" Gillespie shouted at him. "What're you doin'? Ain't nobody dead here, is there? We all going to be doing this again real soon, so mind your manners. And Roach—I see you in the kitchen over there, get your hands off that girl!"

Charlie Parker had slumped back down, and with the mood busted the band shuffled feet and commenced packing up. Ayers wondered idly how the huge double bass got on board, and how Mingus would get it off. But Dizzy had his arm around him again.

"Nice job. Nice whisky, too." He drained the last of one of the bottles. "Say, how much this stuff cost?."

"That one's Yamazakura," Ayers said. "Special deal."

Marika joined them. Dizzy kissed her cheek.

"Pretty Miss Marika. A man needs somebody to listen and you been doing that fine. And a man like him needs to talk." That last was for Ayers. "Let them in, Bobby. Got to do, even if it's hard, got to let them know what's up. That's how I kept my Lorraine from getting distracted and she's still wife Number One. We don't be a mystery, because we ain't."

"I'm taking your advice, Mr. Gillespie, that's the plan."

"And practice more, 'cause you're basically no good yet. How much did you say this whisky cost?"

"Well, that one's about $300 a bottle."

"Three hundred dollars! Damn, you can buy a car for that!

"Not anymore," Ayers said.

It was the last thing he remembered before Marika helped him into his bunk.

CHAPTER NINETEEN

Position

Ayers lay supine in his cabin, hands crossed upon his chest, satisfied. He had been still a long time, and the exhaustion had passed. Effortlessly he rose. Discovering Marika sprawled beside him in the deep sleep of the young, he lifted weightlessly above her and floated to the companionway ladder and the open hatchway above. There rode the morning, toward which he lifted himself rung by rung.

The white fulmar waited, maintaining position in the sky. Their eyes met. When the bird's eyes turned west his followed them, and there on the leeward horizon was a red sailboat, five miles away, jogging under a single sail, paralleling their course. Through the binoculars he could see a self-steering wind vane on the transom. With his forefinger he tapped into his own autopilot a course to converge. It would take a while to get close, but he already knew it was Marika's abandoned boat. A yacht could sail indefinitely, guided by its wind vane. It would sail wherever the breeze commanded, and when the breeze changed it would sail back with never a human hand required.

The sea around him turned silvery then, erupting in flights of glittering fish that were first a bump on the surface, then by the spring of their tail airborne and gliding on translucent wings. A thousand flying fish rose ahead and abeam on either side. For a hundred yards they soared, and as each crashed ignominiously a new one launched, so that the air remained thick with their renewal. They flew like arrows shot from the sea toward a single target dead ahead: Marika's boat.

He sat in his cockpit for an hour, silent, watching the hull ahead grow larger. Sunlight split by tropical clouds warmed his back and stopped the shaking of his hands. He was waiting to be sure, but he was already sure long before the red hull pranced close, its waterline weedy, its mainsail bleached but drawing. He should have called her up on deck at once. Come look, your boat is back. Come look, you are not poisoned, not ended, your future starts anew. Instead, he sat. He was already a singlehander again, and knew it. When much too much time had passed Ayers crawled to the open hatch and called down her name, and when Marika came up the ladder wiping her eyes he pointed ahead.

The red boat was only a hundred yards away. He saw Marika reach out as if to touch it. He felt her grab him, wrap him in her arms, her little feet jumping, her face buried in his neck, her squeals of excitement mixing with the squeaks and squawks of the swooping shearwaters and the petrel chicks bobbing in the troughs of the waves, all come to witness. Her lips startled him. She had never kissed him before, and for a moment so combined was his body with hers, its face and ears and salty scent, that he lost individuation and could not remember himself ever separate. The loss of balance brought him to his knees as a cold shadow ran up his back. He turned to see a rain squall approaching, its gust front a froth of white across the waves to windward.

As a surge of swell brought the two boats nearly side by side Ayers ran a checklist in his mind: need dock lines, fore and aft. They're in the dinghy locker. Need to rig protective fenders too, before the hulls meet. Need to reef our mainsail so we don't overrun her. Need to raft the hulls together and winch them tight, make one boat out of two, or they'll grind each other to death. It was clear in his mind what to do, but he was unable to do it.

"Get the big fenders!" he called. Marika laughed, rain on her face, and moved to obey.

The squall hit them and as it did *Après Vous* heeled and accelerated and the two yachts collided side by side in a crush of fiberglass and gunwales. As they rebounded the red boat heeled and shot forward, luffed suddenly, and was struck amidships by *Après Vous*' sharp bow. They lay entangled, scraping and slamming, sails thundering.

"Marika!" he shouted in warning. But she had already seized the long tail of his staysail sheet where it lay on the deck. Rope in hand she hung out over the lifelines as the vessels rose and fell on separate waves and then, in the level instant, leaped the gap to land on her own boat and throw her line around a stern cleat, tying it fast. Without hesitation she bounded forward to set a bow line. At the foremost point of her tiny boat she stood, barefoot, perfectly balanced, planning her next move. She had a new line in hand and quickly fashioned a loop in it. *Après Vous* loomed above her. Her target was a sturdy cleat on its bow. She flung the loop, and missed. She flung it again, and the loop nearly caught. Ayers knew he should go forward to receive her line, but could not. He lay in the rain, powerless to help. She was so young and lithe, a creature of imagination, a thing from a world of dreams, a perfection of the form of us all. She would do it.

As the loop was cast again the boats veered suddenly apart, dropping her like an elevator, and the stern line she had first set sprang taut. Ayers felt all 60,000 pounds of *Après Vous* resist the strain until with a sound like tearing cloth the cleat on the red boat erupted from its deck, torn out by the roots, flinging bolts and fiberglass shrapnel to spatter the water beneath.

Marika ran aft to seize her steering wheel and as she did the yachts collided again with a resonant crash that shook Ayers to his teeth. This could not go on. Her only course was away, away, away. The yachts must separate at all costs. Marika seemed to know it. Ayers knew it, too. She waved, hesitant and distant.

"Wait!" he called. She had no stores, no food. She could collect water from rain and her fishing pole was still rigged on her fantail, but he had so much more to offer, had always had, so wanted to give so much, so needed to, now.

"Wait!" he cried again in a voice he could hardly hear over the wind.

He dragged himself belowdecks. The hatches were open, rain pouring in. A nuclear blast of light blinded him, followed by a clap of thunder so close he went deaf and ozone soured the air. In the galley he grabbed what he could, a bottle of wine, a pack of frozen berries she had put out to defrost, a bag of rice, a tin of those tomatoes she liked, the special ones grown in the hot soil of Mount Vesuvius itself. He threw the groceries in a paper bag. The stairway back topsides was long, each step an agony. His bag was sodden. When he reached the deck it fell apart in his hands, contents spewing, berries dancing against the bulwarks, the wine bottle spinning overboard.

"Wait!"

All that was left in Ayers' hand was the tin of tomatoes, its label red against the black of the squall, red as her boat, glowing like the lava from which it sprang.

"Here!" Ayers cried, and threw it.

Marika caught the can with one hand as the yachts collided again, hull to hull. She looked at it, puzzled, as the moving waterfall of the squall overwhelmed them both. Ayers, half blinded by the rain, watched her glistening at her helm, sculpted out of air by the torrent. And then with a spin of the wheel she headed her boat suddenly away to be consumed by the clouds overpassing it, engulfed and erased from his sight.

He sat shivering and blank in the cockpit for an unknown time until in the east the wall of black squall cloud rose like a window shade rewinding. It revealed first a bright horizon, then a growing slice of clear sky, and soon thereafter the overarching blue of its sun-beaming dome. *Après Vous* was left becalmed and dripping on a flat and silent sea.

To the west the tumult raged on, lightning flashing. In it was a speck of red trailing a white wake as Marika ran before the wind. To return to him would be a beat against its force, which she would surely not attempt. In another hour she too would lay becalmed, because when a storm was spent it left behind a hole in the air. He waited for the winds to pass beyond her, but they did not. He waited to see the small red sailboat make its way back to him, but it did not. He lay as the sun dried him, and awoke later on the floor of the main cabin, dry and weak. He could still see her, waving, but it was memory now. It was the 129th day of his plan, and he had waited long for this moment and known it would come. He was Bobby Ayers, and it was time for the world to know him again.

The chair of his navigation table was gimbaled, and therefore always level. A piece of chocolate lay upon it. He ate it. The flavor was sharp, the energy coursed in. Before him glowed the big multi-function display of *Après Vous'* integrated navigation systems. The avatar of his boat on the screen lay in the middle of the Pacific, all the South Seas arrayed below. In this uncrossed region he had maintained his position unknown by fellow man. Now all that he would change.

With one finger he called up the hidden waypoints file called "Rarotonga," entered by him a lifetime ago. He touched the single button called "Navigate to." A predicted course appeared on the screen, its magenta line snaking south across the near equator, jogging to avoid the intervening atolls of Penrhyn, Rakahanga and Aitutaki, and onward to the Island of Rarotonga. Immediately he heard the servo motor of his autopilot obey and set the new course.

At the masthead, a weathervane gauged wind direction and speed. Behind the control panel a course computer selected from that data the proper set of his sails. His GPS knew where he was and now the system had been told where to go. Ayers had nothing more to do.

"Marika, bring me a Guinness stout."

Only after he said it did he remember she was no longer there but sailing her own course, away. That seemed right, too. He smiled and opened the waterproof case of the satellite telephone sealed for so long. He was going to enjoy this, and so would everyone else when they heard it. They would call it "typical Bobby Ayers." From the emergency call list he selected a private cellular phone number in Connecticut, and pushed "dial." It would be 10 p.m. in Westport.

"This is James R. Barnet," a stern voice said after five rings.

"Rhymes with garnet?" Ayers said.

"That's right. Who is this"

"It's Bobby Ayers."

"I don't think that's funny," said James Barnet. "Who is this, or I'm hanging up."

"I'm not trying to be funny, Barnet, I'm trying to call my Trust advisor who has power of attorney, and if you're not there I'll call your office manager Phyllis and she can earn your money."

The satellite connection was clear, if a little tinny. A second passed.

"Mr. Ayers? Holy crap! We thought you were dead!"

"Get a pen, I'm changing the will again."

"Wait! I'm in bed, hold the line. Is that really you? You seem very far away!"

Ayers had always enjoyed seeing people jump. You told them what they needed to know, nothing more. If you had the answers, they didn't need questions.

He called the United States Coast Guard in Honolulu and let them know his destination and predicted arrival in nine days. The young rating on the phone said he'd make a note in the log.

He flicked on his Automatic Identification System, removing the cloak of stealth. He ordered the system to begin transmitting his progress as a breadcrumb trail. On the world Internet, that instant, a tiny red dot appeared near the equator for anyone who cared to look. It was the sailing vessel *Après Vous* and Captain Bobby Ayers, their track unfolding for all to see.

For many years Ayers had done business in Rarotonga, the tiny capital of the remote Cook Islands chain. Rarotonga was only 30 miles long, a mountain surrounded by a coral lagoon, a place of dreams remembered and soon to come true. He had never been there before, himself, and hoped everyone would enjoy it.

The swinging navigation chair was designed for comfort in the roughest seas. He lay back in it and waited for sleep to come.

CHAPTER TWENTY

News

Laura was in Maurice's car when she got the call from Mr. Barnet. He said that he had received news of her father. His voice was so uninflected that she directed Maurice to pull to the side of the road, a residential street where the overhanging tree limbs were pale lime with the earliest buds of spring. That impression, of new growth on barren branches, would always contradict the revelation that her father was dead.

Mr. Barnet had received an email moments before from the police department of Rarotonga, a remote island in the South Pacific, seeking the next of kin to Robert Allington Ayers. The email contained a number to call. Mr. Barnet was sorry to give Laura this news on the telephone but felt she should know immediately. He read the call-back number and she wrote it down on the back of a receipt in her purse. Mr. Barnet asked her to read it back, to make sure it was correct. She did. As he gathered himself for condolences Laura hung up and was already dialing an international number.

"He's dead," she said to Maurice.

Maurice put his hand on her shoulder as the phone rang on Rarotonga 6,000 miles away and Laura Ayers, daughter of the deceased American yachtsman Robert Ayers, was connected by a desk clerk to Inspector Dan Solomon of the Cook Islands Police Service. Solomon asked Laura if she had yet chosen a funeral home on the island to receive the body. Maurice turned the car off.

"Inspector," he heard her say into the phone, "is my father dead?" "No, I didn't know." "When did he die?" "How is it possible you don't know when my father died, or how?" "No, I'm calling you from Connecticut, in the United States, this is the first news anyone has heard." "No, you contacted his lawyer, they just called me five minutes ago." "Yes, I'm his only daughter, I'm the right one to talk to." "No, I need to know what happened before I can approve anything like an autopsy." "Look, I'm in a car writing this down, OK? This is new, OK?" "No, it's all right, I'm fine." "What does that mean, he was 'towed in'?" She was writing a phone number down. "I will do all that, yes. Yes, and I appreciate your kindness." She spelled her name and gave Inspector Solomon her phone number and address and hung up.

"How're you doing?" Maurice asked.

"He died on his boat and they towed him in, I think that's what he said."

Maurice had Googled "Cook Islands" on his phone.

"Rarotonga is a small island in the South Pacific in the middle of nowhere, between Tahiti and New Zealand."

Laura nodded. "The inspector gave me the number of the guy who found him. His name is Bruce Tanaka. He's a fisherman or something."

A car cruised slowly by, bumping into a driveway 10 feet ahead. A woman got out to unload groceries and stared at them.

"I need to know if you're OK, Laura," Maurice said.

"I don't feel anything," she said. "Does that make sense?"

"I don't know," Maurice said.

"Let me call this fisherman."

"Let's go home first."

"No, now."

Maurice sat watching the woman unload her car as Laura dialed a new number. It was half an hour before they resumed the journey home, during which Laura read to him from the notes she had taken.

"Mr. Tanaka's a ship captain, not a fisherman," she said. "He thought I was from the insurance company, and when he found out I was the daughter he got all upset."

"I wondered why you were telling him everything was all right."

"He's the one who found my father. He said that a containership reported seeing a yacht adrift a week ago, and they called New Zealand Air Rescue, which was too far away, but they tracked it by satellite, and when it got nearer to Rarotonga they told the police, and the harbormaster said somebody ought to maybe go help out, and Mr. Tanaka is the captain of this 100-foot island barge and he agreed to try."

"For the salvage claim, probably," Maurice said.

"No, he said somebody always has to go out because there's no coast guard and so they all take care of each other. And it took two days, Maurice, and then they found the boat just sailing along looking pretty much normal. And so Mr. Tanaka went aboard and they found my father inside, at the navigation table, just sitting there. And the boat was still on automatic pilot, headed for Rarotonga. He was dead, Maurice. He was dead, and he had been."

"I'm pulling over."

"No. Drive," Laura said.

"OK, but where? Your mother's house, I think."

"No, your house."

"We're the only ones who know," he said gently. "We should tell people."

"What should I tell them? That he's on some island I never heard of? Does anybody know a good funeral home in the Cook Islands? No, I want a map, I want more information, I have to make a lot more calls before I'm telling anybody anything. You can just drop me off and go to work."

"I'm not going to work, Laura."

Light rain began, and in a hiss of tires the cars ahead began to compress like a closing accordion. "And now we're in fucking traffic," Maurice said. The Mercedes stopped, the swish of its wipers blurring the sea of taillights ahead.

He watched tears running down her face.

"I was just hoping you'd get to know him," Laura said.

"Me too."

"I always thought he would come back."

"Me too."

"I always thought, you know, he'd get old, like everybody else's dad."

"How long ago did it happen, did they tell you that?"

"A while," Laura said. She wiped her cheeks with her fists. "Captain Tanaka told me he was covered with mold. He was sitting at his navigation table when they found him, covered in it."

"Do we know for how long?"

Laura had composed herself again, jaw set. "Probably at least a week, Captain Tanaka thinks."

"Jesus Christ," said Maurice. Far ahead red lights flashed over an anonymous accident in the rain.

"Thank god I have you," she said, leaning toward him. He got his arm around her and pulled her as close as the seat belts would permit. The sound of sirens welled up from behind, and in the rearview mirror Maurice could see an ambulance weaving its way toward the wreckage that lay ahead.

* * *

They did not go straight home, but straight to the offices of Barnet and Sons, where Mr. Barnet had agreed to see Laura immediately. They came in wet and accepted coffee. Adam Barnet, introduced to Maurice, winced as his knuckles cracked under Maurice's personal handshake. Mr. Barnet noticed. His own hands were folded, funeral director style.

"My father's dead on the other side of the world and so now what's next?" Laura said.

"Please, sit, everybody" Mr. Barnet said. "This is a time of adjustment, even for us. Laura, I'm not usually called on to bring news as I did and I was clumsy on the telephone. We devise estate plans here, we aren't ordinarily around when they go into effect. I think it would be good to take some time before we go onto Phase Two, which in fact we'll need a few days to complete."

"The Trust anticipated certain events," Adam began.

Maurice palmed the words out of the air. "Excuse me," he said. "It didn't anticipate Laura's dad dying at sea, on his boat, and being towed to an island in the middle of nowhere. Right now we need to make funeral arrangements and tell the family. None of this was foreseen."

"In some respects it was," Adam said with the condescension of superior knowledge. Maurice handed him his coffee cup. Adam looked at it, puzzled.

"Coffee's cold. Help us out, will you, Adam?" He handed him Laura's cup, too. When Mr. Barnet nodded the son rose, confused, said "All right," and carried the cups away.

"What's he mean, anticipated?" Laura asked.

From a rolling cart behind his desk Mr. Barnet pulled several accordion folders, laying them out in preparation for explanation. But the routine client procedures seemed to fail him, and he stopped.

"I didn't really know your father, Laura. He was referred to us and we had three meetings, but that was almost a year ago. I knew him by reputation, of course, and I found him very certain about what he wanted, and we built the Trust to accommodate. I don't ask questions. People should have the living trust they want and our job is to give it to them, but I knew he was an unusual man, an impressive man, sitting right there were you are now. And when my son says 'anticipated,' (this was to Maurice), actually Adam was instrumental in working out many of these details. It seemed to us that Laura's father expected Phase Two of the Trust to be invoked within a certain time period, which is why it was important for his daughter, you, Laura, to become involved immediately, and I'm glad that you agreed, even thought you had certain understandable doubts early on."

"So there's more? There's a Phase Two?"

Phyllis, the office manager, came in with fresh coffee for Laura and Maurice. It was very hot. Nobody wanted it.

"There is," said Mr. Barnet. "Adam can present it best, although I'm happy to." This last was to Maurice, who shrugged.

Hearing his cue, Adam came in pulling a cart with six thick accordion folders arrayed across its surface. "Laura," he said, handing one to her. "Mr. Charles," he said, handing one to Maurice.

"I want to explain," Mr. Barnet continued, "that Mr. Ayers was very clear on the timing of the distribution phases, and that's what Adam means by 'anticipated.' We can reveal what the client intends only when he intends us to."

"You mean he knew he was going to die?"

"He may have known more than we did. Adam?"

"The folders you have are two of six we have prepared on his instructions," Adam Barnet said. "Each is pretty much the same. They contain New Zealand Air tickets to the Island of Rarotonga, beachside reservations, car pickup and delivery, meal plans, and a number of other items including a meeting with the director of South Seas Trust, where Mr. Ayers' major assets are assigned."

"Six?" Laura said. "What six? I know of five sharing beneficiaries—me, my mother, Vivian, Eleanor, and Inge-Lise. Those are the people I talked to. Mr. Sullivan only got a check."

"The most recent name is Miss Marika Heidt, of Auckland, New Zealand," Mr. Barnet said.

"Who's that?"

"We thought you might know her," said Adam.

"When did that come in?"

Adam looked uncomfortable. "About a week ago," he said.

"A week ago? My father has been missing for months and you heard from him a week ago and didn't tell anybody?" Her voice was cold.

"Nine days ago, to be exact," said Mr. Barnet, consulting notes. "He called me at home from his yacht to add Miss Heidt to the distributions under provisions already established. We were not at liberty to reveal the addendum."

"What a shit you are," Laura said to Barnet and son. "Both of you."

"I was not at liberty," the old man repeated. "We didn't know what would happen and he wished to maintain privacy, he was very strong on that. I'm sorry." He seemed unable to look at her.

Maurice said, "So do you think his destination was Rarotonga all along?"

"I don't know if that is so."

"He didn't stop anywhere else, did he?" Maurice said.

"In retrospect, he may have anticipated events," said Adam.

"Like dying." That was Laura.

There was silence.

"Well?" she said.

"In your packet, Laura, is the name of his doctor, Dr. Stein. Arnold Stein, of Westport. I don't know why it's there, but you're the only one who has it. If he was sick he didn't tell us, and from what I recall he was quite energetic and sure of himself, right, dad? Everybody in the office saw it, we were all blown away that he had chosen us."

"We were honored," Mr. Barnet said.

"South Seas Trust, what's that, an offshore bank?" asked Maurice. "Is that why all these plane tickets to this little island? Do people have to go there to collect?"

"Mr. Ayers accounts are at South Seas Trust for protection against creditors," Adam said. "All entirely legal. Rarotonga is under New Zealand law, which is different from the law here and perhaps more considerate. As I understand it, his account is set up so that all withdrawals must be made in person."

"Meaning everybody has to show up," Laura said.

"That's specifically stated, yes."

Laura was sifting through her folders. "All right, then we'll carry it out so they can collect. But it doesn't say what."

"The distribution is to be calculated by the island bank," Mr. Garnet said. "We don't know numbers yet. And Laura, I know this is difficult but your role will end soon. And I think you have done well."

"My role as what?" Laura said. "Phase One, Phase Two, everybody hop on a plane?" She stood up. "Now all I need to do is find a funeral director in the middle of nowhere."

Maurice looked up from his folder.

"It's right here. 'Barata Brothers Funeral home, St. Joseph's Street, Avarua. Request file and memorandum previously discussed.'"

"So, my father thought of everything."

"He did, Laura."

"He left a few things out, like explaining."

She stood up. Maurice thought better than to put his arm around her waist that moment. The Barnets stood up too.

"We'll deliver the packets," Mr. Barnet said. "Adam has to finalize the tickets and so on, you might let us know when it's convenient for the family to travel."

"You think it's a family, Adam?" she said, turning to him. "Tell you what, make it day after tomorrow. No choices. They're on the flight or off it, convenient or not, I don't care. Any problem with that?"

"No, you're the trustee."

Mr. Barnet came out from behind his desk. Awkwardly, he hugged her, and she let him.

"What next," Maurice said in the elevator.

"A goddamned whisky," Laura said.

"And mom."

"And then everybody else, and see who jumps for it."

CHAPTER TWENTY-ONE

Sunday

Laura and Maurice had gone over what they knew, and what to do with it, on the long cross-country flight to Los Angeles. She was the one in charge, he counseled. No, actually her father was still in charge, she countered, eyes flashing.

Now, on the nine-hour leg to Rarotonga, he knew enough to keep silent. Laura let down her Business-Class seat to the sleeping position early, so she wouldn't have to look at him. Or have to look at Inge-Lise, who was reading a paperback across the aisle. Or have to look at Eleanor, who had come over to chat after takeoff and then quickly retreated, seeing the way things were. Her mother and Ed had upgraded to First Class and were on the other side of the purple curtains, drinking champagne. Even in the Air New Zealand lounge at LAX they had seemed to be on vacation, which was irritating. Vivian Liu was somewhere back in Economy, having downgraded her free ticket for the money.

Maurice's unnecessarily large head appeared over the herringbone concourse that separated them. The man didn't smile often, communicating rather with that aura of grace some people fell for, but when he did try to smile, as now, his face turned into a pumpkin and accentuated the gray beginning above his big ears. The head spoke, quietly offering her a sleeping pill. Seeing the frown, however, it dropped from view as if guillotined.

OK, she had carried out the Living Trust plan. "Robert's" plan. She had started calling him that because "my father" got old in the endless phone calls from newspapers and TV and the drivel on Twitter in which she was asked to explain how he had died, and where, and how come. Hanging up was easier than saying she didn't really know. But she couldn't hang up on the gang headed to Mystery Island to collect their share of his fortune because they were all around her.

And they all had had some problem with the quick departure. Eleanor had meetings scheduled. No, the date is final, Eleanor. Inge-Lise declined, claiming a misunderstanding on the part of a man she had known only briefly, and it took Laura a second phone call to convince her that this expedition was not voluntary, but mandatory, and if she didn't show up the whole deal was off for everybody. That wasn't actually stated in the documents, but it worked. As for her mother—well, mom was used to being in charge and now she wasn't. Julia's position was that there was no earthly reason for she and Ed to make this trip, your father is just up to his old tricks again, dear. Right, mom, no 'earthly" reason—how about a reason from beyond the grave? Ed came through in the end, pronouncing it to be Bobby's show, and they were the audience.

That had required a long dinner by the family fire during which Maurice had felt free to ask more questions than she'd ever heard him ask, about her father, about the other wives, about the businesses and about child Laura, complex Laura, difficult Laura, and her mother blabbing on, loving to be asked, delighting to reveal that "there's a lot of Bobby in her, you should always remember that." What did that mean? That running his Trust had been like running his businesses, shrouded in the unexplained and compartmented against uninvited interpretation? When her mother finally agreed to come it was as a lark. What shall we wear?

Neither Laura nor Mr. Barnet had been able to locate this Marika person, who was obviously old daddy's last conquest. Well, fine. That was one subtraction less from the pot of gold, which ought to make everybody happy. Mr. Barnet said the firm would keep trying to locate her, and that, legally, "due diligence" on his part was all that was required. OK, keep billing the Trust, son Adam will need the money for his divorce.

Laura did not plan to sleep because jet lag was reduced if you didn't, but she was out cold when an air hostess touched her arm gently to say that her stepmother back in Economy wanted a glass of wine. Or something like that. The New Zealand accent was hissy and indistinct under the roar of the engines.

"Say it again," Laura demanded.

She had heard it right: Vivian declined to pay for her chardonnay in Economy Class since it was properly the responsibility of the Trust. Laura dug out $20 US.

"*We kin only tick cridit cerds*," the attendant said.

"Then give Vivian this money and tell her to use her own card."

Laura rose from her bunk and went around the console to Maurice, intending to climb into his sleeper with him. His eyes were closed. The plane was cold and she stood shivering in her thin blanket, waiting for him to notice. She kicked his foot. His eyes opened. He wiggled on his side and raised his hand to help her in. There was still no space, he took up all of it. She shook her head 'no' and flopped hard back onto her own bed, pulling a blanket over her eyes.

There were 239 souls on flight NZ18, and Laura was carrying six of them on her back. In her dream the burden made flapping her arms difficult, so that despite her best efforts the huge airplane steadily lost altitude until it skimmed the surface of the Pacific, and she did not how much longer she could keep it from crashing.

* * *

The sign held by the old man in khaki shorts at the Rarotonga airport read "Mr. Ayers," as if the hotel van was waiting for him, not the bedraggled funeral procession of Americans disembarking down the exposed airport ladder in tropical rain. They squeezed into the van over each other, Vivian hissing and Julia laughing and Maurice in the front seat next to the driver, who asked if he were a Maori man, to which Maurice said, "No, I'm a man."

The rain was dense, a downpour that caused the vehicle to slow for floods that carried waves of coconuts across the narrow roadway. Laura could get no sense of the island. It was Sunday, and the few vehicles who passed were puttering scooters with their drivers hunched behind windshields. Humid, dark and green were the only words that came to her. After half an hour the van splashed through puddles to a gravel parking lot and the driver hurried them into the shelter of an open pavilion and Geraldine Van Ness, owner of Reef Haven Luxury Beachside Cottages. Aussie, about 50. Laura had talked to her on the phone. "G'day and welcome."

Geraldine assigned accommodations and the driver, Old Joe, accompanied each to their own rustic villa hidden by blowsy fronds and the gloom of earth-scraping clouds. It was not an arrival but a deposit. Geraldine Van Ness said it was a fine time for a catch-up nap, don't you know, and these showers quickly pass.

Maurice had the key to Cottage 6, "Aitutaki," and both their carry-ons in hand. "Welcome to Devil's Island," he said as they reached the shelter of their windswept deck and pulled closed the rain shutters behind them. Only inside, when Laura had toweled off her eyes, did the scope of the accommodation come clear. It was large, the high ceiling cross-hatched with hewn beams from which massive ceiling fans rotated slowly. A sitting room extended on the left, its rattan furniture perfectly sourced and arranged. The floor was teak boards, smooth underfoot. A modern kitchen lay cleverly to the right, its entrance softened by an arc of coconut shells.

"Not bad," said Maurice.

The bedroom was a museum of Polynesia, stick charts on the walls and a ceiling fan of palm fronds whirring silently, all dominated by a wide bed supported by the hulls of a double canoe. Laura lay down, floating on it, her mind full of lists that recorded what she must do, and in what sequence, and how to do it right or at least in the way her father intended, whatever he really intended, which was hard to know for sure because he was dead. Tears came unexpectedly. Tears because he had been alone. Tears because in the end there was no one there.

"Let's get these wet things off," Maurice said.

She let him undress her. The ceiling fan was cool and so she let him hold her against himself, because he was warm. She let him towel her off and admire her, even though she was two pounds up from 130 and there was nothing she could do about it now. He was a considerate man and she liked that, even though the gallantry was mostly a dislike of being turned down. So he only held her, their bodies together. To settle the matter she kissed him, and in the long kiss he grew closer, one hand pushing aside the wicker tray of chocolates beside her on the bed.

After a few moments she opened herself to him, and when they were finished they slept in each other arms as the rain drummed noisily on the tin roof above.

* * *

Laura had called a meeting for 4 p.m. in the Reef Haven Palm Hut, a long palapa where the group was to be refreshed after their long flight. At 3 o'clock, Maurice still snoring, she made her way down a coral path to the office where Geraldine was on the telephone but quickly got off. The Ayers booking was the largest of the off-season.

Geraldine hoped that everyone was settling in, and said that dinner was at 7, and she happened to know that a large mahi-mahi had been landed only hours ago just for them. Laura learned that her mother and Ed had ordered a rental car for themselves, that Eleanor had booked a SCUBA dive on Wednesday, and that Vivian desired dinner privately in her cottage rather than at the Ayers table. Laura cancelled all the requests.

"Run them through me in the future, if you don't mind," she said. "And let me have a bottle of gin."

Maurice was grateful. She watched him sip his martini over the cottage's diamond-shaped ice cubes.

"Vivian's going to try to skip this 4 o'clock meeting, so go over there and escort her or drag her, everybody needs to be there. She's in the cottage called "Rakahanga.""

"Me?"

"Please. She likes you the best. Let's go."

From the bedroom to the cottage deck was a transit from dark to new, brilliant light. The squalls had passed. Through a fringe of palms lay white sand that seemed to wade into transparent water without a demarcation. The lagoon before them ran toward the lowering sun, occluded by brown coral heads on which shallow waves lapped. The whole shimmering palette ended at a distant reef where curling waves flung violent spray. Beyond that was a cobalt Pacific and a horizon strewn with blossoming cumulus. It was hot. The grass and sand beneath the palms steamed in a litter of frangipani, each cone-shaped flower the perfect imitation of a badminton birdie. Maurice picked one up, marveling.

"I think I'm dressed wrong," he said, sweating in loafers, khakis and Oxford-cloth shirt.

They had been last to emerge, and in fact everyone was dressed wrong except Inge-Lise, whose bikini was in contrast to Eleanor's little black dress and sun hat. The beauty of the beach took even Julia by surprise.

"Perfect Bobby," she said. "Leave it to him."

They gathered under the Palm Hut without much prodding, no doubt curious what Laura had to say. She had rehearsed the speech twice.

"Thank you all for coming in honor of my father, and so here we are. I don't know why he did it this way, but he did, and my plan is to follow his instructions. We're here for a week and we're guests of his Trust. So tonight, dinner is at 7, if we can stay awake, and I think we should. Tomorrow is a visit to the Museum of Polynesia. Tuesday is free. For Wednesday my father has arranged for an island tour and horseback riding. On Thursday the distribution of assets takes place at the offices of South Seas Trust. Friday is his memorial service, it will be a simple Quaker ceremony."

"Your father was an Episcopalian," Julia said.

"Well, mom, he's a Quaker now. After the cremation I will hire a boat, the ashes to be scattered at sea. At midnight Friday we all fly home."

Only now, as Laura completed her speech, did Vivian appear, her face mostly sunglasses, and Maurice with his arm around her as if she were 90 years old.

"Look," Laura said without expression. "I know as well as you do this could have been done by email. But this is where he died, and he wanted us here, too."

"Because he loves to pull our chain," Julia said.

Laura shrugged. "You knew him better than I do."

"None of you knows him at all," Vivian said as heads turned. "Gravediggers," she added.

"Here's Vivian, right on time, and both hands out."

"I loved him, unlike you."

"Well, good for you," Julia said.

"Folks," Ed said, rising. "I think we're going to need a bigger beach."

Inge-Lisa was first to laugh. And then Eleanor, who stood and shook her head, and then even Julia, grinning to see Vivian turn her back and walk away still escorted by Maurice, whose arm she shook off.

Dinner that night was attended, which was all anybody could say about it. Ed drank too much, which he sometimes did, and Laura decided not to seat him next to Inge-Lise again. Vivian showed up as if just to defy expectations, and in a sun blouse and tight jeans. Or maybe she had found a friend in Maurice. Eleanor read a John Grisham novel as she ate, surrounded by candles. Laura's mother commented extensively on the fish, recalling for everyone the cuisine of Bali, the Bahamas and the Seychelles, and then going into the kitchen to tell the chef about the unheralded charms of fresh-caught bluefish if he ever got to Cape Cod. Laura fell asleep in her chair, and at 9 p.m., as custard was being served, Maurice carried her back to their cottage, then went down to the beach with Ed, where he confided that the situation seemed awkward.

"Awkward is when they're shooting at you," Ed said, handing him a cigar. "We're not over the target yet."

CHAPTER TWENTY-TWO

Monday

On Monday Laura arrived at police headquarters in Avarua, near the airport, to accept responsibility for the salvaged yacht and receive a plastic bag of her father's personal effects. That bag would change everything, but not until she opened it in midafternoon.

The morning was glorious. The skies clear, the air on her skin like silk. The van, driven by Old Joe, carried her and Maurice only a few blocks further to Barata Brothers Funeral Home, where the remains of Robert Ayers lay waiting. Solomon Barata, 35 years old, was an easygoing islander in what seemed a good humor at odds with his profession. The body of her father reposed in a temporary coffin and was unexpectedly presentable. His strong chin jutted upright. He was attired in a clean polo shirt obtained from the boat. The shirt reminded her of him more than the waxy skin of his arms. Despite an anticipation of emotion she felt little. By the way Maurice squeezed her hand, he felt more. And then she did look at her father's face, and did cry. Maurice held her as Barata looked on, beaming.

"He looks good," Maurice said.

"Thank you, I'm proud of the job," said Solomon Barata, bowing.

He explained that the body, weeks old when it arrived, had been partially mummified. The salt air tends to preserve, he explained, even under layers of mold. The arteries were strong, and his formula for embalming fluid always restored some normalcy of appearance. Also, the application of a mild solution of the caustic soda his wife used to make soap. Tropical embalming was an art that required old traditions as well as new. The beard they had trimmed and combed, a necessary expedient since it had been quite long. Laura wasn't listening. Barata touched her arm, making her jump.

There was a small issue, he said, with the request for cremation and the scattering of ashes on the sea. Cremation was not a Rarotongan tradition and there was no crematorium on the island. Auckland was the place for that, with shipping of the body required both ways, which could be done, but not in a week. He recited the necessary arrangements in a tone that sounded to Laura like a car dealer describing a car he would never drive himself.

"So what else have you got?" she asked, startling Maurice with her bluntness.

Most Cook Islanders, Barata explained, preferred to be buried on the island, and that was most of his business. Bodies were brought home from far places—New Zealand, Hong Kong, and in one recent case, Jersey City, N.J. Interment was traditionally in vaults above ground. Because it was offensive to cast soil on the departed, the deceased was usually encased directly in concrete, a practice nicely in accord with the climate. The vaults were a way to repose among the ancestors, he said, and to keep memory alive among those who stayed behind.

"We need to speed up the cremation process because we're only here a week," Maurice said.

"Those white vaults, we saw them along the roadway, covered with fresh flowers. Could we do that?" Laura asked.

Yes, but no. The cemeteries of Rarotonga were full, or reserved for local families. But Barata said a cemetery was not really necessary, or even the popular choice. Often a family interred members on their own land. In the backyard, so to speak. His own family was buried that way. He knew the practice seemed unusual to foreigners. "Actually, it weirds them out," he said with a grin.

"So, how could we do that?" Laura said.

Half an hour later the van was negotiating a palm-lined backwoods road to a muddy homestead far above the sea. They were met by Mrs. Hagawa, an elderly aunt of Solomon Barata. Her family had leased the land for a century, she said, and it was dotted with limestone crypts, most green with a patina of mold. As her nephew had predicted, she was open to a discussion of extending her family to include Robert Allington Ayers, whose progenitors were said to have sailed to America on the *Mayflower*, thus making them eligible for inclusion in the Polynesian tradition of pioneer seafaring, and thus for a burial vault on this very land, maybe under those palms over there with a 50-mile view of the South Pacific ocean.

A vault could be constructed in two days, she said, perhaps like that one over there—only bigger. Such a vault, built by the right men, such as her own sons, would stand for a century or more, that is, if some accommodation could be made for the renewal of her family's lease, perhaps by the money of a rich American yachtsman from the *Mayflower*, with the dual mission of preserving not only his own heritage but that of scores of his Maori brethren who were otherwise doomed to fall victim to disinterment by the land-grabber sons of bitches in Avanua who had designs on taking over the lease for themselves when it expired next year. Mrs. Hagawa then showed her tattoos, which were extensive.

Maurice was studying his shoes, which were muddy.

"Done," said Laura. "If the vault can be built by Thursday."

The two women shook hands, and Laura and Maurice headed back down the hill to the van.

"Your dad's family came over on the *Mayflower*?" he said.

"Yes, Maurice."

"Julia says she checked that story out and his grandfather was German and his wife was Jewish, her people were from Minsk."

"We came over on the *Mayflower*, Maurice. All of us. You, too," Laura said, keeping to her stride.

"OK," he said.

* * *

When the van returned them to Reef Haven Cottages it became apparent that Julia and Ed had rented a car on their own dime, with a chauffer who knew how to drive on the wrong side of the road. Also, that nobody else had attended the tour of the Museum of Polynesia which the Ayers Trust had arranged, and which Laura and Maurice had taken alone. Also, that Vivian Liu had requested all flowers removed from her cottage and no maid service permitted. Also, that Inge-Lise and Eleanor had gone off snorkeling on rented motorbikes and not yet returned. Also, that if possible she and Maurice should redo their registration card under one name, either one, it didn't matter, as long as it said, "Mr. and Mrs."

OK, let everybody have it their way. Laura was not a sheep herder or Trust-enforcer, she had gotten them all here and that was enough. Which, in saying that to Maurice, was in fact a load off her mind. He agreed and proposed a swim. She declined, feeling groggy. He put on his suit and went off with Ed and Julia, who were carrying paddleboards to the lagoon.

Glad to be alone, Laura went to get some Advil from her purse and discovered instead the plastic bag of her father's personal effects. Inside were a wristwatch, a moldy wallet with a few credit cards and some Mexican 500-Peso bills, a folded photocopy of the ship's Documentation, a pair of scratched prescription sunglasses and a very large pill bottle prescribed to Robert Ayers from a pharmacy in San Diego.

The prescription was dated 14 months before. The pills were a drug called Riluzole, which she had never heard of. She Googled it and her breath left her in a rush. This could not be true. She would have known it. Vivian would have known it. Everybody should have known it. She had spent a week with her father after this date—yes, they had gone to New Orleans, and he had been fine. He had mentioned that he and Vivian were separating, and that "it was for the best." She had not pressed. It had been Mardi Gras and they had danced, father and daughter. They had walked the old quarter, trying to find the jazz he liked, which was anything but Dixieland. They had bought tickets on the Mississippi paddlewheel steamboat and watched its machinery churn. He had mentioned recently buying a sailboat. He had mentioned someday taking her for a sail. She had told him about Maurice, and her mother, and Ed, and looking for a job, and what else? Everything else. He had listened, looking at her the way he did, with that look of approval she had always known from him, the silent acknowledgement, the private thing that meant they didn't need words.

The prescription was for 100 pills, and the container was marked "3 of 3," meaning 300 pills—a year's worth or more. She thought of Vivian, who had been with him then. Vivian, whom she had never thought about except as a third wife or a nut job. Vivian, who had been there when these pills had been prescribed and who was now here, in the cottage next door, with the shades drawn.

Moments later she was pounding on Vivian's door. When it opened she pushed in, wielding the jar of Riluzole.

"Do you know about this?" Laura said.

Vivian withdrew.

"This medicine is only prescribed for one disease, Lou Gehrig's disease, and it means you will die. You knew he would die and you didn't tell anyone?"

"You should have known."

"I didn't know! Nobody did!"

"Because he didn't tell you. Not an accident."

"If he had amyotrophic lateral sclerosis, ALS, didn't you know what that means?"

Vivian's face was composed. Her eyes flashed, unblinking.

"Did I know? Ha! I was there for the diagnosis and the tests. He didn't want me, but I came. The clinic had to tell me, I was his wife, no matter what he said."

"Didn't you think I had a right to know?"

"We discussed it."

"Discussed what? What was there to discuss—"

"Him. You. Me. Yes me, who took his divorce. That's right, like a knife in my stomach. My husband? Goodbye. My life? Goodbye. My family? —I don't have one, as you see, only enemies all around. He said I would be taken care of, like the rest of you, that I should start over, ha! Like a business deal, and now time to get out. Like he was an old contract no longer acceptable to both parties and so I should exercise my exit clause. Where were all of you? You were nowhere, I was there. I was the goodbye so he could go off alone again. The doctors told him, Mr. Ayers, you die. You need to put your house in order, sir. He put in order the end of me, and I knew why. He's Robert, he was getting out. Everybody taken care of and don't worry about it, Vivian. And don't tell anybody. Who am I going to tell? You? Ha!"

"Yes, Vivian, me."

"You, I don't even know. Robert I know. I tried what I could try, but I don't cry like babies. He was walking away from a bad deal like he taught me to do. I could keep him maybe with a hammer and a nail. I tried to. I would have kept him in a chain if I could keep him! I would kill somebody! I kill everybody!"

Vivian's English, usually guarded but precise, deteriorated in the heat of emotion and the accusations of the aggrieved daughter.

"You loved him, I know that," Laura said.

"You thought I am a stone?"

"You're not a stone."

"I know what he was thinking. He was thinking, Vivian Liu OK, she have money, she move on, she take the world by storm. But it's not true, your father was wrong! I am finished too. No more left. I honor him because he chose me to know he would die, and because I am strongest."

Laura offered her arms as tears ran on Vivian's cheeks.

Vivian stepped back. "No," she said.

"We're family now."

"No."

"Don't you know why we're here, in this stupid place, all of us?"

"That nobody should be poor." Vivian said it with a flash of bitterness, chin high.

"No, that's not it. My father never gave a damn about money and we both know it. Listen, I've got to tell everyone about this and I want your help."

"No."

"Yes," Laura said, "and you'll do it because he wanted us to know why we're here together."

"I am here alone," Vivian said.

"Oh, you are not. Dad told me you were elegant and beautiful and the smartest woman he had ever met. He's dead, so don't make him wrong."

Going out the door Laura let the screen door slam behind her and didn't look back.

* * *

As the group gathered, a barman named Priest circulated taking drink orders. Ed already had a mai tai, and Inge-Lise and Eleanor were showing sunburn from their morning on the water. The palms sang overhead and beyond them the lagoon gleamed. They knew by Laura's arrival with a handful of notes that something was up.

"Did any of you know that my father was sick?" she asked.

"What, sick?" said Julia. "You're not crazy if it works."

That got a laugh which quickly died.

"I mean that he was diagnosed almost a year and a half ago with amyotrophic lateral sclerosis, ALS, which is Lou Gehrig's Disease."

"My god," Julia said.

"We did not know that," Ed said.

Laura saw movement. It was Vivian, walking to join them. She carried a sun umbrella and underneath it wore the multi-colored sarong provided each guest in their cottage. Maurice, who was on the phone again with the Mayo Clinic, cleared a bench for her to sit down.

"I knew him only a few months ago," Inge-Lise said carefully. "He said nothing about that. But he had tremors. And there were times he would disappear for days, and never say why."

"Vivian knew," Laura said. "She was the only one of us who did." Vivian sat silent.

Laura described her father's recent history, confirmed only that afternoon. He and Vivian had gone to the Mayo Clinic for confirmation of the diagnosis more than a year ago. He had been given a course of treatment, or palliation, which he rejected. He had been advised to limit his activities, which he had rejected. He had been told that the disease had already progressed, and that his current remission was temporary. He had been told that many patients lived three years with his disease, that five was not unusual, but that physical and mental issues were to be expected and that no cure was at present possible although urgent research continued. Laura said that she had discovered his pills, and gone to Vivian, and learned from Vivian the extreme difficulty she had faced, knowing what none of them knew, and how her father in his characteristic and eccentric and sometimes brutal way had insisted on a divorce, and a bond of silence, so that he could proceed, alone, wherever he was going, which was here to Rarotonga, knowing that he would die alone at sea. That had been his plan all along in the Trust of which she was executor. And only one of them had known the reason why, and that was Vivian.

Vivian rose. "I could not tell you," she said, chin high. "It was not permitted by Robert that anyone knew."

"Which if you ask me is a burden none of the rest of us had to bear," Laura said.

As Vivian began to tremble Laura was surprised to see her mother spring to her side and wrap her in her arms. Vivian reacted as if struck, but Julia held on. Inge-Lise and Eleanor came to, pressing close. Laura couldn't hear what they were saying, but her mother was crying, too. Ed watched, shaking his head. Priest, arriving with a tray of drinks, thought better of it and retreated 10 paces away. The group had compressed, deflated by lost presumption, the shock of the diagnosis, and the release of tension that had kept them unaligned. As the women locked arm in arm, Ed noticed a figure approaching on the beach sand.

It was a 26-year-old woman in a two-piece bathing suit, deep-tanned, her shoulders decorated in dolphin tattoos. She seemed hesitant, and paused before the thatch roof of the Palm Hut and the intimate group there.

"Excuse me," she called out. "I'm Marika. Is this the Robert Ayers Funeral party?"

CHAPTER TWENTY-THREE

Tuesday

The young woman's story was so preposterous, even offensive, that Laura was on the phone in minutes to Mr. Barnet, who confirmed it as fact. The identification presented—a New Zealand driver's license in the name of Marika Heidt, age 26, resident of Auckland, N.Z.—matched that of the beneficiary added by Mr. Ayers' transmission of nine days before, his last transmission.

Marika Heidt was to receive one-sixth of the Ayers estate. In accordance with his wishes, she had been provided air transport to Rarotonga like the rest of them, and with the same accommodation. That was all Mr. Barnet knew. He had located Miss Heidt only a few days before, by a search of a yacht registration database that identified her as the owner of a 29-foot sailboat named *Gone Girl*. All Mr. Ayers had given him was the name of the boat, and a first name. But it was enough.

Marika was lithe, young, hair cut short probably by herself, Laura surmised, and with dolphins leaping in three colors. Her attitude was skeptical, but no more so than that of the Ayers party, who were not unaware that her presence cut their share of the estate substantially. Not, as they all said later, that it mattered. What mattered was that what she said made no sense at all, even to her.

The interrogation was so heated, at first, that Priest retreated to the bar with his tray of frozen margaritas until Maurice begged him to come back, and quickly, as Laura bore in.

"So you weren't ever actually on my father's boat?"

"I already said I wasn't," Marika said, her Kiwi accent cutting the air.

"How old are you?" said Julia.

"She's 26, mother, Mr. Barnet already told us that."

"You must have known him before, then?" said Inge-Lise.

"Well, I didn't. Sorry!" said Marika.

"And he just threw you a can of tomatoes, that's it?" Laura was exasperated and didn't know what else to say.

"Forgive us if this sounds like some kind of scam," Ed said.

"Yes, I'll say it does," said Marika, hands on hips. "I thought that before I came, but your tickets were good, so what the hell. If it's a time-share you're selling, nice try. I haven't got a dime, but the booking was free so here I am. Go ahead, make your pitch and I'll listen." She laughed. To Priest she said, "I think I'll have a margarita, if you don't mind."

It was Laura who intercepted, sat her down, and asked her to begin all over again, so they could sort it out. Mr. Ayers was her father, Laura said. Mrs. Newman there, with Ed, were her mother and stepfather. Maurice was her boyfriend, Eleanor and Inge-Lise and Vivian were friends of the family. Please indulge us, we're as confused as you are.

Marika was a singlehander. In this entire world she owned only her boat. She was single, independent and a bad prospect for any trickery or traps. She had defied her parents, her teachers, and everybody she knew to sail alone to Indonesia, and she planned someday to sail alone around the world. She required no explanations of anything by anybody, and did not plan to give any about herself, and frankly the whole idea of a time-share condo on this island, nice as it probably was, was ridiculous, because, what, you would have to go back to the same place every year for your two weeks and do what, just sit there?

"There is no time-share!" Laura shouted at her, followed by Maurice asking her to continue, please, so they could try to get things straight.

All right, she had been on a beam reach, whatever that was, checking Gribs by shortwave, whatever Gribs were, when she stood up in her companionway and saw another yacht on the horizon. That was unusual. She had not seen a yacht or any other vessel since leaving the shipping lanes weeks before. She had first tried to hail the other sailboat on VHF radio, but gotten no response. She checked her Automatic Identification System, but the other yacht had its system turned off, like it didn't want to be found. She could see that the name of the other boat was *Après Vous,* and it was huge, 60 feet long, and that their courses were slowly converging. Then after a while the other boat actually turned to intercept her, which was very nice, as she would have liked to greet another boat and it was traditional to say hello, on the radio at least, since she had not seen another human being in a while and was pretty knackered from being in the wop wop so long and living in her togs, so she even hauled on some pants for the occasion.

As her audience waited Marika paused to gulp down half her margarita and gag.

"Careful, they freeze your throat," Ed said.

"Shut up, Ed," Julia said.

So the big yacht, which was only under partial sail, got very close and for a while they were sailing along side by side, Marika continued. It was a nice afternoon, only about 10 knots of wind, and she saw that it was a very expensive boat with a lot of barnacles on its hull and slime on the sides, which meant to her it had been out there a long time, and it was obviously sailing on autopilot. Abandoned, she thought. Or, maybe a ploy to get her to come nearer, because out there you never know, and you are responsible for your safety and not just from falling overboard but from all kinds of things and not the least of them, men. And although she did not have firearms on board, she did have a bag of rocks and a strong throwing arm, don't try her out.

So about then she noticed a guy in the cockpit of the boat, just his head. And she thought, *ahkay thyn*, be careful. They were only about 10 feet apart, the two boats, hers much smaller and bouncing around like it always did, when he sort of reared up and she saw he had long dirty hair and a scraggly beard, and he was making gestures. Her impression was he was really old, like almost a skeleton, and maybe or certainly in some kind of distress, which naturally at sea when that happens you would normally come to their aid.

His fingernails she noticed were about this long, weird, and he kept waving come closer, come closer like. Or whatever, it wasn't clear. Are you all right, sir? she said to him, are you in need of assistance? But he just kept motioning to come closer. She saw that there were old clothes on the lifelines and junk on the decks, but the sails were set right, even though some of the lines were ragged. Waves brought them almost touching as they sailed along, but the guy had disappeared. She kept hollering, are you in need of assistance? and like that, and pretty soon all of a sudden he reappeared, in tattered shorts and nothing else, and something big in his hand. She got a rock and showed him and told him she'd clobber him, sir, and then the boats came crashing together and bounced off each other, and she saw what he had in his hand, it was a can of tomatoes.

She told him her name was Marika, and did he need any help? And he started saying stuff you couldn't understand, so she got worried and steered away, but then he got all agitated and waved her back. So she steered back and he reached out with his arm which was shaking and handed her the can of tomatoes. She had to drop her rock to take it.

"He handed you a can of tomatoes," Eleanor repeated.

She took it, Marika said, because she didn't know what else to do. And she thought it was not a good idea to stick around, because he was acting all wobbly and crazy, so maybe there were other people hiding down below, waiting to come up, and he was the decoy, right? And so she decided it was not a survival situation except maybe for her, and so she altered course and put up her biggest sail and went off downwind. She kept sailing that way for a long time, checking behind her to see if she was being chased, but no she wasn't, so the next morning she resumed course for Auckland. And they're telling her that guy on the boat was Mr. Ayers?

"If the boat was called *Après Vous*, yes," Laura said.

"What is he, a millionaire or something?"

"Yes," said Laura.

"And he put me in his will?"

"Yes."

"Gee," said Marika. "Why?"

"Nobody ever knew why Bobby did anything," Julia said. "He liked it that way."

"And you're all his family?"

"You too, looks like," Ed said.

"But I didn't even know him," Marika said.

It was Maurice's opinion that the story was impossible on the face of it, and that a more logical explanation was that Marika and Mr. Ayers had met on a prior occasion, perhaps in another port, and that aspects of the relationship between them had been left out.

"Like what?" Marika asked.

"She wasn't in Mexico," Inge-Lise said, her tone cool. "I'd know that. Were you in Ensenada with us?" she asked the young woman directly.

"What? No way. You think it's all *sus*, don't you. But I was there and you people weren't. You haven't sailed *ei-deen* days without another living creature to talk to, no radio, no ships to pass. I was pretty far gone myself when that other boat showed up, and a couple days afterwards it seemed like I was having one of those hallucinations you get out there with nobody to talk to but yourself. I could of put the whole thing down to imagining it, like you do to keep yourself company, except I had those tomatoes he gave me. I ate them, too. Best ones I ever tasted. They came from some volcano in Italy, it said that right on the label. You can't get tomatoes like that where I'm from, no way in the world."

Priest arrived with more margaritas, which were welcomed.

"Well, I have some papers for you to sign," Laura said. "We're all here for the funeral and the dispensations, that's

Thursday, and in the meantime I'm sure you probably want to get out of those travel clothes."

"These are my clothes," said Marika.

"That's all you brought? Come back to my cottage, I can help you with that."

Maurice stood to join the two women as they headed off.

"Not you," Laura said.

So Maurice went down to the beach to smoke another cigar with Ed and discuss the topic of Laura, who was their usual subject. The former wives and the fellow intimate Inge-Lise remained in the Palm Hut, sipping cocktails in the moonlight and comparing notes about the events of the day, and about themselves, and about what they had heard about each other. It was Vivian, in her blunt way, who broached a small relief they conceded upon finding it shared: At least Ayers had not bedded that beautiful child, who despite her looney accent and unfortunate tattoos could have been his granddaughter, and although they had come to accept each other as having shared him, separated by years but bound by his inexcusable past, all agreed that that would be a bit much, even for Bobby.

CHAPTER TWENTY-FOUR

Wednesday

The next morning Old Joseph asked Maurice if he were coming with Laura and Marika to the harbor to inspect Ayers' yacht.

Oh? Well, of course he was.

He sat in the front seat while the two women behind him went over the police inventory report for *Après Vous*, Marika rattling off things to look for such as towing damage, lost equipment and pilferage. At breakfast, the women had a long conference call with the insurance company about the salvage claim, for which as trustee of the estate Laura was apparently responsible. The harbormaster wanted the claim resolved because the yacht could not stay at its temporary mooring, and there was no haul-out facility on the island for such a large vessel.

In the van between errands Maurice talked about rugby with Joseph, who had last played when he was 55 but still could show the boys how to do it, although not for very long. He had heard that Maurice was a college basketball star, and asked to shoot some hoops with him that afternoon.

Maurice said that he no longer played basketball. Joseph asked why. Maurice, who was trying to listen to what was being said at the women's table, said he didn't have time anymore. Old Joseph said, how much time does it take to play a little basketball? Maurice said, what? Old Joseph said Maurice was on vacation, wasn't he? Did he know what a vacation was? So Maurice gave up trying to hear what Laura and Marika were talking about, and told Old Joseph he would be glad to shoot some hoops with him.

"You got any Maori blood in you at all?" Joseph asked, seeing how Maurice's head touched the roof of the van every time they hit a bump.

"I don't think so," said Maurice.

"I don't think so either," said Old Joseph. "No offense."

The harbor was a small indentation only somewhat protected by the prevailing trade winds and not what Laura had expected. Shipping containers lined the commercial docks and heavy inter-island vessels rose and fell in the backwash of entering swells. There was only one sailboat, and it was her father's. She'd never seen it before. *Après Vous* lay moored by a bow anchor, her stern fastened to shore by two long lines. The boat was elegant and sleek, her teak decks gray with salt. Lines lay uncoiled on deck, and the hull was heavily marked by contact with the old truck tires that lined the quay. Loose halyards rattled. The cockpit was littered with empty soda cans, which was not her father's style. There seemed no way to get aboard until Marika drew an inflatable dinghy to a rusty ladder on the seawall and gestured them in. Just climbing down into the dinghy was difficult. Once aboard, its rubber sides flexed in the confused harbor waves and the 10-foot voyage to the side of the yacht was across an oily, bumptious expanse.

Following Marika's lead they climbed a mahogany boarding ladder aboard.

The yacht was certainly not at sea. Three fisherman stood 20 feet away in the parking lot, casting their baits. From the commercial yard heavy clanging resounded amid the roar of forklifts at work. Yet the boat rolled and pitched, yanking so suddenly at its restraining lines that it took both hands to hold on. Maurice sat down on the dirty cockpit seats. Laura moved forward, hand over hand along the lifelines to the bow pulpit, which rose and fell like an amusement park ride.

Maurice had his head in his hands. Marika dropped next to him, conferred, and immediately pulled the dinghy close again. Big Maurice, natty in pressed khaki shorts and Hawaiian shirt, dropped into it like a sack of turnips and was propelled by Marika's push back to the rusty dock ladder, up which he climbed to kneel quickly over the nearest grass.

"Where's Maurice?" Laura asked, returning hand over hand to the cockpit.

"Seasick," said Marika. "Only took him one minute. That's OK, he'll take a taxi home. I told him we'd be here a while."

"Oh."

"You OK?

Laura was. She followed Marika below, imitating her sure handholds down the companionway stairs, and was surprised by the expanse of the main salon. A few blankets lay strewn about and the smell was musty, but the space was larger than she expected. Varnish shined and the lights of the instrument panel glowed as if ready to depart. Her father had died here, and his presence remained. The sinks were full of dirty plates and the brass of the enormous espresso machine had corroded green. The cabin moved as if alive, although down here the motion was less accentuated than on deck. She heard under her feet a continual clicking. That was shrimp talking, Marika said. You ought to hear whales singing, it gets so loud it wakes you up.

They found Ayers' saxophone on the bunk in the guest cabin. A book of music exercises, much thumbed. Empty bottles of beer. Filthy shorts and T-shirts, dozens of them, which Marika quietly began to stuff into plastic bags she had found in a cabinet. The floor was wet toward the front of the boat, which Marika said was called the 'bow.' At the main electrical panel she flicked a switch and a bilge pump hummed. The ventilation hatches were all dogged tight, and a thermometer at the navigation station read 89 degrees Fahrenheit. They went around opening them. Sunlight and a warm breeze flushed the interior.

Laura was fascinated by the way Marika moved, fluid and effortless. How she turned slightly through doorways, how her balance seemed to absorb the yacht's motion, how she knew where everything was, or should be, from the stop-latches on drawers to the dogs on hatches to the exotic items of equipment she pointed to and named as they explored the cabins and compartments of her father's home, escape, and yes, chosen place of death. She imagined him cooking at the swinging stove, sleeping in the master's bed, alone and self-sufficient far from the land of people.

"You doing all right?" asked Marika.

Laura nodded, balancing against the constant movement. "Is your boat like this?"

"God no," she said. "I'm a little teeny 30 feet long. This is a couple of million bucks worth, and all the gear the finest there is. He knew what he was doing, tell you that. It's weird for me, because he scared me away. But I'm sure he was much different, you know, before. Did you sail together a lot, your dad and you?"

"Never once," said Laura.

"Too bad."

"I never knew he had a boat, but now it makes sense."

They set to cleaning. First the mold, to be wiped away with vinegar and peroxide from the ship's supply. Then the inspection of the engineering compartments, Marika confirming the oil level of the diesel and the generator and checking the filters and sacrificial zincs and the circuit breakers of the instrument panels. They collected sheets and socks and scattered clothes, and when Marika discovered with envy a fully functional washer-dryer in its own cabinet, began a wash load immediately. Much of the food on board was still preserved, frozen or in unopened packages in the lockers. They emptied the refrigerator of spoiled stuff and hauled their trash bags to the cockpit in a growing pile. The aft cabin, which Marika said was the owner's accommodation, remained pristine, as if hardly used. After hours of work they discovered an auxiliary refrigerator there, and from it Laura pulled two icy Mexican long-neck beers. Marika popped their tops with a rigging knife and they climbed to the helm cockpit to open a year-old bag of her father's potato chips.

The sun was hot, so Marika rigged the cockpit canopy. In the shade they went over the afternoon's project. They would install chafing gear for the dock lines, which already showed signs of wear. Then scrub the decks to remove its new stains of shore-side industrial grime. Re-furl the mainsail, which took a while because Marika had never encountered motorized winches or automatic furling, but together they figured out what buttons to push. Wrenches in hand they surveyed the hydraulic systems that made everything work, tightening fittings, wiping away fluids, making notes.

While tracing wires with a headlamp on her forehead Marika asked about Connecticut and college and Laura asked about Auckland and Marika's family and how a girl got away with having her own boat and sailing off alone, which Marika said had been opposed by everyone. Even her father disapproved, which proved that your basic Kiwi dad is stuck in the 19th Century, because if her brother wanted to do it he would've said, good on ya, lad, and what do you need? Of men in their lives, for Marika there was currently none, so their investigation of the topic was all Maurice. What was his nationality? American, said Laura. As to how they had met, it had been awkward since she was living with somebody else at the time. Awkward, but necessary. Marika approved. Her own experience was that men were periodically necessary but generally, for a woman under 30, just mostly not. She did intend to get one, but not until necessary.

It was five o'clock before they finished, but without diving to inspect the bottom, which Marika said they could do tomorrow. Laura hired a fisherman to offload the trash bags and summoned Old Joseph to fetch them with the van. Maurice was waiting at the cottage when she returned. He had not been seasick, he said, but had some business calls to make and they had seemed to be doing fine without his help.

Maurice could pout, but Laura put that out of her mind.

* * *

It was that night that the discussion turned to whether Robert Ayers had ever killed a man, a topic brought up out of the blue by Julia after three of Priest's margaritas. Killed a man in Philadelphia, when he was with Eleanor. And had not Eleanor been interviewed by the police about it?

Eleanor said she was certain Robert had not killed anybody, and that the interview had been pro forma, having to do with a fatal explosion involving one of the contractors that Bobby's company worked with.

Marika seemed delighted, and looked at Laura with new interest. "Mr. Ayers killed somebody?"

Ed laughed, and said that Bobby let these things be said about him. Encouraged them, even. It was all part of the Bobby Ayers lore.

"He was quite capable of it," said Julia.

"It that possibly true?" said Inge-Lise.

"No," said Eleanor.

Vivian, who didn't drink, said, "You're crazy."

"You know, Marika, he had a tattoo, like you do," said Julia. "Not fish on his chest, though."

"Mom, stop." That was Laura.

"Bobby's tattoo said 'Three Things,' and we all know where it was, on his back, down here." Julia put her arm behind her back. "Nobody ever asked him what it meant? Oh, come on."

"What did it mean?" said Marika.

Nobody said anything.

"I'm just curious," she added. "Don't forget, I didn't even know him."

"Three things to do in life," Eleanor said.

"Which three?"

"You don't tell anybody which three," Inge-Lise said. She laughed suddenly. "I did ask him."

"The three things were never to be spoken about," said Vivian. "I honor that."

"We all honor it," Julia said. "But I was with him the longest, and I had a daughter with him who's sitting right there, and Ed here was his best friend, and I think he got that tattoo as a psychological justification for all the stuff he did, the disappearing act, the money, anything he wanted to, killing somebody even. It justified who he was. He could look in the mirror and say, my Three Things, that's what I was put here to do."

"In the mirror it would be backwards," Ed said.

"Enough from you," Julia said.

"Robert didn't hide it," said Vivian. "In the gym of the Singapore Hilton all his colleagues saw the words, and do you know, they bowed down to him. He had 'Three Things.' What they were he would never say, but he had them. On that trip the distributor of the Caterpillar equipment company, who was a weightlifter, he got one. Also, the biggest concrete man in Asia, he had that same tattoo put on. The big men saw what Robert was, and understood it, and gave us contracts. The mark on him raised him up. He had Three Things in life to do. I used to say to other men, do you know yours? Ha!"

"I've heard these stories all my life," Laura said.

"From who?" said her mother.

"From your cocktail parties, mom. I think when I was growing up you told everybody you met about the tattoo, the Three Things, the murder. I was in the Ninth Grade when I asked Ed if it was true, and what did you say, Ed? "Don't believe everything you hear about your dad.""

"Which is true," Ed said.

"You were big listener, but that was not for a child's ears," Julia said.

Eleanor said: "Folks, I was there. He didn't kill anybody. He was depressed and at that time everything fell apart for him and he just checked out. And all the police wanted from me was, was I OK? Because they gave Mr. Sullivan a guard until this Mafia guy they were looking for died, and the cause was not a mystery at all, he blew himself up by accident. That was in the papers, it's a matter of record."

"That 'by accident' got Bobby a lot of mileage," said Ed.

"He got mileage out of everything," Julia said. "For example, you can't sue somebody who is mentally incompetent. It can be very useful to be hospitalized when you're being hounded by creditors and that was as good a place to hide as in a pill bottle or a booze bottle, which he also did, and as good a place to leave everything for somebody else to clean up."

"One past the limit," Ed said.

"That is unfair," Vivian said.

"Mr. Ayers was in the Mafia?" Marika said.

"I don't think that's what Eleanor said," Inge-Lise said.

"Gee, I really wish I had known him," said Marika.

Maurice had been watching Laura. He felt not part of it. He felt ignored. He felt Laura participated to gain information, when in fact she had more information than they did. He felt that the same apparent passivity that freed her pretty face from the smile lines others had was also a mask she had worn since childhood. It was a mask she took off and put on. It was a mask that Ed had confirmed. It was how she dealt with her mother and everyone else and even with him. He hoped she was not dealing with him now, and he suspected that she could, if animated by this same cold spirit, break him like a stick.

"Do you want to know what the Three Things are?" Laura asked. "Because I know what they are."

Yes, Maurice thought, and he would never see it coming.

"And I'll tell you," Laura said, "to relieve this endless fascination with my father as the Wizard of Oz or Machiavelli or Al Capone. Here they are, as stitched forever on his backside.

"Number One: 'Marry a woman you truly love.' I think all of you got a piece of that one.

"Number Two: 'Make a million dollars.' OK, he made it and lost it and made it again, that was the game, I think.

"Number Three: Are you ready? 'Kill a man who truly deserves to die.'

The Palm Hut was silent. Even priest put down his tray.

"My father was an autodidact, as you all know. Dropped out of school, self-educated all the way. Eleanor sent me his books, almost 100 of them. He only cared about people's autobiographies, you know, to find out how they got successful. I've been reading them, mostly for his notes, which are pure daddy on every page. 'Never let them see you weak.' 'They explain, you don't.' 'Every victorious army is hungry and tired.' It goes on and on. My father didn't learn from the past, he stole it, and that's what made him Bobby Ayers and that's the man we loved.

"Three Things? He took that from a business guy you never heard of, his name was E.W. Scripps, and his book is called 'Damned Old Crank.' Maybe that's what daddy's autobiography ought to be called, if anybody actually writes it. Mr. Scripps did marry a woman he loved, and he did make a million dollars, but I hate to disappoint you, when it came to the third thing he couldn't do it. He said he never could find a man who truly deserved to die because they all had a story that was true for them even if it wasn't true for anybody else. So mom, and everybody? Guess what. So does my father."

Laura sat down hard. Marika put her arm around her. Priest looked confused, but Ed gestured him in.

"Freshen up all around," he said.

Julia opened her mouth, but Ed put his hand on her shoulder and said quietly, "Here's to Bobby Ayers, who never killed anybody, not even us."

The toast was grave, each to their own thoughts, except for Marika, who said, startlingly loud, "Righto, to Bobby!"

In the moment that followed Laura kissed Maurice lightly on the cheek, too lightly he thought, and led Marika off to their cottage to go over documents from the boat.

It was Wednesday night, the night on Rarotonga it became the Reef Haven Cottages' turn to host a beachside band. From the parking lot streamed a line of strangers, barefoot couples who were already dancing as Priest departed to man the public bar on the sand. The strains of "Rum and Coca-Cola" filled the humid air redolent of hibiscus and coconuts.

Julia stood up: "Calypso? In the South Pacific?"

Ed put his arm around her waist and led her to the music.

Maurice felt exposed. Vivian sat beside him, stiff in her sarong. He took her hand.

"No," Vivian said.

"Yes," said Maurice, dragging her toward the beach.

As it happened, Vivian danced very well.

CHAPTER TWENTY-FIVE

Thursday

At breakfast Maurice sat apart, reading a newspaper on his laptop. The beachside Palm Hut was cool and the Wi-Fi powerful, an exception on an island made remote by lack of television and cell towers. Others of the group arrived, most a little hung over, to do the same, conscious of a bond together. The bond was not confined only to their meeting at 2 p.m. at the offices of South Seas Trust, where Bobby Ayers' money would be distributed among them. They seemed also to have accepted each other as contradictions to presumptions. Marika was a hoot. Ed and Julia, well, they were a pair, all right. Eleanor and Inge-Lise, the one ironic and skeptical and some kind of scientist, the other, after what had seemed like initial embarrassment among the legitimized former wives, probably the most socially secure and the most travelled.

Vivian's attitude had certainly changed. Formerly she had seldom spoken first, and when she did it was corrective. Now she seemed almost at ease, though still guarded, and strangely protective of her late ex-husband. Also, she had started eating. Must be the free food, Julia said. Or that

Vivian knew something they didn't. As for Ed, he had been Ayers' best friend, whatever that meant. Hadn't he married Julia out from under him in conditions of grave duress? The group bond was recognized for what it was: after a certain age, new companions become increasingly rare, and these companions were new. Here they were in each other's laps, all expenses paid, with opportunity to confide and gossip and with clean towels every day, all present on account of Robert Ayers, who had passed through, altered or ruined each life, depending on what day of it you looked at, and so they shared each day the way a season is shared, or the flu. His funeral was tomorrow. Today at 2 o'clock they would divide his assets. That topic wasn't discussed, of course. Too tacky. The topic being discussed at the moment was Maurice, his head down in the news.

Something was wrong between those two, and it was apparently Laura. What about Laura? Yes, what about Laura? The theories were tentative. She did remind everyone of her father. She had that provocation of distance, as in, what is she thinking? Maurice was a find, wherever she got him from. And where she got him from was the place Ayers had gotten them all from: the world of the curious and interested, the ranks of the easily bored, the list of those who in the fundament of the predictable found something lacking and were drawn toward trouble, or challenge, or whatever you call it, some spark, some break in the pattern. Poor Maurice. Nobody survives regularity long. Poor Maurice. Big and strong and in the hands of the only daughter of Bobby Ayers.

"Anything in the news?" Inge-Lise said, sliding next to him with a fresh croissant for both.

"What?" said Maurice, looking up.

* * *

In mid-morning Ed and Maurice took a taxi to the harbor looking for the girls, as Ed called them. He said he sort of enjoyed not having instant communication by cellular phone. Ed could remember a time, in his first marriage, when people were glad to see each other at the end of the day. Now you were tracked by bloodhounds wherever you went and "unavailable" was the same as being dead. Had Maurice noticed that Laura often didn't answer her phone, and that a bell ringing in her pocket did not automatically open the door to her inner life? Unusual in the current generation. Ed had kids by his first marriage, grown and successful, but just between the two of them, Laura was the most interesting. He admired how she was not wrapped up in evanescent concerns, but sort of above it all. Frankly, how lucky it was that Maurice had come along. Julia loved him. Ed, not to get girly about it, liked hanging out with him and wanted it to continue. However, and this was the point, Laura was hard to figure. The best women were a lot of work, of course. They were a career. Julia had been a career. Laura, Ed predicted, would be a career.

Well, Maurice confided, he would not have gone into the insurance business if he thought it were easy, or just lucrative. He went into it because he wanted to learn it.

That's the thing, Ed said, we have to learn them, especially somebody like Laura. Because if there's nothing there to learn you get bored, which was the case with his golf partners who had married these trophy dolls with fish lips. But anyway, Maurice, a sexy woman, a desirable wife, is all in your head. And if Laura's in yours, well, his advice was to get into hers. Find out what's going on in there, and take action. Because whatever has come up between you two, action is required.

"Nothing has come up," Maurice said.

"A strong hand, if it's a loving hand," Ed said as the cab pulled onto the parking lot of Avenua harbor. "A deciding hand."

"Nothing has come up," Maurice repeated.

They got out of the taxi onto the grass in front of a line of charter fishing boats tugging at their mooring lines. "So where's this big sailboat of Bobby's?" said Ed, looking around.

"Used to be right here," said Maurice.

The waves still bounced confusedly against the quay, but *Après Vous* was gone. Maurice strode up and down the grass, searching. Ed had to trot to keep up as Maurice headed for the harbormaster's office across the road, where he took the wooden stairs two at a time.

The harbormaster said that the two women had decided to make a sea trial before signing the salvage inventory papers. They had departed a few hours before, through surf in the reef entrance. He had warned them of six-foot seas outside and a westerly wind, which made the harbor a lee shore. But he had kept an eye on them from his window and somebody knew what they were doing, because they had slipped the anchor smartly and motored out without a hitch and then set sail. He imagined they would return before nightfall, and he hoped they were not heading to another island without a departure clearance.

Maurice said very little on the ride back to the cottages. Ed said it was not unusual for Laura to be, well, Laura. And that Marika was an experienced sailor, and she had seen Bobby's ghost, and if that didn't scare her nothing Laura did would.

* * *

Julia was the only one not concerned that Laura and Marika had failed to return for the reading of the will. Typical Laura, she said. Maurice paced. Ed went on some more about the simplicity of life without cell phones while holding a luncheon martini out of sight on his thigh. The others were overdressed and suddenly formal in their exchanges in preparation for the important financial event to come. At quarter to two Old Joe piled them into the van, pulled shut the door, and headed up the coast road toward South Seas Trust in the island center of Avarua.

The office was up a flight of concrete exterior stairs which they climbed, clothes blowing, to find Laura and Marika waiting, newly sunburned and in shorts still wet with salt. Apologies. Had to inspect the hull. Decided on a quick sail. Blowing 20 out there. Laura was beaming.

Her mother took her aside and discretely thrust a hairbrush in her hand. When Laura came out of the women's room Maurice was waiting.

"You're supposed to be in charge," he said.

"I am," Laura said, and kissed him on the lips. She pointed Marika toward a plastic chair, motioned for the others to sit down, and nodded toward an unmarked door.

"Folks, Mr. Johnson will be out in a minute. He said all there is to it is some paperwork to sign and then we can all go back and toast my father on the beach and enjoy the glorious ocean Marika and I just came from and which got us all wet."

"I'm dry already," Marika said.

"Well, I'm going to sit down," Laura said. "Come on Maurice, it's not really a formal occasion."

One by one, Ed last, they sat. It was 20 minutes before Lee Johnson came through the door with a cardboard box of envelopes. He was in his 30s, in a short-sleeved dress shirt, close-cropped hair and clip-in bicycle shoes. The shoes clicked on the linoleum floor.

"This is Mr. Johnson," Laura said.

"Oh, forgot to introduce myself," said Johnson. "Well, I'm glad we're all here. Mr. Ayers was a client of ours for 27 years, and I'm sorry I never got a chance to actually meet him. But I do recall what he said to me on the phone once, and that was that there is US law and then there is Napoleonic law, and he wanted to have the canons on his side. And we do, here." He laughed, but the timing was off. "That's because in the Cook Islands we have New Zealand law, which is based on the Napoleonic Code, which is quite different from the American system of federal and state laws, which tend to be different and contradictory." Then, brightly: "The Cook Islands are more protective of assets, Mr. Ayers believed. And he was right."

"Also, it's hard to sue somebody in Rarotonga if you live in the States," added Ed, who had been a lawyer once.

"Anyone like some water?" Johnson asked. But the eyes before him were fixed on the box in his arms as if to burn holes in it, and so he said quickly, "Well, then," and began to read off the names on the envelopes inside.

The names had hands, and the hands reached for the envelopes. When they were distributed, Johnson said that he would get the forms for wire transfer and such, and left the room through his unmarked door. The Ayers beneficiaries sat, unmoving. The protocol of the envelopes was unclear. You looked at a business card when somebody handed it to you. But you didn't open the gift envelope at a wedding or a bar mitzvah. Julia handed her unopened envelope to Ed, but it was too large to fit in his jacket pocket.

"Oh, all right," said Laura, tearing hers open.

Marika gasped when she opened hers, then lowered her head in imitation of the Ayers family around her, who, examining their shares, nodded respectfully as if the deceased were watching. Ed solemnly passed their envelope to Julia, who glanced at the document inside and burst out laughing.

"I knew it!" 'Glee' was the tone as the group would characterize it later.

"Mother!" said Laura.

"Sorry, but I knew he'd be almost broke! It just rounds Bobby out to a perfect square, doesn't it? I know I shouldn't laugh, but really, this is just icing on the cake."

"Broke?" said Eleanor. "My check is for $398,117."

"We all got the same amount," said Laura. "Marika, too."

Marika had her award in hand and was bent over it, sobbing. She kept repeating that she was rich. Laura had her hand on her back, as if consoling.

"Except Vivian. Vivian gets two envelopes," Laura said.

"This is a large amount of money," said Eleanor. I don't even really need it. I feel bad to take it."

"Take it," said Ed.

"Vivian gets two envelopes," Laura continued, "because Maurice and I learned only the day before yesterday that my father lost his case in tax court. For three years, the IRS has been after her for the judgement, which they owed together, and they were coming after the estate to collect. My father fought them tooth and nail but he also stipulated that if the judgement went against him he would make good and get Vivian off the hook. And it was a big hook,

Vivian, and I'm sorry you had to go through all this, but I think it's all right now. Isn't it?"

Vivian was frightened, they all agreed later. She was as guarded as an interloper and looked guilty as a thief. She stood rigid, clutching the envelopes to her chest.

"Not my fault," said Vivian, her voice stone. "I so sorry, but not my fault."

"I always said the IRS would have its day," said Julia, "scum-sucking bastards that they are."

"What was the judgement?" That was Ed.

"All I can say is sorry one hundred times," Vivian said. "I did not want this, I need nothing. But my sons in China would have to pay and they would be ruined for sure. Robert said we would fight the Internal Revenue, I didn't want to but he said we would win, and I knew we wouldn't, you can never win against them."

"To be clear," Laura said, "The assets were divided six ways, no favorites. Vivian's share is just the same as the rest of ours. The second check she got is to the IRS for $3.9 million, which is the amount they owe. I don't think any of us has a problem with that."

"Three point nine mil?" said Ed. "Whoa!"

"I'm so sorry to take so much from everybody's money," Vivian said, tears running,

"Are you nuts?" Julia was the first to rush her, grab her shoulders and shake her like a child. The others joined, reaching through each other to touch her, congratulate her, finding her tears contagious, finding themselves entwined in a sea of arms and scraping chairs that dissolved the awkwardness until just the slightest smile drew across Vivian's face and she stood among them in pride of self again, released only slowly from the burden of four helpless debtor years. Only Marika still sat, head down, staring at her piece of paper. Laura went and drew her up.

"I shouldn't be here," Marika said.

"Yes," Laura said, "my father wanted you to be."

Johnson returned then, shoes clicking, with six clipboards and six pens.

"Oh, one other thing," he said, handing a thick folder to Laura. "You also get the boat."

On the drive back the van resounded with admissions of how odd the scene had been; how funny Mr. Johnson; how marvelous that the awards were net gifts, the tax already paid for; how generous the amounts and how nice the equitable sharing; how deserving Vivian was of the IRS grant; how remarkable Bobby Ayers' bringing them all together; how pretty the day; how bumpy the ride and how disconcerting it was, they all agreed, to be driving on the wrong side of the road and thank goodness Old Joseph was at the wheel.

By the time the vehicle bounced through the puddles in front of Reef Haven Cottages they were singing La Marseillaise in honor of Napoleon and Bobby Ayers, and when they got out Priest was waiting with a half dozen bottles of Dom Perignon provided by the Ayers estate.

Vivian could dance even while crying, it turned out. She danced so well with Ed that after a while Julia bumped her out of the way and took over, and Vivian went back to writing a letter to her sons in China telling of her continued good fortune in the United States.

Laura and Maurice did not dance. They were down at the beach in the moonlight, arguing. The gestures that could be seen were emphatic and disturbing, so much so that the other celebrants didn't want to look, although they did.

Julia started to take a bottle of champagne down to them, but Ed held her arm. Whatever it was, they were the only ones who could work it out.

"If she screws this up I'll kill her," Julia said.

"It only works when it works," said Ed.

So together they turned away, back to the dance floor, where Bobby Ayers had bought the drinks.

CHAPTER TWENTY-SIX

Friday

The interment of Robert Ayers was scheduled for 11 a.m., and at breakfast Laura was missing again. So were Maurice and Marika. The others sat at the Palm Hut table being served papaya and waffles.

"What's going on?" Julia said. "Does anybody know the schedule?" No one did.

"I'm concerned that this must be done right," Vivian said.

"I agree. We may have to step in, Vivian."

"Do we even know where he's being buried?" asked Inge-Lise.

"Joseph!" said Julia as he passed. "Where is it you're taking us all at 11 o'clock?"

Old Joseph pointed to the massive volcanic mountain behind them, its green peak rising into a shroud of clouds, then shuffled on.

"Laura and Marika headed for the harbor early this morning," said Eleanor. "I think she has to deal with the boat before we all leave."

"And Maurice?"

"He wasn't with them," Eleanor said.

Inge-Lise was studying the papers in her Trust packet. She broke the momentary silence as Priest poured more of the rich, dark coffee that they all deemed best in the world.

"I want to say," she began, "as the one who wasn't married to him, and the one who almost didn't come, how strange it is to be here but also unexpectedly nice, and to have met you all, and heard about Bobby, because he sure didn't tell me much in Mexico and the truth is a lot would be unresolved for me if I hadn't come. I wanted to say that out loud instead of just thinking it." A smile intruded in her voice, or maybe it was just the accent. "And I wonder if you all have noticed, in the packets we got, that the estate provides this same accommodation for us every year, the cottages, the airline tickets, the van, every year from now on, for all of us, in perpetuity. It's in the codicil in Appendix 3."

"I did notice that," Eleanor said.

"Just what we need, perpetual Bobby," said Julia.

"He wished that we would know each other," said Inge-Lise.

"He wished to be remembered," said Vivian.

"And now every year he'll come back to life," Julia said. "The man cooked up his own resurrection."

"All I know," Inge-Lise said, "is that he planned this a long time. In Mexico we were all convinced he was sailing the southern route, like everyone else. That's what he wanted us to think, that we'd all sail together to Tahiti. He was our leader, he had the biggest boat, he was enthusiastic. And of course, I was going to be his crew. But none of it was ever true. He intended all along to run straight west into the open Pacific beyond the shipping lanes where nobody else ever goes and hide out there. And that's what he did, no goodbyes at all."

"Don't take that part personally," Eleanor said.

"He never said 'goodbye,'" said Vivian.

"But then when you almost forgot, 'Hello again!' Right, Ed?" said Julia.

"He's dead, leave him alone."

"I was completely unaware that he was sick," said Inge-Lise, "Looking back, I should have been, but nobody was because his manner was always so certain and persuasive. I don't blame him for not wanting a wheelchair and then worse, because it's a terrible disease. But it's terrible to die all by yourself, and he knew he would, and I really don't get that. But then, he didn't want me to."

"Robert chose to be alone," Vivian said.

"I don't think he was ever alone," Julia said. "In his head he had all of us there like little puppets, dressing us up in clothes and probably undressing us, too, whenever he felt like it. We were strings to pull and he could make us dance or cry or just wonder where he was. He owned us, and he still does. Right, Ed?"

Ed laughed. The others didn't. Inge-Lise passed Julia Appendix 3 from her packet.

"I read it, I know what it says," Julia responded. "It really takes gall to bring us back here every year and what, put flowers on his grave and tell stories about him."

"Gotcha," said Ed.

"To me, it's an honor," Vivian said quietly.

"All I know is that it's going to take me a while to understand what happened here," said Inge-Lise. "And that includes being a lot richer than I was. Which I'm the first person to bring up, I think."

The ensuing silence left a hole that might have been filled with gratitude or sarcasm, but no one had the heart for either. No one had the heart for anything except to follow the Ayers schedule, whatever it turned out to be. They were leaving tonight at midnight. In the meantime they had a family funeral to go to and the family was apparently their own, circumstance replacing genealogy, absurdity and contradiction the ties that bound, and would in perpetuity on a South Sea island where every year they would grow older together until oblivion took the last. Unless, as Julia pointed out, there were grandchildren to keep the memories alive.

"So what's going on with Laura and Maurice?" she asked. "Somebody tell me, I'm not blind. Is the whole thing over and I just don't see it?"

"They seem to have made an accommodation," Inge-Lise volunteered.

"After considerable negotiation," Eleanor added.

"That's what I'm worried about," Julia said.

* * *

Mrs. Hagawa met the mourners at the foot of the burial site as they stepped out of the van into the mud. Better to go barefoot from here, she advised, collecting their shoes and piling them on a chicken coop. They followed her, single file, up a slippery trail to the plateau of the Hagawa estate until the banana trees stopped and a panorama of the Pacific ocean opened suddenly far below and wreathed in steamy clouds. The gasps of surprise were audible.

Low, white funeral vaults were scattered across the hillside and it quickly became apparent that they were climbing to the highest, newest and biggest of them, where a dozen islanders were waiting with a man in black, the Rev. Alexander Wight of the Christian Ministry of Cook Islands. He was going over some documents with Maurice and having trouble with his reading glasses. Under a cluster of palms some distance away Marika and Laura were chatting animatedly, as if time were short and their list of things to do was long.

Mrs. Hagawa stood before the vault, which was strewn with frangipani and palm fronds, as from behind her the air filled with rhythmic chanting. It was the *Imene tuki*, she said, the traditional Polynesian hymn being performed by her brothers. They sang unaccompanied, grunting in complex rhythms and harmonies punctuated by staccato bursts of undecipherable Maori. The effect was to pin the small party in place before the tomb in which Robert Ayers lay. Julia watched Laura under the palms, and was relieved to see Maurice direct her to a prominent place and to shoo Marika away to join the others. He then peremptorily advanced upon Rev. Wight, pulling him to the fore by his sleeve, as if he might slip away.

"Thank you all for coming," the minister said, "uh, on this day when we are in the presence of, ah, both darkness and the light, and Mr. Maurice Charles would like to lead us now in prayers for the deceased."

Maurice kissed Laura on the lips—"Oh?" Julia said to Ed—and displaced Rev. Wight, who seemed grateful to step aside.

"I'm Maurice, whom some of you just met this week. I myself only met Robert Ayers once, but here we all are at his vault on the hill, and from what I know he would like this view very much. Laura says he wasn't a religious man in the usual sense, and thank you Rev. Wight for appreciating that. I was raised Quaker and so I asked to make some remarks today on the pattern of my own mother's funeral. The Quakers aren't much for ceremony, the idea is plain and simple, but one thing they do is let the people who come to say goodbye stand up in their pew and talk about the deceased, who they were and how their lives fit together. The idea is that by listening to other folks you see where you fit in, too." Maurice paused. Wind rustled the palm fronds on the limestone vault behind him.

"But I don't think we need to do that today, because we already have. We have testified all week to each other about who Robert Ayers was to us, and how it came to be that we are part of his story on earth. A man is known by the people he knows, even if he can never know himself. And so we celebrate who Bobby Ayers was, each to himself, and in that way he lives on in us. In the end, memory is the only god we have."

At that Rev. Wight shifted uncomfortably and looked to Mrs. Baraka for correction. She was beaming, however, having been a good deal more impressed by the tall, brown American than the bumblers around him, even the strong-willed daughter.

"He's doing all right, isn't he?" Julia whispered to Ed.

"Relax," Ed said.

"I want grandchildren," Julia said.

Maurice cleared his throat and read from a sheet of paper what he said were the words of William Penn, founder of the State of Pennsylvania.

"I should have figured Maurice for a Quaker," Eleanor said.

"Where's Pennsylvania?" Marika said.

And this is the comfort of the good, that the grave cannot hold them, and that they live as soon as they die. For death is no more than a turning of us over from time to eternity.

Let us not cozen ourselves with the shells and husks of things, nor prefer form to power, nor shadows to substance. This world is a form; our bodies are forms. But our souls being of another and nobler nature, we should seek our rest in a more enduring habitation.

"Habitation" was the cue for the Hagawa brothers to surround the heavy limestone vault and launch again into the *Imene tuki*, louder this time and more celebratory. The rhythm was infectious but foreign, and when Ed tried to join in with his clear tenor he was lost in an instant.

Laura now appeared with a bright lei of flowers around her neck, which she somberly removed and draped over her father's resting place as Maurice guided her by the waist.

Vivian poked Julia hard in the ribs.

"Too native!" she said under her breath. "Robert not a native!"

"Believe me, this wasn't my idea," Julia said. "We're Episcopalians."

Rev. Wight now stepped forward with a new folder in his hands. He seemed to be doing the best he could under circumstances that did not have the benefit of rehearsal or familiar liturgical sequence.

"We will now switch ceremonies in the interest of time and airline schedules, because, ah—."

"Hold on a minute," Maurice said. "Laura and I have announcement to make. We're going to be married, here and now. I think her father would be good with that, and Rev. Wight has kindly agreed. I managed to get the license just this morning, which wasn't easy, but I guarantee it's legal and binding." He grabbed Laura, who was grinning, and pulled her too his side. "I had to make a deal to make this happen, but it's a good deal, and Laura agrees."

"I do." said Laura.

"Not yet!" Julia called out.

Maurice gestured the minister nearer, holding him with a massive hand.

"On this happy occasion," Rev. Wight began, and then stopped as Maurice squeezed his arm. "Oh yes, I have agreed to 'streamline.' Therefore I ask you, Laura, do you take this man to be your lawful wedded husband?"

"I do," she said.

And Maurice, do you—"

"I do," said Maurice.

"Then what God had made together let no man put asunder, and you can kiss the bride."

They kissed, and when they had, Maurice seized her waist and lifted her weightless aloft for all to see as the *Imene tuki* resumed, jubilant now. Stunned congratulators pressed in with grins and hugs. Julia watched as Laura, set down, retrieved the lei of frangipani off the funeral vault and put it over Maurice's head and hers, too.

"Bobby would like seeing them dance on his grave," Ed said to Julia as Laura hugged her, surrounded by the Barata clan, friends, gardeners, chickens, running dogs and Rev. Wight, who was passing around a bottle of Black & White Scotch.

"So what's the deal?" Ed said. "We know you two made one," Ed said.

"I buy our house," Maurice said. "She gets to sail her father's boat home."

"What?" said Julia. "Are you serious?"

"I want to do it singlehanded, like dad," Laura said, Maurice's arm around her. "Don't worry, Marika's going to teach me, she has to sail the boat to New Zealand anyhow, for the refit. I'll be her crew at first, until I know what I'm doing. Maurice knows that's what I want to do, I knew it first time I stepped aboard, and he says I should, as long as we got married first.

"That was the deal," Maurice said.

"So we're staying here another week for our honeymoon and then we'll be back home. Marika says we have to wait for the seasons to change anyhow before we leave. So come on, let's everybody come back to the beach for dinner, you don't have to get on the plane till midnight."

Maurice had his long arms around both Laura and Julia as hands clapped and dogs barked.

"I think we should all say goodbye to Bobby before we celebrate," Ed said.

"We can try, but it won't work," Julia said, following him toward the sunlit grave up the hill.

* * *

As island custom dictated, a photo of Bobby Ayers was placed on the vault.

It was still there when they all returned the next year, and everyone agreed the eyes followed you whenever you passed.

###

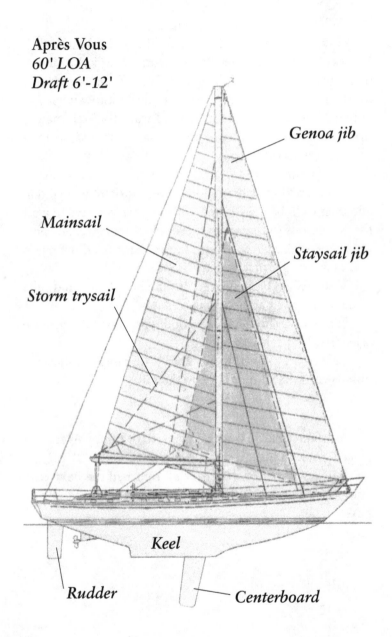

Après Vous
60' LOA
Draft 6'-12'

Genoa jib

Mainsail

Staysail jib

Storm trysail

Keel

Rudder

Centerboard

Nautical Terms Used

A

Aback. A sail is aback when sheeted to the windward side, where it tends to stop progress.

Abeam. Ninety degrees from the heading.

AIS. Automatic Identification System. Transponder instrumentation that provides location, course, speed and other information. Installation is mandatory for large commercial ships but voluntary for yachts.

Aloft. Above the deck.

Alternator. A device attached to the engine to make electricity to charge batteries.

Alto Stratus. Mid-altitude clouds that suggest an approaching storm.

Amidships. In the middle of the boat.

Anemometer. A device for measuring the speed of the wind, usually by a paddlewheel at the top of the mast.

Aneroid barometer. A device for measuring atmospheric pressure without the use of fluids.

Apparent wind. Wind created by movement of the vessel. For true wind, apparent wind is added or subtracted.

Autopilot. Motorized steering capable of programmed courses.

Astern. Behind the yacht.

B

Back. The wind is said to back when it changes direction counter-clockwise.

Backstay. The wire that supports the mast from stern to masthead.

Batten. A flexible strip of wood or metal. In sails, they are inserted in a pocket on the leech to extend the area and prevent curling.

Beam reach. To sail with the wind abeam. A fast and pleasant course.

Beam. The width of a boat.

Bear off. To alter course away from the wind.

Becalmed. Without wind.

Beneteau. A French manufacturer of popular sailboats.

Berths. Bunks for sleeping.

Bilge. The lowest part of the yacht, where water and spillage collects. A pumping system is required, usually automated.

Binnacle. A mount to bring the compass to convenient height for the helmsman and to hold instruments.

Binnacle Guard. Handholds on the binnacle.

Block. Nautical term for pulley. There are many specialized types.

Boom vang. A device, solid or of block and tackle, to hold the boom down when sailing off the wind.

Boom. The horizontal spar at the bottom of a sail.

Bow roller. An assembly on the bow to hold an anchor and facilitate its deployment and retrieval.

Bow. The front end of a boat.

Bow thruster. A propeller in a transverse tunnel at the bow to provide sideways thrust for docking.

Broach. When sailing downwind, to be turned sideways to the seas and wind.

Broad reach. A course between downwind and a beam reach. Often the fastest point of sail.

Bulkhead. A partition separating one part of a vessel from another.

Bulwark(s). On a yacht, a raised section of the outboard deck designed to deflect seas and assist footing.

Bunk board. A wooden device installed to restrain sleeping crew.

Bunk. A boat bed.

C

Carbon fiber. A reinforced polymer that is stiffer, lighter and stronger than steel.

Centerboard. A retractable keel. *Après Vous* has a centerboard within a fixed keel.

Chafe. To wear away, as by friction. Also, the result of such wear.

Chafing gear. Devices of rubber or cloth for the protection of lines or sails against chafe.

Chartplotter. A GPS instrument that contains electronic charts displayed on a screen, and provides position, course, time to destination and other data.

Circuit breaker. A switch designed to protect against electrical overload.

Cirrus. High-altitude ice clouds suggesting deterioration of weather. They often appear as wispy "mares' tails."

Cleat. A fitting for the securing of a rope.

Clew. The outer corner of a sail, and its fitting.

Clock. The wind is said to clock when it changes direction clockwise.

Close-hauled. A yacht is close-hauled when sailing as close to the wind as possible. Sailed are trimmed hard and heel is maximized.

Coaming. The side of the cockpit extending above deck level.

Cockpit(s). Recessed seating areas on deck. *Après Vous* has a large center cockpit and a smaller aft cockpit. Both can be accessed from below.

Companionway. The deck opening to the cabin, protected against weather by a sliding hatch.

Companionway stairs. The means of access between cockpit and cabin floor. Sometimes called a ladder.

Compartment. A room on a boat or ship.

Containership. A commercial ship designed for the transport of shipping containers, which are stacked on deck.

"Cement boat". A vessel made using a composite of steel mesh and thin cement.

Cumulus. Puffy fair-wind clouds typical of the trade winds.

D

Deck. The top of the boat. The sides of a boat are called topsides.

Degrees magnetic. A course stated as 360°M (Magnetic) refers to the magnetic compass.

Diaphragm pump. A pump which utilizes a bellows to move fluids, rather than a spinning impeller.

Dodger. A protective shield over the companionway to provide protection against wind and spray.

Downhaul. A rope for pulling or holding a sail down.

Drogue. Any device dragged behind a vessel to slow forward speed and keep the stern to following seas.

Draft. A measure of the vertical distance between the waterline and the keel.

Dyneema. A brand name for Ultra High Molecular Weight Polyethylene (UHMWPE) used as the core of low-stretch ropes.

E

EPIRB. "Emergency Position Indicating Radio Beacon." Current models have GPS. When deployed, an EPIRB transmits its position to guide rescue.

F

Fantail. The fan-shaped afterdeck of a vessel.

Fathom. A fathom is six feet.

Fender. A pneumatic cushion used to prevent damage when one vessel lies alongside another or a dock.

Fiddles. The raised edges of a table designed to keep objects from sliding off.

Folkboat. A small sailboat of Nordic tradition.

Forepeak. A storage area under the deck of the bow.

Foresail. Any sail forward of the mast.

Forestay. The wire, or stay, running from bow to top of the mast.

Foul Weather Gear. Personal waterproof gear usually consisting of bibbed trousers and an overhanging coat.

Foul. A line or sail which is tangled, jammed, or stuck.

Fulmar. Any of large tube-nosed seabirds of the family Procellariidae distinguished by gliding flight and curiosity.

G

Gale. A wind of 32-63 mph.

Genoa jib. A large foresail extending aft of the mast.

Gimbals. An arrangement of pivots for keeping a lamp or stove level against the movements of a vessel at sea.

Generator. A secondary diesel engine to provide electrical power.

GPS. The Global Positioning System satellite-based navigation system is a free international service operated by the United States Air Force.

Grib. Contraction of GRIded Binary weather file, a wind prediction chart.

Gulf Stream. A warm Atlantic Ocean current which influences weather from the east coast of North America to Northern Europe.

Gunwale. The upper edge of a vessel's side. Often pronounced "gunnel."

H

Halyard. A line for the hoisting of a sail.

Headlamp. A battery-powered light worn on a head strap. A miner's light.

Heave to. To position the boat with one sail aback and reduced forward motion, as for riding out a storm.

Heel. A vessel is heeled when the force of wind inclines the boat to one side.

Helm. The rudder control, usually a steering wheel or tiller. To "take the helm" is to steer the boat.

Hove to. The state that exists after heaving to.

Hull. The body of a vessel exclusive of her masts and gear.

I

International 14 dinghy. A venerable small racing boat considered demanding to sail well.

Isobar. Contour lines on a chart revealing difference in atmospheric pressure. Converging isobars mean high winds.

J

Jackline. The fore and aft line of a harness and tether safety system. The jackline lies taut on the deck, allowing the tether to slide unimpeded.

Jib. A triangular sail set on the forestay.

Jordan Series Drogue. A drag line containing many small cones deployed from the stern to provide a constant slowing effect on a vessel riding out a storm. Named for Don Jordan, the aeronautical engineer who advanced the design.

K

Keel. A central weighted fin to provide righting force against the wind on the sails and also hydrodynamic lift to windward.

Ketch. A two-masted sailboat with the mizzen mast stepped forward of the steering position.

Knot. One nautical mile per hour. A knot is 1.15 statute miles per hour.

L

Laser. A one-design planing dinghy and rite of passage for competitive sailboat racers.

Latitude. Distance north or south of the equator expressed in degrees and minutes of arc.

Lazarette. A storage compartment under a deck. Also, lazaretto.

Leeward. Opposite of windward; downwind of the observer.

Leeway. The sideways movement made through the water by a vessel.

Lifeline. A stainless steel guard wire held by stanchions on the rail.

Lines. Ropes.

Longitude. Distance east or west of the meridian of Greenwich.

Luff. To bring the vessel's bow closer to or into the wind.

M

Mainsail. On a sloop, the sail on the boom.

Marine railway. Tracks constructed from land to water for launching or hauling out vessels on a sliding cradle.

Mast. A vertical spar on a sailboat.

N

Nautical mile. One-sixtieth of a degree of latitude, about 1.2 statute miles.

Nimbostratus. Multi-level rain clouds.

NOAA. The acronym for the National Oceanic and Atmospheric Administration, purveyor of charts and weather products.

O

Off the wind. Not close-hauled.

On the wind. Sailing close-hauled.

P

Puddle jump. The sail from North America across the Pacific. Ironic understatement, since the distances are great.

Puddle jumpers. Crews of transpacific yachts.

Port tack. Sailing with the wind from the port side.

Port. The left side of a boat when facing forward.

Portlight, porthole, port. An opening, fixed or hinged, for light or ventilation.

R

Reach. A point of sail with the wind abeam or forward of the beam, but not so far forward as to make the vessel close-hauled.

Reef. To reduce the area of a sail by partially lowering it or furling it on a roller.

Reeve. To pass a rope through a block, fairlead, or hole.

Regulator. In scuba, the device that meters air from the pressurized air tank.

Rigging knife. Any small folding knife, usually also with a spike, carried for use in common deck tasks.

Roller furler. A device which reefs a headsail by furling it around the forestay. *Après Vous* also has a self-furling mainsail which retracts into the boom.

RPM. Revolutions Per Minute is a measure of the rotation speed of an engine.

Rudder. The hydrofoil which turns the boat when swung by a wheel or tiller.

Running lights. Navigation lights. For the bow of sailing craft, 112.5° red on the port side and 112.5° green on starboard; and one 135° white light at the stern.

Running rigging. The sheets, halyards, topping lifts and such which control the sails.

S

Safety harness. Reinforced webbing worn on the chest to which a tether can be attached.

Sail. Mainsail, jib, genoa jib, spinnaker and so on. Sails are never called "sheets," that term is reserved for their control lines.

Salon. The main cabin.

Sacrificial zinc. Replaceable anode that prevents galvanic corrosion of nearby components.

Seaway. The ocean offshore.

Self-steering vane. A weathervane on the stern connected to a mechanism designed to steer a sailboat on a chosen course. Requires no electricity. Marika's boat has one.

Settee. A seat in a cabin which also can serve as a berth.

Shackle. A quick-release fitting for the attachment of lines and tackles.

Shake out. To let out a reef.

Shearwater. A long-winged sea bird named for its characteristic flight "shearing" wave faces.

Sheave. The wheel in a block over which a rope runs.

Sheet. A line by means of which a sail is trimmed. Sails are never called sheets.

Ship alarm. A feature of AIS that when enabled sounds a warning when another vessel approaches.

Shrouds. The stays that support the mast.

Singlehander. One who ventures offshore as sole crew.

Skipjack. A historical sail-powered oyster dredger with characteristic raked mast and long boom.

Sloop. A sailboat with one mast.

Solar panels. Photovoltaic modules that generate direct current from sunlight for the charging of yacht batteries.

Spectra. A brand name for high strength line of ultra-high-molecular-weight polyethylene. See also, *Dyneema.*

Spinnaker. A downwind sail, usually large, flown from a pole.

Squall. A sudden, localized increase in wind often accompanied by rain.

Stanchions. Uprights along the outer deck to hold lifelines.

Standing rigging. Permanent shrouds and stays which support the mast.

Starboard tack. Sailing with the wind from the starboard side.

Starboard. The right-hand side of a vessel when facing forward.

Staysail. A small jib set on its own forestay. Convenient when the large genoa jib is not required.

Spreaders. Crosstrees on a mast to hold the shrouds.

Stern. The back of the boat. Opposite of bow.

Storm petrel. A small seabird typically seen to dart among troughs in the waves. Also called "Mother Carey's chickens."

Storm trysail. A narrow, heavyweight triangular sail set in place of the mainsail for storm conditions.

Surface analysis chart. A small-scale weather chart showing areas of high and low pressure, fronts and storms.

Swell. Long, easy waves with crests that don't break.

T

Tack. To alter course so the bow passes through the eye of the wind. Also called "coming about."

Taffrail. The rail across or around the stern.

Teak and Holly. A veneer of two woods often used for the cabin sole.

Teak. An oily wood with good sea properties widely used before teak forests became depleted.

Tether. The line or strap connecting a chest harness to a jackline or other strong point.

Topsides. The sides of a boat between the deck and the water. The top of the boat is called the deck.

Transom. The transverse hull section where the two sides of a yacht meet at the stern.

Trim (v). To correct the position of a sail by means of a sheet.

Trim (n). A yacht is said to be in trim if it lies appropriately on its waterline while at rest.

Trysail. A small heavy-weather sail set in place of the mainsail. Also *Storm trysail.*

Turning block. Any block which changes the direction of a line.

V

Veer. A clockwise change in wind direction. A wind changing direction counterclockwise is *backing.*

Vane. The weathervane of a self-steering system.

VHF. Very High Frequency radio. Range is limited to line of sight.

W

Wake. The path of disturbed water left astern of a moving vessel.

Watermaker. A device to convert sea water to potable water by reverse osmosis.

Warm front. Warm, moist air pushing over a cooler mass. It rises, condenses, and often showers.

Waypoint. A navigation point entered on an electronic chart by the user.

Weatherfax. Facsimile delivery of weather prognostications.

White squall. A squall which appears without a visible cloud.

Winch handle. A lever used to crank a winch.

Winch. A mechanical device consisting of a drum on an axle, usually with gearing, to give increased power when hauling on a line. *Après Vous* has motorized winches which can also be hand-cranked.

Windmill electricity generator. A large propeller mounted on a stanchion at the stern to charge yacht batteries by its rotation.

Acknowledgements

A novel is unknown territory both for reader and writer. The best we can both do is muddle on, hoping the thing knows where it's going and will lead us there.

But the stuff in a story ought to be right, a pound still weigh a pound and a mile just as long as ever. For that I asked help from bright people. Jacob Epstein, for structural insight, Jeffrey Lewis for wisdom and Carl B. Feldbaum, for worldly experience. On weather, Joe Buck and Skip Allan. For music, Thomas Newman and Bill Bernstein. On the vagaries of living trusts, Adam Gauthier, and for trust law and IRS matters, John D. Faucher, JD. In Rarotonga, John Jesse, Harbor Master, and Antony B. Will on offshore trusts. Insofar as I did not always take their advice, they stand blameless wherever the temple is despoiled.

Tracy Olmstead Williams, after 30 years of marriage, remains my haven in storm and calm, and thank goodness for her.

About the Author

Christian Williams was an editor and reporter for The Washington Post from 1972 to 1986. He later wrote and produced television dramas from "Hill Street Blues" to "Six Feet Under" before retiring in 2010. He has four children and lives in Pacific Palisades, CA, with his wife, Tracy Olmstead Williams.

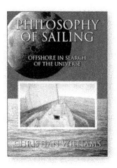